THE DRAMATISTS GUILD RESOURCE DIRECTORY™

2014

The Writer's Guide to the Theatrical Marketplace™

20th Edition

Focus Publishing
R. Pullins Company

The Dramatists Guild Resource Directory
© 2014 The Dramatists Guild of America Inc.
The Dramatists Guild Resource Directory and The Writer's Guide to the Theatrical
Marketplace are trademarks of The Dramatists Guild.

Published by
Focus Publishing/R. Pullins Company
PO Box 369
Newburyport, MA 01950
www.pullins.com

ISBN 13: 978-1-58510-715-5

Cover image: Joey Stocks
Cartoons: Mark Krause

For more information, contact Rebecca Stump, Editor of the *Resource Directory* at
rstump@dramatistsguild.com.

10 9 8 7 6 5 4 3 2 1

1213V

Contents

Editor's Note

Welcome to the 20th printed edition of The Dramatists Guild Resource Directory — a springboard for every dramatist in the submission process. On the cover of this printed edition you'll see two writers using our new Dramatists Guild Resource Directory Online. We are excited to move towards a more accurate way to offer submission information to members. The Dramatists Guild Resource Directory Online (affectionately known as the RDO) makes it easier for you to find opportunities while we provide you with current or updated information.

Through the RDO, Guild members have a fully searchable database of nearly 900 submission opportunities which you can sort by genre, submission deadline, geographic region, preferred length or special interests. We've also built in features like *Bookmark It*, to help keep track of opportunities to pursue by storing them to your own personal list; *Remind Me*, for sending you an email about those time-sensitive deadlines; and *Post It*, to share a resource to our Member Bulletin Boards.

New technology and electronic media allow us to stay current with the most up-to-date resources for all dramatists, and to keep you current as well. Because of this, it is no longer necessary to produce a paper copy of the RD. **Therefore, this is the last printed version we intend to publish.** Instead, the RDO will supply members with much more accurate information that will be will be updated each week – rather than once a year. This will mean that the listings opportunities will increase and we are hopeful, there-fore, that more theatres /festivals/contests will list with our online directory. Our RDO is primed to be your one-stop-shop for submission opportunities.

A strong word of advice about this book: by the time we go to press, a number of the opportunities listed may have new staff, updated deadlines, or may no longer exist. Such is the nature of the field; the landscape is constantly changing. It is essential that you verify the information we provide by going directly to the website of the theatre, contest, festival, etc. Please review each organization's policies carefully to ensure that all authorial rights are upheld. If you find a listing you believe is inaccurate or misleading please contact us here at the Guild. Remember, though, listings by their nature are never complete, and any listing or omission doesn't constitute approval or disapproval by the Guild, its Council, officers, employees, agents, or affiliates. Please be responsible with your submissions.

1. When submitting to a particular program within a contest, theatre, etc., cite the specific program to which you're submitting. Many groups sponsor multiple programs.
2. Include a self-addressed stamped envelope (SASE) with sufficient postage. Most organizations won't return material without one, and some organizations don't return material at all.

3. It's always a smart (and economically sound) choice to discover whether organizations take electronic submissions. If electronic submissions are not noted on their website, it's worth an inquiry directly to the theatre.
4. Include your contact information in a query letter, since some organizations prefer blind submissions with no identification on the script itself.

Finally, many thanks to the Assistant Editor, Jennifer Bushinger, as well as Seth Cotterman, Gary Garrison, Tari Stratton, Joey Stocks and Roland Tec for their invaluable contributions to this resource.

"What is not started today is never finished tomorrow." ~Johann Von Goethe

—Rebecca Stump, Editor

Bill of Rights

The Dramatists Guild is America's professional association of playwrights, librettists, lyricists and composers, with over 6,500 members around the world. The Guild is governed by our country's leading dramatists, with a fifty-five member Council that includes such dramatists as Edward Albee, Stephen Sondheim, John Patrick Shanley, Tony Kushner, Marsha Norman, Lynn Nottage, Emily Mann and Christopher Durang.

Long before playwrights or musical theatre writers join the Dramatists Guild, they often struggle professionally in small to medium-sized theatres throughout the country. It is essential, therefore, that dramatists know their rights, which the Dramatists Guild has defended for nearly one hundred years. In order to protect the dramatist's unique vision, which has always been the strength of the theatre, s/he needs to understand this fundamental principle: dramatists own and control their work.

The Guild recommends that any production involving a dramatist incorporate a written agreement in which both theatres/producers and writers acknowledge certain key rights with each other.

In Process and Production

1. ARTISTIC INTEGRITY. No one (e.g., directors, actors, dramaturgs) can make changes, alterations, and/or omissions to your script — including the text, title, and stage directions — without your consent. This is called "script approval."

2. APPROVAL OF PRODUCTION ELEMENTS. You have the right to approve the cast, director, and designers (and, for a musical, the choreographer, orchestrator, arranger, and musical director, as well), including their replacements. This is called "artistic approval."

3. RIGHT TO BE PRESENT. You always have the right to attend casting, rehearsals, previews and performances.

Compensations

4. ROYALTIES. You are generally entitled to receive a royalty. While it is possible that the amount an author receives may be minimal for a small- to medium-sized production, some compensation should always be paid if any other artistic collaborator in the production is being paid, or if any admission is being charged. If you are a member of the Guild, you can always call our business office to discuss the standard industry royalties for various levels of production.

5. BILLING CREDIT. You should receive billing (typographical credit) on all publicity, programs, and advertising distributed or authorized by the theatre. Billing is part of your compensation and the failure to provide it properly is a breach of your rights.

Ownership

6. OWNERSHIP OF INTELLECTUAL PROPERTY. You own the copyright of your dramatic work. Authors in the theatre business do not assign (i.e., give away or sell in entirety) their copyrights, nor do they ever engage in "work-for-hire." When a university, producer or theatre wants to mount a production of your play, you actually license (or lease) the public performance rights to your dramatic property to that entity for a finite period of time.

7. OWNERSHIP OF INCIDENTAL CONTRIBUTIONS. You own all approved revisions, suggestions, and contributions to the script made by other collaborators in the production, including actors, directors, and dramaturgs. You do not owe anyone any money for these contributions.

   If a theatre uses dramaturgs, you are not obligated to make use of any ideas the dramaturg might have. Even when the input of a dramaturg or director is helpful to the playwright, dramaturgs and directors are still employees of the theatre, not the author, and they are paid for their work by the theatre/producer. It has been well-established in case law, beginning with "the Rent Case" (Thompson v. Larson) that neither dramaturgs nor directors (nor any other contributors) may be considered a co-author of a play, unless (i) they've collaborated with you from the play's inception, (ii) they've made a copyrightable contribution to the play, and (iii) you have agreed in writing that they are a co-author.

8. SUBSIDIARY RIGHTS. After a small- or medium-sized production, you not only own your script, but also the rights to market and sell it to all different media (e.g., television, radio, film, internet) in any commercial market in the world. You are not obligated to sign over any portion of your project's future revenues to any third party (fellow artist, advisor, director, producer) as a result of a production, unless that production is a professional (i.e., Actor's Equity) premiere production (including sets, costumes and lighting), of no less than 21 consecutive paid public performances for which the author has received appropriate billing, compensation, and artistic approvals.

9. FUTURE OPTIONS. Rather than granting the theatre the right to share in future proceeds, you may choose to grant a non-exclusive option to present another production of your work within six months or one year of the close of the initial production. No option should be assignable without your prior written consent.

10. AUTHOR'S CONTRACT: The only way to ensure that you get the benefit of the rights listed above is through a written contract with the producer, no matter how large or small the entity. The Guild's Department of Business Affairs offers a model "production contract" and is available to review any contracts offered to you, and advise as to how those contracts compare to industry standards.

We realize that making demands of a small- to medium-sized theatres is a difficult task. However, you should feel confident in presenting this Bill of Rights to the Artistic Director, Producer, Literary Manager, or university administrator as a starting point for discussion. At the very least, any professional in the dramatic arts should realize that it is important for writers to understand the nature of their work — not just the artistic aspects, but the business side, as well — and that they stand together as a community, for their mutual benefit and survival, and for the survival of theatre as a viable art form in the 21st century.

Suggested Formatting for Plays and Musicals

Included in this document are suggested formats for plays and musicals drawn from suggestions of distinguished dramatists, literary managers, teachers of dramatic writing, producers, professional theatres and publishers. It is the Guild's belief that these formats present a standard that will work for most professional opportunities. A few additional elements to consider:

1. Formatting works towards two purposes: easy reading and the ability to approximate the performance time of the written story. For plays, we've given you a traditional and a more modern format to choose from. Admittedly, not all stories or styles of writing will work within a standard format. Therefore, use your better judgment in deciding the architecture of the page.

2. There is an industry standard (though some may say old-fashioned) of using the 12-point Courier-New font; we've also noted that Times New Roman is used in more modern formatting. With the proliferation of computers and word-processing programs, there are literally hundreds of fonts to choose from. Whatever your choice, we recommend that you maintain a font size of 12 points—thereby assuring some reliable approximation of performance time.

3. Though you wrote the story, someone has to read it before anyone sees it. Therefore, make your manuscript easy to read by employing a standard format with clearly delineated page numbers, scene citations and act citations. Headers and footers are optional.

4. If you're using a software program, such as Final Draft, to format your work, be aware that you have the ability to create your own format in these programs that can be uniquely named, saved and applied to all of your manuscripts.

5. Usually, between the title page and the first page of the story and/or dialogue, there is a page devoted to a character break-down. What's important to note on this page is the age, gender and name of each character. Some dramatists write brief character descriptions beside each name.

6. While it is cost-effective for both xeroxing and mailing, realize that some institutions prefer that you don't send double-sided documents. We recommend that you inquire about preference.

7. There is no right or wrong way to signify the end of a scene or act. Some writers do nothing but end the scene; others write "black out", "lights fade down", "End Act 1" or some other signifier that the scene or act has concluded.

8. The binding margin should be 1.5 inches from the edge. All other margins (top, bottom, right) should be 1.0 inch from the edge.

Sample Title Page

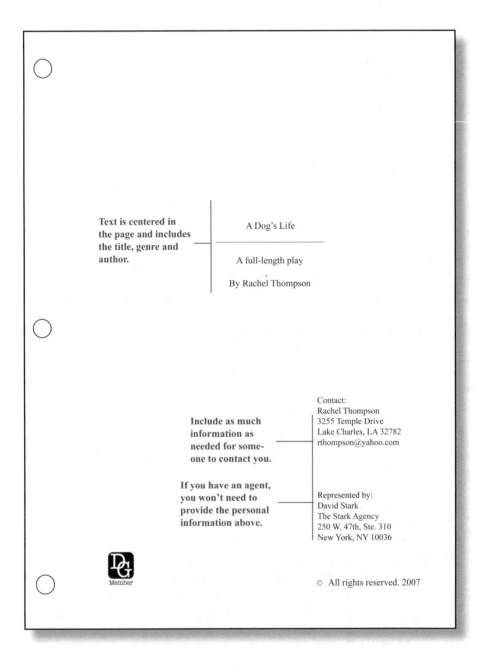

Text is centered in the page and includes the title, genre and author.

A Dog's Life

A full-length play

By Rachel Thompson

Include as much information as needed for someone to contact you.

Contact:
Rachel Thompson
3255 Temple Drive
Lake Charles, LA 32782
rthompson@yahoo.com

If you have an agent, you won't need to provide the personal information above.

Represented by:
David Stark
The Stark Agency
250 W. 47th, Ste. 310
New York, NY 10036

Member

Modern Play Format

From Tennessee Williams' *Not About Nightingales*

Essential page numbering
16.

Dialogue begins 1.5 inches from left side to account for binding. Dialogue is single-spaced.

BOSS

You've probably come here to question me about that ex-convicts story in that damned yellow sheet down there in Wilkes county – That stuff about getting Pellagra in here – Jimmy, hand me that sample menu!

JIM

She's not a reporter.

Character name in all caps; in the center of the page.

BOSS

Aw. – What is your business, young lady?

EVA

I understand there's a vacancy here. Mr. McBurney, my landlady's brother-in-law, told her that you were needing a new stenographer and I'm sure that I can qualify for the position. I'm a college graduate, Mr. Whalen, I've had three years of business experience – references with me – but, oh – I've – I've had such abominable luck these last six months. – the last place I worked – the business recession set in they had to cut down on their sales-force – they gave me a wonderful letter – I've got in with me.

Dialogue extends to 1.0 inch from right margin

She opens her purse and spills contents on floor.

BOSS

Anybody outside?

EVA

Yes. That woman.

BOSS

What woman?

EVA

The one from Wisconsin. She's still waiting –

BOSS

I told you I don't want to see her.

(talking into phone)

How's the track, Bert? Fast? Okay.

Stage action begins in the center of the page and scans to the right margin. A blank line is inserted before and after.

Standard font for this formatting is 12.0 point, New Times Roman.

Stage action reliant on the proceeding dialogue is indented to the left of the character name.

Sailor Jack's mother, MRS. BRISTOL, has quietly entered. She carries a blanket.

MRS. BRISTOL

I beg your pardon, I – You see I'm Jack Bristol's mother, and I've been wanting to have a talk with you so long about – about my boy!

Musical Format

From *APPLAUSE*, Book by Betty Comden, Adolph Green.
Music by Charles Strouse, Lyrics by Lee Adams

Essential page numbering**

56.

KAREN
(to Margo)
Margo, you've been kicking us all around long enough. Someone ought to give *you* a good swift one for a change!

(She leaves.)

EVE
Miss Channing . . . if I ever dreamed that anything I did could possibly cause you any unhappiness, or come between you and your friends . . . please believe me.

MARGO
(in a low, weary voice)
Oh, I do. And I'm full of admiration for you.
(stands, approaches Eve)
If you can handle yourself on the stage with the same artistry you display off the stage . . . well, my dear, you are in the right place.

(She speaks the following lines as the music
of WELCOME TO THE THEATRE begins.)

Welcome to the theater, to the magic, to the fun!

(She sings.)

WHERE PAINTED TREES AND FLOWERS GROW
AND LAUGHTER RINGS FORTISSIMO,
AND TREACHERY'S SWEETLY DONE!

NOW YOU'VE ENTERED THE ASYLUM,
THIS PROFESSION UNIQUE
ACTORS ARE CHILDREN
PLAYING HIDE-AND-EGO-SEEK . . .

SO WELCOME, MISS EVE HARRINGTON,
TO THIS BUSINESS WE CALL SHOW,
YOU'RE ON YOUR WAY
TO WEALTH AND FAME,
UNSHEATH YOUR CLAWS,
ENJOY THE GAME!
YOU'LL BE A BITCH
BUT THEY'LL KNOW YOUR NAME
FROM NEW YORK . . . TO KOKOMO

WELCOME TO THEATRE,
MY DEAR, YOU'LL LOVE IT SO!

Annotations (left margin):

Dialogue begins 1.5 inches from left side to account for binding. Dialogue is single-spaced.

Character name in all caps; in the center of the page.

Stanzas are separated by a blank line and distinguish themselves by dramatic thought and/or changes from verse to chorus to bridges, etc.

Annotations (right margin):

Stage action is indented 3 inches from left; put in parentheses. A blank line is inserted before and after.

Dialogue extends to 1.0 inch from right margin

Stage action reliant on the proceeding dialogue is indented to the left of the character name.

Lyric are in all CAPS, separated line to line by either musical phrasing and/or the rhyming scheme and clearly indented from the left margin.

For duets, or characters singing counter-point, create two columns side by side, following the same format here.

**There are many ways to paginate your play, from the straight forward numerical sequence of 1, 2, 3 to an older format of 1-2-16, (meaning Act 1, Scene 2, Page 16).

Sample Letter of Inquiry

Though there is no right or wrong way to write a letter of introduction to your work, realize an effective submission letter should be short, professional and with just enough information so the reader knows you've submitted exactly what was called for in the solicitation. And while it's tempting to entice the reader to want to read the script with an overly expressive narrative in your submission letter, consider that this is the first exposure to your writing (of any kind) that will be read by someone in the producing organization . Be mindful, then, how you represent yourself on paper, and allow your play or musical to speak for itself.

A common question is often asked when writers construct a production resume: what do you do if you don't have a lot of readings or productions to list on your resume? Whatever you do, don't misrepresent yourself; don't say you've had a reading or a production of a play at a theatre that you haven't had. You'll eventually be found out and look worse than someone who has a thin resume. If you don't have a lot of production experience with your writing, write a brief synopsis of each of the plays you've written, cite any classes or workshops you've taken as a playwright and detail any other experience you have in the theatre (as stage manager, director, actress, dramaturg, etc.). People are more likely to be sympathetic to you being young in the theatre than they are to you being someone who misrepresents themselves.

A more accomplished playwright's resume should list the productions or readings of plays (by theatre and date), awards, grants, writers colonies attended, workshops, festivals invited to and any special recognition received as a writer. Give the reader a sense of the whole of your writing career, including memberships in theatre groups, professional organizations and related writing work. Include your address and phone number at the top or bottom of your resume, cover sheet of your play and obviously on the return envelope. Again, there are any number of variations on how to construct a writer's resume, but a template to inspire your thinking can be found on the following page.

Sample Letter of Inquiry

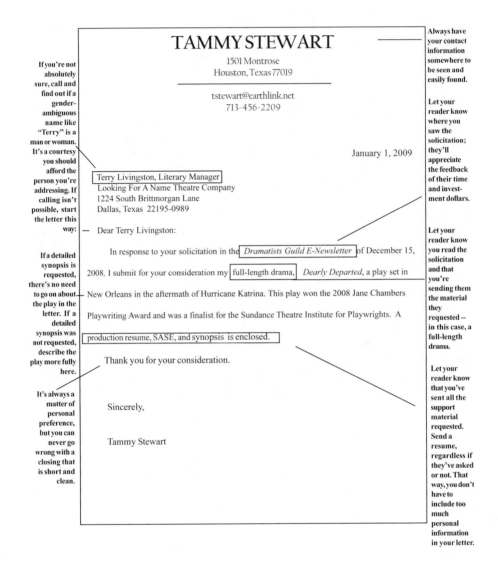

Always have your contact information somewhere to be seen and easily found.

If you're not absolutely sure, call and find out if a gender-ambiguous name like "Terry" is a man or woman. It's a courtesy you should afford the person you're addressing. If calling isn't possible, start the letter this way:

TAMMY STEWART

1501 Montrose
Houston, Texas 77019

tstewart@earthlink.net
713-456-2209

January 1, 2009

Terry Livingston, Literary Manager
Looking For A Name Theatre Company
1224 South Brittmorgan Lane
Dallas, Texas 22195-0989

Dear Terry Livingston:

In response to your solicitation in the *Dramatists Guild E-Newsletter* of December 15, 2008, I submit for your consideration my full-length drama, *Dearly Departed*, a play set in New Orleans in the aftermath of Hurricane Katrina. This play won the 2008 Jane Chambers Playwriting Award and was a finalist for the Sundance Theatre Institute for Playwrights. A production resume, SASE, and synopsis is enclosed.

Thank you for your consideration.

Sincerely,

Tammy Stewart

Let your reader know where you saw the solicitation; they'll appreciate the feedback of their time and investment dollars.

Let your reader know you read the solicitation and that you're sending them the material they requested -- in this case, a full-length drama.

Let your reader know that you've sent all the support material requested. Send a resume, regardless if they've asked or not. That way, you don't have to include too much personal information in your letter.

If a detailed synopsis is requested, there's no need to go on about the play in the letter. If a detailed synopsis was not requested, describe the play more fully here.

It's always a matter of personal preference, but you can never go wrong with a closing that is short and clean.

The DG Statement on Submission Fees

The Dramatists Guild of America denounces the practice by festivals, play contests and educational events of charging excessive fees to dramatists who submit their work. Any request for submission fees should be accompanied by a complete explanation of how those fees are to be spent. The Guild also insists that contests and festivals announce the names of all finalists and winners to all participants.

It is important that members understand that submission fees are not the norm and, when required, the festival should offer something significant in return for the writer's investment, such as a large cash prize, a residency or a production. Reading fees are in no case acceptable, as most festivals receive that money from other grant sources. In no case should playwrights have to pay to simply have their work read.

The Guild also strongly disapproves of a festival's placing any encumbrances on the work as a result of the play being chosen a finalist or a participant. Any future participation in the life of the play must be earned by the festival by producing the work, and should never be granted by the writer without consultation with the Guild. If the festival expects any subsidiary income from the plays, that information should be stated clearly in all of the organization's printed and electronic materials related to the event.

The Council of the Guild feels that its members should be made aware of all legitimate opportunities available to them, and so we have listed in this section those particular contests and festivals that charge fees and have provided explanations regarding how their submission fees are spent, as well as full disclosure of any encumbrances they place on a selected writer's work, when offered by the sponsor.

Agency, from the desk of Gary Garrison

This article originally appeared in the Dramatists Guild e-newsletter on April 18, 2008

On the average, I get three to four phone calls or emails a day that go something like this: "I need an agent. I know everyone needs an agent, but I *really need* an agent. Why can't the Guild help get me an agent or a director or anyone who can help promote my work? And why can't the Guild get more theatres to respond to playwrights and new plays? We need more opportunities!" Look, I just want to get square with you once and for all: we are a member-service and advocacy organization. And while I don't want to downplay the importance for some of you to be professionally represented by an agent (or your work placed in a theatre), it is not one of the mandates of this organization to help you secure representation or production.

It doesn't matter what anyone has to say about writers and agents, the truth is having an agent is perceived — right or wrong — as a benchmark of success that comes with certain positive opportunities and a healthy amount of validation. The desire in most of us, then, is never likely to go away. But if you really want to pursue the agent thing, I want you to take a good, honest look at simple facts and figures to help you make sense of what's ahead of you.

- The numbers: talking to my colleagues here at the Guild, and then making a few phone calls around town to some very respectable agents, to our best estimation there are approximately thirty-five agents dedicated to promoting dramatic writing for the theatre. That's thirty-five agents *total* — throughout the whole country — that represent every playwright you know by name, and then the many hundreds you don't know (yet). The simple numbers alone show the odds are against most of us having an agent.

- Most agents that I've spoken with are rarely interested in representing a single piece of work and are far more interested in representing (and helping you grow) a body of work. To approach an agent to represent a single play or musical is not likely to get you anywhere. Agents, like all theatre business people, are as interested in the present as they are the future.

- Twenty years ago, maybe even ten years ago, a hit production of a play or a musical and a good New York Times review (or any major newspaper review) would almost ensure that you'd have an agency knocking at your door. That's not true any longer; there's a glut of material and writers out there that remain unrepresented. Theatre, like most arms of the entertainment industry, is ageist.

Jeeeeeez, Gary, did you have to be so...honest? In a word, yes, because so many of us are singularly obsessed about getting an agent. Are there exceptions to any of the points above? Of course there are exceptions; that's what makes this life interesting. Can you have a productive, successful career in the theatre without professional representation? You bet, and a heck of a lot of people do.

Please understand that we provide a list of working literary agents as a convenience for you — nothing more. By listing these agents (which is not a comprehensive list), we do not intend to suggest that they are seeking new clients or that we are particularly endorsing them as agents. Unless indicated otherwise, send a query and synopsis to one agent at a time.

Career Development Professionals

WE'RE LOOKING FOR SOMETHING A LITTLE LESS YOU.

Accountants

Kimerling and Wisdom
Ross Wisdom, Managing Partner
150 Broadway, Room 1105
New York, NY 10038
Phone: (212) 986-0892
rwisdom@kwllc.us
www.kwllc.us
Notes: Est. 1970.
Submission Fee: No
Agent Only: No

Marks Paneth & Shron LLP
Mark A. D'AmbrosiPartner
685 3rd Ave.
New York, NY 10017
Phone: (415) 430-1140
Fax: (415) 430-1145
dale@theatrebayarea.org
www.markspaneth.com
Notes: Est. 1907. Nationally ranked, full-service public accounting firm for individuals and companies in the entertainment industry.
Submission Fee: No
Agent Only: No

Agents

Abrams Artists Agency
275 Seventh Avenue, 26th fl.
New York, NY 10001
Phone: (646) 486-4600
Fax: (646) 486-0100
mgrossman@abramsartny.com
www.abramsartists.com/literary.html
Notes: Agents: Sarah L. Douglas (Department Co-Head), Charles Kopelman (Department Co-Head), Beth Blickers, Max Grossman, Ron Gwiazda, Leah Hamos, Steve Ross, Amy Wagner. Professional recommendation required.
Submission Materials: professional referral only
Submission Fee: No
Agent Only: No

Barbara Hogenson Agency, Inc.
165 West End Avenue #19C
New York, NY 10023
Phone: (212) 874-8084
Fax: (212) 595-6748
Bhogenson@aol.com
Notes: Est. 1994. Response time: 2 months.
Preferred Genre: All genres
Preferred Length: Full-length
Submission Materials: professional referral only
Submission Fee: No
Agent Only: No

Bret Adams Agency
448 W. 44th Street
New York, NY 10036

Phone: (212) 765-5630
morsini@bretadamsltd.net
www.bretadamsltd.net
Notes: Est. 1953. Staff: Bruce Ostler, Mark Orsini; Alexis Williams; Colin Hunt (Literary); Margi Rountree, Ken Melamed (Acting). Query must include professional recommendation.
Preferred Genre: All genres
Submission Materials: query letter
Submission Fee: No
Agent Only: No

Farber Literary Agency Inc.
Ann Farber, President
14 East 75th Street
New York, NY 10021
Phone: (212) 861-7075
Fax: (212) 861-7076
farberlit@aol.com
Notes: Est.1990. Response: 1 month.
Preferred Genre: All genres
Preferred Length: Any length
Submission Materials: full script, query letter, S.A.S.E., synopsis
Submission Fee: No
Agent Only: No

Fifi Oscard Agency, Inc.
110 West 40 Street
Suite 2100
New York, NY 10018
Phone: (212) 764-1100
Fax: (212) 840-5019
agency@fifioscard.com

www.fifioscard.com
Notes: Est. 1956.
Preferred Genre: All genres
Preferred Length: Any length
Submission Materials: see website
Submission Fee: No
Agent Only: No

Gage Group Inc.
14724 Ventura Blvd
Sherman Oaks, CA 91403
Phone: (818) 905-3800
Fax: (310) 859-8166
gagegroupla@gmail.com
Notes: Est. 1975. Submissions not returned.
Response: 3 months.
Submission Materials: professional referral
only
Submission Fee: No
Agent Only: No

Gersh Agency (NY)
Kate Navin, Theater Department
41 Madison Ave
33rd Floor
New York, NY 10010
Phone: (212) 634-8169
Fax: (212) 391-8459
knavin@gershny.com
Notes: Must be submitted through
professional recommendation.
Submission Fee: No
Agent Only: No

Harden Curtis Associates
214 W. 29th Street, Suite 1203
New York, NY 10001
Phone: (212) 977-8502
Fax: (212) 975-8420
maryharden@hardencurtis.com
www.hardencurtis.com
Notes: Est. 1995. Response: 2 mos.
Preferred Genre: All genres
Preferred Length: Any length
Submission Materials: professional referral
only
Submission Fee: No
Agent Only: No

International Creative Management (ICM)
[CA]
10250 Constellation Blvd.
Los Angeles, CA 90067
Phone: (310) 550-4000
books@icmtalent.com

www.icmtalent.com/
Notes: Talent & literary agency.
Preferred Genre: All genres
Preferred Length: Any length
Submission Materials: see website
Submission Fee: No
Agent Only: No

International Creative Management (ICM)
[NY]
825 8th Ave.
New York, NY 10019
Phone: (212) 556-5600
Fax: (212) 556-5665
books@icmtalent.com
www.icmtalent.com/
Notes: Talent & literary agency.
Preferred Genre: All genres
Preferred Length: Any length
Submission Materials: see website
Submission Fee: No
Agent Only: No

International Creative Management (ICM)
[UK]
4-6 Soho Sq.
London W1D 3PZ United Kingdom
Phone: (442) 074-3208 Ext 00
books@icmtalent.com
www.icmtalent.com/
Notes: Talent & literary agency.
Preferred Genre: All genres
Preferred Length: Any length
Submission Materials: see website
Submission Fee: No
Agent Only: No

Judy Boals Inc.
307 W. 38th St., #812
New York, NY 10018
Phone: (212) 500-1424
Fax: (212) 500-1426
info@judyboals.com
www.judyboals.com
Notes: Submit via personal recommendation.
Response : 1 month.
Submission Materials: query letter, S.A.S.E.
Submission Fee: No
Agent Only: No

Kerin-Goldberg Associates
155 E. 55th St., #5-D
New York, NY 10022
Phone: (212) 838-7373
Fax: (212) 838-0774

kgatalent@nyc.rr.com
Notes: Est. 1989. Staff: Ron Ross, Ellison
Goldberg, Chris Nichols.
Agent Only: No

Paradigm (NY)
360 Park Ave. South
16th Floor
New York, NY 10010
Phone: (212) 897-6400
Fax: (212) 575-6397
jtantleffasst@paradigmagency.com
www.paradigmagency.com
Notes: Agents: William Craver, Lucy Stille,
Jack Tantleff. Response: 6 months. We do not
accept unsolicited submissions.
Submission Materials: query letter, S.A.S.E.
Submission Fee: No
Agent Only: Yes

Peregrine Whittlesey Agency
Peregrine Whittlesey, Agent
279 Central Park West
New York, NY 10024
Phone: (212) 787-1802
Fax: (212) 787-4985
pwwagy@aol.com
Submission Materials: query letter, S.A.S.E.
Submission Fee: No
Agent Only: No

**Robert A. Freedman Dramatic Agency,
Inc.**
1501 Broadway, suite #2310
New York, NY 10036
Phone: (212) 840-5760
Fax: (212) 840-5776
RFreedmanAgent@aol.com
Notes: Est. 1928. Response: 4 months.
Agents: Robert Freedman, Selma Luttinger,
Marta Praeger.
Preferred Length: Full-length
Submission Materials: query letter, S.A.S.E.
Submission Fee: No
Agent Only: Yes

Soiree Fair Inc.
Karen Gunn, President
133 Midland Ave., #10
Montclair, NJ 07042
Phone: (973) 783-9051
Fax: (973) 746-0426
Soireefair@yahoo.com
www.soireefair.com

Notes: Est. 1995. Material must be
unoptioned, unpublished, unproduced and be
submitted with professional recommendation.
Preferred Genre: Plays or Musicals
Special Interest: LGBT
Preferred Length: Full-length
Submission Materials: query letter, synopsis
Submission Fee: No
Agent Only: No

Susan Schulman, A Literary Agency
Susan F. Schulman, Agent
454 W. 44th St.
New York, NY 10036
Phone: (212) 713-1633
Fax: (212) 581-8830
schulman@aol.com
Preferred Genre: All genres
Special Interest: Theatre for Young
Audiences
Preferred Length: Full-length
Submission Materials: see website
Submission Fee: No
Agent Only: No

The Marton Agency, Inc.
1 Union Square West
#815
New York, NY 10003
Phone: (212) 255-1908
Fax: (212) 691-9061
info@martonagency.com
Notes: Specializes in brokering foreign-
language rights to US theater works.
Promotes plays to associates abroad,
generally after a production has been
mounted in the US.
Submission Fee: No
Agent Only: No

The Shukat Company Ltd.
340 W. 55th St., #1A
New York, NY 10019
Phone: (212) 582-7614
Fax: (212) 315-3752
staff@shukat.com
Preferred Genre: All genres
Preferred Length: Full-length
Submission Materials: 10-pg sample, query
letter, S.A.S.E.
Submission Fee: No
Agent Only: No

William Morris Endeavor (NY)
1325 Avenue of the Americas
New York, NY 10019
Phone: (212) 586-5100
jbz@wmeentertainment.com
Notes: Staff: John Buzzetti, David Kalodner, Derek Zasky, Susan Weaving, Jonathan Lomma, Scott Chaloff.
Submission Materials: professional referral only
Submission Fee: No
Agent Only: No

Writers & Artists Agency [CA]
8383 Wilshire Blvd., #550
Beverly Hills, CA 90211
Phone: (212) 767-7800
Fax: (212) 582-1909
strell@sunshinesachs.com
Submission Fee: No
Agent Only: No

Attorneys

Daniel Aharoni & Partners LLP
Lauren DeBellis Aviv, Arts Immigration Attorney
575 Madison Ave
New York, NY 10022
Phone: (212) 605-0415
lauren@danielaharoni.com
Notes: Immigration for artists and entertainers.

Brooks & Distler
Marsha Brooks, Partner in Law Firm
110 E. 59th Street, 23rd fl.
New York, NY 10022
Phone: (212) 486-1400
Fax: (212) 486-2266
brookslaw@aol.com

Peter S. Cane, Esq.
230 Park Avenue
Suite 1000
New York, NY 10169
Phone: (212) 922-9800
Fax: (212) 922-9822
peter@canelaw.com

Case Arts Law LLC
53 West Jackson Blvd
Suite 209
Chicago, IL 60604
Phone: (312) 234-9926
Fax: (312) 962-4908
www.caseartslaw.com
Notes: A boutique law firm providing sophisticated representation to classical musicians, performers, and fine arts clients.

Cowan, DeBaets, Abrahams & Sheppard LLP
41 Madison Ave., Fl. 34
New York, NY 10010
Phone: (212) 974-7474
Fax: (212) 974-8474
fbimbler@cdas.com
www.cdas.com

Law Office of Gary N. DaSilva
Gary N. DaSilva, Esq,
111 N. Sepulveda Blvd., #250
Manhattan Beach, CA 90266
Phone: (310) 318-5665
Fax: (310) 318-2114
mail@garydasilva.com

Day & Koch LLP
Portland, OR
Phone: (503) 224-4900
info@dayandkoch.com
http://www.dayandkoch.com/
Notes: Day & Koch LLP represents creative companies, individuals, and entrepreneurs in business and corporate transactions, entertainment, and intellectual property law. Day & Koch is an "AV" rated law firm, the highest rating attainable in the Martindale-Hubbell Law Directory.

Drinker Biddle & Reath LLP
Janet Fries, Of Counsel
1500 K Street, MW
Suite 1100
Washington, DC 20005
Phone: (202) 842-8800

Law Offices of Gordon P. Firemark
Gordon P. Firemark, Attorney at Law
10940 Wilshire Blvd, 16th Floor
Los Angeles, CA 90024
Phone: (310) 243-6251
Fax: (310) 477-7676
gfiremark@firemark.com
www.firemark.com
Notes: Additional websites:
www.theatrelawyer.com and
www.theatreproduceracademy.com.

Fitelson, Lasky, Aslan, Couture and Garmise
551 5th Ave., #605
New York, NY 10176
Phone: (212) 586-4700
Fax: (212) 949-6746

Frankfurt, Kurnit, Klein and Selz
S. Jean Ward, Attorney
488 Madison Ave.
New York, NY 10022
Phone: (212) 980-0120
Fax: (212) 593-9175
sjward@fkks.com
www.fkks.com

Franklin, Weinrib, Rudell & Vassallo PC
Elliot H. Brown, Esq, Partner
488 Madison Ave.
New York, NY 10022
Phone: (212) 935-5500
Fax: (212) 308-0642
ehb@fwrv.com
www.fwrv.com
Notes: No submissions accepted from agents or anyone else.

David H. Friedlander, Esq.
David H. Friedlander
81 Park Dr.
Mount Kisco, NY 10549
Phone: (914) 241-1277
Fax: (914) 470-2244
david@dfriedlander.com
www.dfriedlander.com
Notes: Does not accept play submissions.

Law Offices of Jeffrey L. Graubart, P.C.
100 Corson Street, Third Floor
Pasadena, CA 91103
Phone: (626) 304-2800
Fax: (626) 304-2807
info@jlgraubart.com
www.entertainmentlaw.la
Notes: Est. 1970.

Roberta L. Korus, Attorney at Law
Roberta L. Korus, Attorny at Law
Three Emmalon Ave
North White Plains, NY 10603
Phone: (914) 269-8120
Fax: (914) 831-2174
robertakorus@gmail.com

Ronald A. Lachman
468 N. Camden Dr. #200
Beverly Hills, CA 90210
Phone: (323) 655-6020
ron@ronaldlachman.com

Leavens, Strand, Glover & Adler, LLC
Jerry W. Glover, Partner
203 North LaSalle Street
Suite 2550
Chicago, IL 60601
Phone: (312) 488-4173
jglover@lsglegal.com
www.lsglegal.com
Notes: An entertainment, media, & intellectual property law firm concentrating our practice on matters involving creative industries and endeavors. Our clients include content providers and creators, media companies, television and radio broadcasters, authors, songwriters, recording artists, musicians, advertisers and brands, television and film writers, independent record labels, distributors, independent film producers and documentarians, web site operators and developers, publishing companies, and film, television and music production companies.

Miller Korzenik Sommers LLP
Eric Rayman, Attorney
488 Madison Ave
New York, NY 10022
Phone: (212) 254-6531
Fax: (212) 228-5130
erayman@mkslex.com
www.mkslex.com

Paul, Weiss, Rifkind, Wharton & Garrison
Charles H. Googe, Chair of Entertainment
Deptartment
Att: C.Googe
1285 Avenue of the Americas
New York, NY 10019-6064
Phone: (212) 373-3345
cgooge@paulweiss.com
www.paulweiss.com

Robert S. Perlstein, Esq.
Robert S. Perlstein, Attorney
1501 Broadway
Suite 703
New York, NY 10036
Phone: (212) 832-9951
Fax: (212) 831-9906
rspesq@judgedee.net
Notes: Clients: major performers, conductors,
singers, actors, musicians (pop, classical,
etc.), arrangers, orchestrators, screenwriters,
television producers, authors, music
coordinators, models, and fashion industry
personnel, designers.

**Robinson, Brog, Leinwand, Greene,
Genovese & Gluck**
Richard M. Ticktin, Partner
875 Third Avenue
9th Floor
New York, NY 10022
Phone: (212) 603-6308
Fax: (212) 581-5981
rmt@robinsonbrog.com
www.robinsonbrog.com

Saper Law
Aaron Midler, Associate Attorney
505 North LaSalle
Suite 350
Chicago, IL 60654
Phone: (312) 527-4100
Fax: (312) 527-5020
amidler@saperlaw.com
saperlaw.com/blog
Notes: Saper Law is an intellectual property,
social media, and business law firm with
headline grabbing clients and cases.

Law Office of Susan J. Steiger, Esq.
Susan J. Steiger, Attorney
60 East 42nd Street, 47th floor
New York, NY 10165
Phone: (212) 880-0865
Fax: (212) 697-0877

Law Office of John J. Tormey III, Esq.
John J. Tormey, Attorney-at-Law
1324 Lexington Avenue, PMB 188
New York, NY 10128
Phone: (212) 410-4142
Fax: (212) 410-2380
brightline@att.net
www.tormey.org
Notes: Entertainment Transactional Legal
Work and General Law Practice.

Volunteer Lawyers for the Arts (VLA)
1 E. 53rd St., Fl. 6
New York, NY 10022
Phone: (212) 319-2787
Fax: (212) 752-6575
vlany@vlany.org
www.vlany.org
Notes: Est. 1969. Provider of pro bono legal
and mediation services, educational programs
and publications & advocacy to the arts
community in NYC. Fees: based on client's
finances.

Commercial Producers

Araca Group
545 W. 45th Street
10th floor
New York, NY 10036
Phone: (212) 869-0070
Fax: (212) 869-0210
creative@araca.com
www.araca.com
Notes: Est. 1997. Broadway/off Broadway
productions.
Preferred Genre: Plays or Musicals

Preferred Length: Full-length
Submission Materials: agent-only
Submission Fee: No
Agent Only: Yes

Boyett Ostar Productions
268 West 44th Street
4th Floor
New York, NY 10036
Phone: (212) 702-9779
Fax: (212) 702-0899

Submission Fee: No
Agent Only: No

Cameron Mackintosh Inc.
Shidan Majidi, Production Associate
1650 Broadway, #800
New York, NY 10019
Phone: (212) 921-9290
Fax: (212) 921-9271
smajidi@camack.com
www.cameronmackintosh.com
Notes: Mary Poppins, Les Miserables, The
Phantom of the Opera, Oliver!, Oklahoma!,
My Fair Lady, The Witches of Eastwick,
Miss Saigon, CATS.
Preferred Genre: Musical theatre
Preferred Length: Full-length
Submission Materials: agent-only
Submission Fee: No
Agent Only: Yes

Dodger Properties
311 W. 43rd St., #602
New York, NY 10036
Phone: (212) 575-9710
info@dodger.com
www.dodger.com
Notes: Est. 1978. Jersey Boys.
Preferred Genre: All genres
Preferred Length: Full-length
Submission Materials: agent-only
Submission Fee: No
Agent Only: Yes

Jane Harmon Associates
Jane Harmon
One Lincoln Plaza, Suite 28-0
20 West 64th Street
New York, NY 10023
Phone: (212) 362-6836
Fax: (212) 362-8572
harmonjane@aol.com
Notes: Est. 1979. Agent submissions,
industry recommended and unsolicited.
Submit via email or mail. Response: 2-4
weeks.
Preferred Genre: Plays (No Musicals)
Preferred Length: Full-length
Submission Materials: query letter, resume,
synopsis
Submission Fee: No
Agent Only: No

Margery Klain
Margery Klain, Producer
2107 Locust St.
Philadelphia, PA 19103
Phone: (212) 869-1112
Fax: (212) 730-0381
office@margolionltd.com
Notes: Est. 1985. Material must be
unoptioned. Response: 2 months.
Preferred Genre: Plays or Musicals
Preferred Length: Full-length
Submission Materials: professional referral
only
Submission Fee: No
Agent Only: Yes

Margo Lion Ltd.
246 W. 44th St., Fl. 8
New York, NY 10036
Phone: (415) 499-8350
Fax: (415) 499-8537
marinarts@marinarts.org
www.margolionltd.com
Notes: Email submissions preferred.
Response: 1 year.
Preferred Genre: All genres
Preferred Length: Full-length
Submission Materials: agent-only
Submission Fee: No
Agent Only: Yes

Nederlander Organization
1450 Broadway, Fl. 6
New York, NY 10018
Phone: (212) 840-5577
Fax: (212) 840-3326
kraitt@nederlander.com
www.nederlander.com
Notes: Est. 1912.
Preferred Genre: All genres
Preferred Length: Full-length
Submission Materials: agent-only
Submission Fee: No
Agent Only: Yes

Shubert Organization
D.S. Moynihan, VP, Creaive Projects
234 W. 44th St.
New York, NY 10036
Phone: (212) 944-3700
vincer@shubertticketing.org
www.shubertorg.com
Notes: Est. 1900.
Preferred Genre: All genres
Preferred Length: Full-length

Submission Materials: agent-only
Submission Fee: No
Agent Only: Yes

Stephen Pevner, Inc.
Stephen Pevner, Producer
382 Lafayette St., Fl. 8
New York, NY 10003
Phone: (212) 674-8403
spidevelopment@gmail.com
Agent Only: No

Vienna Waits Productions
John Breglio, Esq, Producer
1285 Avenue of the Americas
32nd Floor
New York, NY 10019
Phone: (917) 584-8341
jbreglio@paulweiss.com
Submission Fee: No
Agent Only: No

Publishers

Anchorage Press Plays Inc.
617 Baxter Ave.
Louisville, KY 40204-1105
Phone: (502) 583-2288
Fax: (502) 583-2288
applays@bellsouth.net
www.applays.com
Notes: Est. 1935. Educational, professional
and amateur venues. Response Time: 6 -9
months.
Preferred Genre: All genres
Special Interest: Theatre for Young
Audiences
Preferred Length: Any length
Submission Materials: see website
Submission Fee: No
Agent Only: No

Asian Theatre Journal
2840 Kolowalu St.
Honolulu, HI 96822
Phone: (888) 847-7377
Fax: (800) 650-7811
uhpjourn@hawaii.edu
www.uhpress.hawaii.edu/journals
Notes: Dedicated to performing arts of Asia,
traditional and modern, including original
and translated plays.
Special Interest: Asian-American
Submission Materials: query letter
Submission Fee: No
Agent Only: No

Big Dog Publishing
Dawn Remsing, Editor, Publisher
P.O. Box 1401
Rapid City, SD 57709
Fax: (605) 791-0186
info@bigdogplays.com
www.bigdogplays.com

Notes: Est. 2005. Plays for family and school
audiences (K-12). Publishes 25-40 plays/year.
Response time: 2-3 months. Prefer
produced/award-winning work. No email
submissions please.
Preferred Genre: Plays or Musicals
Preferred Length: Any length
Submission Materials: see website
Submission Fee: No
Agent Only: No

Broadway Play Publishing Inc. (BPPI)
56 East 81 Street
New York, NY 10028-0202
sara@broadwayplaypubl.com
www.broadwayplaypubl.com
Notes: Est. 1982. Response time: 2 months
query, 4 months script.
Preferred Genre: All genres
Preferred Length: Any length
Submission Materials: query letter
Submission Fee: No
Agent Only: No

Callaloo
4212 TAMU
Texas A&M University
College Station, TX 77843
Phone: (979) 458-3108
Fax: (979) 458-3275
callaloo@tamu.edu
http://callaloo.tamu.edu
Notes: Quarterly journal devoted to creative
work by and critical studies of the work of
African-Americans and peoples of African
descent throughout the African Diaspora.
Response time: 6 months.
Preferred Genre: All genres
Special Interest: African-American
Preferred Length: Any length

Submission Materials: full script (3 copies), query letter, S.A.S.E.
Submission Fee: No
Agent Only: No

Capilano Review TCR
2055 Purcell Way
N. Vancouver, BC V7J 3H5 Canada
Phone: (604) 984-1712
Fax: (604) 990-7837
contact@thecapilanoreview.ca
www.thecapilanoreview.ca
Notes: Est. 1972. Unpublished poetry, drama, visual arts. Response time: 4 months. Please use Canadian postage for SASE.
Preferred Genre: Verse
Preferred Length: Any length
Submission Materials: see website
Submission Fee: No
Agent Only: No

Confrontation
Joana Semeiks, Editor
CW Post Campus English Dept.
Brookville, NY 11548
Phone: (516) 299-2720
Fax: (516) 299-2735
mtucker@liu.edu
www.cwpost.liu.edu/cwis/cwp/culture
Notes: Material submitted must be unpublished.
Preferred Genre: Plays (No Musicals)
Preferred Length: 10-min./10pgs.
Submission Materials: full script, S.A.S.E.
Submission Fee: No
Agent Only: No

Currency Press
Deborah Franco, Acting Publisher
PO Box 2287
Strawberry Hills 02012 Australia
Phone: (029) 319-5877
Fax: (029) 319-3649
proposals@currency.com.au
www.currency.com.au
Notes: Publisher/distributor of performing arts books on Australian drama, film, music (including play and film scripts) in Australia & New Zealand.
Preferred Genre: Plays (No Musicals)
Preferred Length: Full-length
Submission Materials: full script, S.A.S.E.
Submission Fee: No
Agent Only: No

Dramatic Publishing Company
Linda Habjan, Submissions Editor
311 Washington St.
Woodstock, IL 60098
Phone: (800) 448-7469
Fax: (800) 334-5302
plays@dramaticpublishing.com
www.dramaticpublishing.com/
Notes: Est. 1885. Response: 8 months.
Preferred Genre: All genres
Preferred Length: Any length
Submission Materials: full script, S.A.S.E.
Submission Fee: No
Agent Only: No

Dramatics Magazine
Don Corathers, Editor
2343 Auburn Ave.
Cincinnati, OH 45219
Phone: (513) 421-3900
Fax: (513) 421-7077
dcorathers@schooltheatre.org
schooltheatre.org
Notes: Est. 1929. National monthly magazine for High School theater students & teachers, printing 7 one-acts and full-lengths/year. Response: 5 months. Buys one-time, non-exclusive publication rights only.
Preferred Genre: Plays (No Musicals)
Preferred Length: Any length
Submission Materials: full script
Submission Fee: No
Agent Only: No

Dramatists Play Service, Inc.
Attn: Michael Fellmeth
440 Park Avenue South
New York, NY 10016
Phone: (212) 683-8960
fellmeth@dramatists.com
www.dramatists.com
Notes: Performances licensed. All venues except commercial. Response: 6 months.
Preferred Genre: Plays or Musicals
Preferred Length: Full-length
Submission Materials: query letter, synopsis
Submission Fee: No
Agent Only: No

Eldridge Publishing Company Inc.
Nancy S. Vorhis, Senior Editor
Box 14367
Tallahassee, FL 32317
Phone: (850) 385-2463
Fax: (850) 385-2463

info@95church.com
www.histage.com
Notes: Est. 1906. Performances licensed, all venues. Material for non-denominational religious market. Email work to newworks@95church.com. Response, 2 months.
Preferred Genre: Plays or Musicals
Special Interest: Theatre for Young Audiences
Preferred Length: Any length
Submission Materials: audio CD, full script, query letter, S.A.S.E.
Submission Fee: No
Agent Only: No

Empire Publishing Service
Joseph W. Witt
Box 1344
Studio City, CA 91614
Phone: (818) 784-8918
empirepubsvc@att.net
Notes: Est. 1960. Publishes performing arts books, including sheet music. Plays must have been produced. No email submissions please. Response: from 3 days to 1 year.
Preferred Genre: All genres
Preferred Length: Any length
Submission Materials: query letter, S.A.S.E.
Submission Fee: No
Agent Only: No

Meriwether Publishing Ltd./Contemporary Drama Service
Mark Zapel, President
885 Elkton Drive
Colorado Springs, CO 80907
Phone: (719) 594-4422
Fax: (719) 594-9916
editor@meriwether.com
www.contemporarydrama.com
Notes: Theatre arts books written by drama educators and professionals, plus DVDs, CDs and videos for classroom use. Submit by US mail.
Preferred Genre: Plays or Musicals
Preferred Length: Any length
Submission Materials: see website
Submission Fee: No
Agent Only: No

Moose Hide Books
Richard Mousseau, Publisher
684 Walls Rd.
Sault Ste. Marie, ON P6A-5K6 Canada

Phone: (705) 779-3331
Fax: (707) 779-3331
rmousseau@moosehidebooks.com
www.moosehidebooks.com
Notes: Response: 1 month.
Submission Materials: query letter, S.A.S.E.
Submission Fee: No
Agent Only: No

Music Theatre International (MTI)
421 W. 54th St.
New York, NY 10019
Phone: (212) 541-4684
Fax: (212) 397-4684
www.mtishows.com
Notes: Est. 1952. Performances licensed, all venues. MTI is a secondary licensing agency and prefers musicals that have been produced.
Preferred Genre: Musical theatre

NewMusicals.com
R. J. Chiarappa, Submissions Editor
22 Grenhart Street
West Hartford, CT 06117
Phone: (860) 236-0592
Fax: (860) 236-5762
info@newmusicals.com
www.newmusicals.com
Notes: Please Note: We are not accepting any submissions at this time. Please check our website for updates.
Preferred Genre: Musical theatre
Preferred Length: Full-length
Submission Materials: see website
Submission Fee: No
Agent Only: No

Norman Maine Publishing
Dawn Remsing, Editor, Publishing
P.O. Box 1401
Rapid City, SD 57709
Fax: (605) 791-0186
info@normanmaineplays.com
www.normanmaineplays.com
Notes: Est. 2005. Plays for community, professional and university theatre. Response: 2-3 months. Prefer produced/award-winning work. No email submissions please.
Preferred Genre: Plays or Musicals
Preferred Length: Any length
Submission Materials: see website
Submission Fee: No
Agent Only: No

Original Works Publishing
Jason Aaron Goldberg, President
1637 N. Las Palmas Ave
Los Angeles, CA 90028
info@originalworksonline.com
www.originalworksonline.com
Notes: Est. 2000. Submitted material must
have been produced. Response: 3-6 months.
Preferred Genre: Plays (No Musicals)
Preferred Length: Any length
Submission Materials: see website
Submission Fee: No
Agent Only: No

PAJ: A Journal of Performance and Art
Bonnie Marranca, Editor
Box 532, Village Station
New York, NY 10014
Phone: (212) 243-3885
Fax: (212) 243-2885
pajpub@mac.com
www.mitpressjournals.org/paj
Notes: Est. 1976. Response: 2 months query,
2 months script. Preferred length: Under 40
pages. Prefer experimental or plays in
translation.
Preferred Genre: Plays (No Musicals)
Submission Materials: query letter, synopsis
Submission Fee: No
Agent Only: No

Players Press Inc.
Box 1132
Studio City, CA 91614
Phone: (818) 789-4980
playerspress@worldnet.att.net
Notes: Est. 1960. Response: 2 weeks query, 6
months script. Only plays and/or musicals
that have been produced. A reading is not a
production. One production is acceptable if
under an Equity contract (professional) or
winner of a playwriting contest. Two
productions are required if they are
community, school or any form of amateur
production.
Preferred Genre: Musical theatre
Preferred Length: Any length
Submission Materials: query letter, S.A.S.E.
Submission Fee: No
Agent Only: No

Playscripts, Inc.
450 Seventh Ave.
Suite 809
New York, NY 10123

Phone: (866) 639-7529
Fax: (888) 203-4519
submissions@playscripts.com
www.playscripts.com/submit
Notes: Est. 1998. Acting editions sold and
performances licensed to
amateur/professional venues worldwide.
Musicals by agent submission only.
Preferred Genre: Plays (No Musicals)
Preferred Length: Any length
Submission Materials: see website
Submission Fee: No
Agent Only: Yes

Poems & Plays
Gaylord Brewer, Editor
MTSU English Dept.
Murfreesboro, TN 37132
Phone: (615) 898-2712
Fax: (615) 898-5098
gbrewer@mtsu.edu
www.mtsu.edu/english/poemsandplays
Notes: Est. 1993. Work must be unpublished.
Response: 3 months.
Preferred Genre: Plays (No Musicals)
Preferred Length: 10-min./10pgs.
Submission Materials: full script, S.A.S.E.
Submission Fee: No
Agent Only: No

**Rodgers & Hammerstein Organization
Theatricals**
Lissi Borshman, Amateur Licensing
Representative
229 W. 28th St., Fl. 11
New York, NY 10001
Phone: (212) 564-4000
Fax: (212) 268-1245
theatre@rnh.com
www.rnh.com
Notes: Titles must be returned within 2
weeks after closing in perfect condition.
Quotes expire 3 months after created.
Submission Materials: application
Submission Fee: No
Agent Only: No

Samuel French Inc.
Amy Rose Marsh, Literary Manager
45 W. 25th St.
New York, NY 10010
Phone: (212) 206-8990
Fax: (212) 206-1429
publications@samuelfrench.com
www.samuelfrench.com

Notes: Est. 1830. We are the largest play publisher and licenser in the world, with a catalogue of over 5,000 active plays. Recently published plays include 4000 Miles by Amy Herzog and Seminar by Theresa Rebeck. Average response time: 6 months.
Preferred Genre: All genres
Preferred Length: Any length
Submission Materials: see website
Submission Fee: No
Agent Only: No

Smith and Kraus
Lawrence Harbison, Editor
Box 127
Lyme, NH 03768
Phone: (603) 643-6431
Fax: (603) 643-1831
lharbison1@nyc.rr.com
www.smithkraus.com
Notes: Smith & Kraus, theatrical trade publisher, seeks ten-minute and full length plays for its annual anthologies, edited by Lawrence Harbison. Plays must be produced between May 1, 2013 and April 30, 2014 and must include a title page with contact information for the author or agent. Email submissions only.
Preferred Genre: Plays (No Musicals)
Preferred Length: Any length
Submission Materials: E-mail only
Submission Fee: No
Agent Only: No
Deadline(s): March 1, 2014

Speert Publishing
New York, NY
Phone: (212) 979-7656
espeert@speertpublishing.com
www.speertpublishing.com
Notes: Self-publishing services for acting editions of original plays. Response: 1 week.
Preferred Genre: Plays (No Musicals)
Preferred Length: Any length
Submission Materials: query letter
Submission Fee: No
Agent Only: No

Steele Spring Theatrical Licensing
Samantha Levenshus, Director of Licensing
3845 Cazador Street
Los Angeles, CA 90065
Phone: (323) 739-0413
Fax: (818) 232-9158
submissions@steelespring.com

www.steelespring.com
Preferred Genre: All genres
Preferred Length: Full-length
Submission Materials: see website
Submission Fee: No
Agent Only: No

Tams-Witmark Music Library Inc.
Sargent L. Aborn, President
560 Lexington Ave.
New York, NY 10022
Phone: (212) 688-2525
Fax: (212) 688-3232
saborn@tamswitmark.com
www.tams-witmark.com
Notes: Classic Broadway musicals for stage performance around the world.
Preferred Genre: Musical theatre
Preferred Length: Any length
Submission Materials: see website
Submission Fee: No
Agent Only: No

Theatrefolk
Craig Mason, Publisher
P.O. Box 1064
Crystal Beach, ON L0S-1B0 Canada
Phone: (866) 245-9138
Fax: (877) 245-9138
tfolk@theatrefolk.com
www.theatrefolk.com/submissions
Notes: We publish plays specifically for student performers. Production: simple. Response: 6-8 weeks. Please review our submission policy before submitting.
Preferred Genre: All genres
Preferred Length: Any length
Submission Materials: see website
Submission Fee: No
Agent Only: No

TheatreForum
9500 Gilman Dr.
MCO344
La Jolla, CA 92093
Fax: (858) 534-1080
ashank@ucsd.edu
www.theatreforum.org
Notes: Plays must have been professionally produced. Submit via email.
Preferred Genre: Plays (No Musicals)
Preferred Length: Full-length
Submission Materials: query letter
Submission Fee: No
Agent Only: No

Theatrical Rights Worldwide
Steve Spiegel, President & CEO
570 Seventh Avenue, Suite 2100
New York, NY 10018
Phone: (646) 736-3232
Fax: (212) 643-1322
licensing@theatricalrights.com
www.theatricalrights.com
Notes: Est. 2006. Work must be unpublished.
Response: 3-6 months.
Preferred Genre: Musical theatre
Preferred Length: Any length
Submission Materials: audio CD, full script,
query letter, S.A.S.E.
Submission Fee: No
Agent Only: No

YouthPlays
Jonathan Dorf, Partner
7119 W. Sunset Blvd. #390
Los Angeles, CA 90046
Phone: (424) 703-5315
info@youthplays.com
www.youthplays.com
Notes: We publish plays for young actors
and audiences. Particular needs include:
Flexible to large cast, One-Act (30-35
minutes) comedies for high school and
middle school actors, adaptations, and
profession theatre for young audience scripts.
Deadline is ongoing for regular submissions.
Preferred Genre: Theatre for Young
Audiences
Preferred Length: Any length
Submission Materials: see website
Submission Fee: No
Agent Only: No

Career Development Opportunities

AND THE HONORABLE MENTION AS A
THIRD RUNNER-UP TO THE SEMI-FINALIST
IN THE PRELIMINARY ROUND GOES TO . . .

Colonies & Residencies

Altos de Chavon
66 5th Ave., #819D
New York, NY 10011
Phone: (212) 229-5370
Fax: (212) 229-8988
altos@earthlink.net
www.altosdechavon.com
Notes: Est. 1981. 3 1/2 month residencies in
La Romana, Dominican Republic, for visual
artists, writers, musicians, and architects.
Summary of work, critiques of previous work
required.
Submission Materials: query letter, synopsis
Submission Fee: Yes
Agent Only: No
Deadline(s): August 15, 2014

Atlantic Center for the Arts
1414 Art Center Ave.
New Smyrna Beach, FL 32168
Phone: (386) 427-6975
Fax: (386) 427-5669
program@atlanticcenterforthearts.org
www.atlanticcenterforthearts.org
Notes: Est. 1982. Residencies of 3 weeks
with master artists. Workspace includes black
box theater, music/recording studio, dance
studio, art & sculpture studios, digital lab and
resource library.
Submission Materials: see website
Submission Fee: Yes
Agent Only: No

Bellagio Center Creative Arts Residencies
Rob Garris, Managing Director, Bellagio
Programs
Villa Serbelloni, Via Roma 1
Bellagio 22021 Italy
Phone: (212) 852-8431
Fax: (212) 852-8438
bellagio_ny@rockfound.org
www.rockfound.org/bellagio
Notes: The Residency Program offers
scholars, artists, thought leaders,
policymakers, and practitioners a serene
setting conducive to goal-oriented work as
well as opportunities for establishing new
connections with fellow residents and other
professionals from around the world. The
Bellagio Creative Arts Fellows high profile
program awards fellowships to visual artists
who have demonstrated exceptional

originality, work that is inspired by or related
to global social issues, and who share in the
Foundation's mission of promoting the well-
being of humankind. The Creative Arts
Fellows are nominated by an international
selection committee of leading arts
professionals. The Fellows are given a cash
award and are invited for a residency for two
months to work on a project.
Preferred Genre: All genres
Submission Materials: see website
Submission Fee: Yes
Agent Only: No

Blue Field Writers House
17136 Fairfield Street
Detroit, MI 48221
Phone: (313) 646-9964
sallyjane77@hotmail.com
www.bluefieldwritershouse.com/favicon.ico
Notes: Blue Field Writers House is a
nurturing and supportive communal residence
where writers can come to spend
concentrated time completing their writing
projects. Writers can apply for residencies
from two weeks to two months in length, and
they will be provided with a private room,
24/7 access to the fully-stocked community
kitchen, Wi-Fi, laundry facilities, parking,
and, most importantly, uninterrupted time to
write. Located in the University District of
Detroit, writers will have the opportunity to
explore all the cultural and artistic events that
Detroit has to offer. Blue Field Writers House
will also provide each of its residents the
opportunity to do a public reading of their
work-in-progress.
Submission Materials: see website
Submission Fee: No
Agent Only: No

**Byrdcliffe Arts Colony Artist-in-Residence
(AIR) Program**
34 Tinker St.
Woodstock, NY 12498
Phone: (845) 679-2079
Fax: (845) 679-4529
info@woodstockguild.org
www.byrdcliffe.org
Notes: Est. 1980 Catskill Mountains,
Woodstock, NY. Four, 4-week sessions per
season. Application on website. Additional

phone number May - September ONLY (845)-679-8540. The Byrdcliffe Artist in Residence Program provides uninterrupted time, creative space and an inspiring environment to artists of exceptional talent. Month long residencies are available to visual artists, composers, playwrights/screenwriters, and writers of fiction, nonfiction and poetry in the months of June-September.
Preferred Genre: Plays or Musicals
Preferred Length: Any length
Submission Materials: see website for application
Submission Fee: Yes
Agent Only: No
Deadline(s): March 1, 2014

Camargo Foundation
Cindy Gehrig, President
1 Ave Jermini
Cassis 13260 France
Phone: 0 (113) 344-2011 Ext 157
Fax: 0 (113) 344-2013 Ext 657
apply@camargofoundation.org
www.camargofoundation.org
Notes: Interdisciplinary residency program includes thirteen furnished apartments, a reference library and three art/music studios. Residencies are one semester. See website for complete online application requirements.
Preferred Genre: All genres
Preferred Length: Any length
Submission Materials: see website
Submission Fee: Yes
Agent Only: No
Deadline(s): January 12, 2014

Centrum Artistic Residencies Program
Box 1158
Port Townsend, WA 98368
Phone: (360) 385-3102
lisa@centrum.org
www.centrum.org/residencies
Notes: Est. 1980. Awarded in one week blocks, residencies may be of any duration, time and space permitting. Submit proposal of work focused on with resume and work sample. Submissions accepted year-round.
Preferred Genre: All genres
Submission Materials: see website
Submission Fee: Yes
Agent Only: No

Dorland Mountain Arts Colony
Jill Roberts, Colony Manager
Box 6
Temecula, CA 92593
Phone: (909) 302-3837
Fax: (951) 582-4973
info@dorlandartscolony.org
www.dorlandartscolony.org
Notes: Est. 1979. Secluded retreat on a scenic Nature Preserve in southern California 300 acres near Wine Country,
Submission Materials: application
Submission Fee: Yes
Agent Only: No
Deadline(s): December 1, 2014

Emlenton Mill
201 Main Street
Emlenton, PA 16373
Phone: (724) 867-0277
www.emlentonmill.com
Notes: The Emlenton Mill Foundation is a non-profit art and historic education center. Our mission is to support, inspire and celebrate art and history by providing unique educational and artistic experiences. The Foundation strives to fulfill its mission by offering a variety of art classes, concerts, lectures, artist retreats, art shows and camps. The Artist-in-Residence program seeks to host and serve visual artists, writers and composers giving them valuable time to create and immerse themselves in their crafts.

Gell Center of the Finger Lakes
Kathy Pottetti, Director
Operations/Programming
740 University Ave.
Rochester, NY 14607
Phone: (585) 473-2590
Fax: (585) 442-9333
Kathyp@wab.org
www.wab.org
Notes: Writers & Books promotes reading and writing as lifelong activities for people of all ages, through educational programs, publications, community events and author appearances. For thirty-two years our programs, held at our Rochester and Finger Lakes facilities, have reached a growing audience of thousands, making us one of the largest and oldest literary organizations in the country. Our programs have received nationwide recognition while inspiring generations of Rochesterians to make

literature a part of their everyday lives. The Gell House provides an inspirational setting in which to write, and an ideal setting for small conferences.
Submission Materials: see website
Submission Fee: No
Agent Only: No

Hawthornden Retreat for Writers
Hawthornden Castle
Lasswade EH18 1EG Scotland
Phone: 0 (131) 440-2180
Fax: 0 (131) 440-1989
office@hawthornden.com
Notes: Est. 1982. Residencies of 4 weeks (February-July, September-December) in 17th-century castle, 40-minute bus ride to Edinburgh. Residents housed in study bedrooms. Author must be produced or published.
Submission Materials: 10-pg sample, application
Submission Fee: No
Agent Only: No
Deadline(s): June 30, 2014

Headlands Center for the Arts
Holly Blake, Residency Manager
944 Fort Barry
Sausalito, CA 94965
Phone: (415) 331-2787
Fax: (415) 331-3857
hblake@headlongs.org
www.headlands.org
Notes: Est. 1987. Hosts 40 residencies for artists of all disciplines per year from 1 to 3 months. Response: 4-5 months.
Submission Materials: see website
Submission Fee: Yes
Agent Only: No

Hedgebrook Women Writers in Residence
Kathryn Preiss, Residency Associate
PO Box 1231
Freeland, WA 98249
Phone: (360) 321-4786
Fax: (360) 321-2171
hedgebrook@hedgebrook.org
www.hedgebrook.org/page.php?pageid=21
Notes: Hedgebrook retreat for women writers is on Whidbey Island, about thirty-five miles northwest of Seattle. Situated on 48-acres of forest and meadow facing Puget Sound, with a view of Mount Rainier, the retreat hosts women writers from all over the world for

residencies of two to six weeks, at no cost to the writer. Our selection process occurs once a year, in the fall. Through a completely anonymous, two-round process, approximately forty writers are invited for residencies of two weeks to six weeks. Our residency season runs from February through October in 2014. Please visit our website for more information.
Special Interest: Women's Interest
Submission Materials: see website
Submission Fee: Yes
Agent Only: No

Helene Wurlitzer Foundation of New Mexico
P.O. Box 1891
Taos, NM 87571
Phone: (575) 758-2413
Fax: (575) 758-2559
HWF@taosnet.com
www.wurlitzerfoundation.org
Notes: Est. 1956. Rent and utility fee free rsidences of 3 months (January-November) for visual artists, writers and composers. See website for submission guidelines.
Submission Materials: application
Submission Fee: No
Agent Only: No
Deadline(s): January 18, 2014

International Writing Program (IWP)
Christopher Merrill, Director
430 N. Clinton St.
Iowa City, IA 52242
Phone: (319) 335-0128
Fax: (319) 335-3843
iwp@uiowa.edu
http://iwp.uiowa.edu
Notes: Est. 1967. For published writers of fiction, poetry, drama, or screenplays who are not US residents but are proficient in English. August-November, 3 month residency.
Submission Materials: see website
Submission Fee: No
Agent Only: No

La MaMa Playwright Retreat
74-A E. 4th St.
New York, NY 10003
Phone: (212) 475-7710
web@lamama.org
http://lamama.org/programs/umbria/playwrightretreat
Notes: Est. 2007. Come with nothing and leave with a play; participants are asked to

arrive with a clean slate, and over the course of the workshop, writers will develop new, complete scripts. The fee is $2,300. Fee includes workshop, housing and meals for 10 days, ground transportation from the Rome airport to and from La MaMa Umbria, and excursions by bus, van or car. Space is extremely limited. Please visit our website for submission deadlines and information.
Submission Materials: application, resume
Submission Fee: Yes
Agent Only: No

Lanesboro Residency Program Fellowships
103 Parkway Ave. N., Box 152
Lanesboro, MN 55949
Phone: (507) 467-2446
Fax: (507) 467-4446
Info@lanesboroarts.org
www.lanesboroarts.org
Notes: Retreat space also available for rent.
Submission Materials: see website
Submission Fee: No
Agent Only: Yes
Deadline(s): June 30, 2014

MacDowell Colony
Courtney Bethel, Admissions Director
100 High St.
Peterborough, NH 03458
Phone: (415) 441-8822
Fax: (415) 771-5505
dorij@magictheatre.org
www.macdowellcolony.org
Notes: Est. 1907. Residencies/studios for up to 8 weeks (Jun-Sep, Oct-Jan, Feb-May). Multiple deadlines: September 15, January 15, and April 15. Financial assistance available. Response: 10 weeks
Preferred Genre: All genres
Preferred Length: Full-length
Submission Materials: see website
Submission Fee: Yes
Agent Only: No

McKnight National Playwriting Residency and Commission
Amanda Robbins-Butcher, Artistic Administrator
2301 Franklin Ave. E
Minneapolis, MN 55406
Phone: (612) 332-7481
info@pwcenter.org
www.pwcenter.org

Notes: Commissioning and production of new works from nationally recognized playwrights. Recipient in residence at Center while play is in development. Please include a work sample with your application.
Submission Materials: application
Submission Fee: No
Agent Only: No
Deadline(s): November 14, 2014

Millay Colony for the Arts
454 East Hill Rd, Box 3
Austerlitz, NY 12017
Phone: (518) 392-3103
Fax: (518) 392-4944
apply@millaycolony.org
www.millaycolony.org
Notes: Est. 1973. Month-long residencies (April-November) on former estate of Edna St. Vincent Millay for writers, visual artists, composers. No cost for residency. See website for submission guidelines.
Submission Materials: see website
Submission Fee: Yes
Agent Only: No
Deadline(s): October 1, 2014

Shenandoah International Playwrights
Box 1
Verona, VA 24482
Phone: (540) 248-1868
Fax: (540) 248-7728
theatre@shenarts.org
www.shenanarts.org
Notes: Est. 1977. Up to 12 playwrights (from around the US and the world) work with dramaturges, directors and actors in July-August, culminating in invited readings. Visit this site for more information: http://worldvoices.pen.org/grants-and-awards/shenandoah-international-playwrights-writers-retreat
Preferred Genre: All genres
Preferred Length: Full-length
Submission Materials: see website
Submission Fee: Yes
Agent Only: No

Sundance Institute Playwrights Retreat at Ucross
180 Varick St.
Suite 1330
New York, NY 10014
Phone: (646) 822-9563
Fax: (310) 360-1969

theatre@sundance.org
www.sundance.org/programs/ucross
Notes: Est. 2001. 18-day retreat for 5
playwrights and 1 theater composer at Ucross
Foundation, Clearmont, Wyoming. Artists are
selected by invitation only.
Submission Materials: see website
Submission Fee: No
Agent Only: No

The Edward F. Albee Foundation
Jakob Holder, Secretary
The Edward F. Albee Foundation
14 Harrison St.
New York, NY 10013
Phone: (212) 226-2020
Fax: (212) 226-5551
info@albeefoundation.org
www.albeefoundation.org
Notes: Est. 1966. Residencies of 4 - 6 weeks
(mid May -- mid October) in Montauk, NY,
for writers and visual artists. Office hours are
Mondays through Thursdays 12-6pm EST.
Submission Materials: see website
Submission Fee: No
Agent Only: No
Deadline(s): March 1, 2014

**The Field Artward Bound Residency
Program**
Pele Bauch, Associate Director, Programming
161 6th Ave., Fl. 14
New York, NY 10013
Phone: (212) 691-6969
Fax: (212) 255-2053
pele@thefield.org
www.thefield.org
Notes: This residency program (free to Field
Members) provides individual performing
artists the opportunity to enjoy a creative
retreat with a group of fellow artists. Retreats
are set in beautiful, rural settings so that
participants can unplug from the daily grind
and focus on their creative process or career
development while connecting with peers in
an encouraging community. Open only to
current Field Members who demonstrate a
history of art making, participants are
selected via lottery.
Preferred Genre: All genres
Preferred Length: Any length
Submission Materials: application
Submission Fee: No
Agent Only: No

Tyrone Guthrie Centre
Annaghmakerrig
Newbliss Ireland
Phone: (353) 475-4003
Fax: (353) 475-4380
info@tyroneguthrie.ie
www.tyroneguthrie.ie
Notes: Est. 1981. Year-round residencies of
varying duration in private rooms, studios,
self-catering farmyard cottages. Response: 1
month.
Submission Materials: application
Submission Fee: Yes
Agent Only: No

U.S. - Japan Creative Artists' Program
Margaret P. Mihori, Associate Executive
Director
1201 15th St. NW, #330
Washington, DC 20005
Phone: (202) 653-9800
Fax: (202) 418-9802
jusfc@jusfc.gov
www.jusfc.gov
Notes: Est. 1979. 3-month residency in Japan
for produced professional US artists with
financial assistance.
Submission Materials: application
Submission Fee: Yes
Agent Only: No
Deadline(s): March 1, 2014

Ucross Foundation Residency Program
Ruth Salvatore, Residency Manager
30 Big Red Ln.
Clearmont, WY 82835
Phone: (307) 737-2291
Fax: (307) 737-2322
info@ucross.org
www.ucrossfoundation.org
Notes: Est. 1981. Residencies of 2 weeks to
6 weeks (February-June, July-November)
near Big Horn Mountains. Residents are
provided living & studio space plus meals.
Submission Materials: see website
Submission Fee: Yes
Agent Only: No

**VCCA (Virginia Center for the Creative
Arts)**
Sheila Pleasants, Director of Artists' Services
154 San Angelo Dr.
Amherst, VA 24521
Phone: (434) 946-7236
Fax: (434) 946-7239

vcca@vcca.com
www.vcca.com
Notes: Est. 1971. Residencies of 2 weeks-2 months on a beautiful and secluded hilltop in the foothills of the Blue Ridge Mountains near Sweet Briar College. Residencies includes private studios, private bathrooms and all meals. Dinner is in the dining room with up to 25 other writers, artists, and composers. Does not accept scholarly projects. Response time: 2 months.
Submission Materials: application, full script
Submission Fee: Yes
Agent Only: No

William Inge Center for the Arts
Peter Ellenstein, Artistic Director
Box 708
1057 W. College Ave.
Independence, KS 67301
Phone: (620) 331-7768
Fax: (620) 331-9022
info@ingecenter.org
www.ingecenter.org
Notes: Est. 2002. Residencies of 8-9 weeks at William Inge's family home in small Midwestern town; private bedroom in historic 1920s-era house; shared bath. Each playwright receives a week-long professional play development workshop, which culminates in rehearsed reading of a playwright's script. Resident playwrights also teach playwriting 10-12 hours a week at a college and/or high school class. Financial arrangement: stipend of approximately $4,000, plus travel; meals not provided, but housing has a full kitchen. Guidelines: playwrights should have work that has had several professional productions; teaching experience also desirable. Application: send writing sample, description of the project you would like workshopped, resume, references (including in regards to teaching experience), one-page bio, availability over next two years and letter of inquiry. Open Deadline.

Notification: 4 months. Submissions accepted year-round.
Preferred Genre: Plays (No Musicals)
Preferred Length: Full-length
Submission Materials: see website
Submission Fee: No
Agent Only: No

Writers Omi at Ledig House
Art Omni Ledig House
55 5th Ave., Fl. 15
New York, NY 10003
Phone: (847) 242-6001
Fax: (847) 242-6011
literary@writerstheatre.org
www.artomi.org
Notes: Est. 1992. Residencies (March-June, September-November) in Catskill Mountains. Residents provided with separate or combined work/bedroom areas. All meals included. See website for submission guidelines:
www.artomi.org/writers/application.php
Submission Materials: see website for application
Submission Fee: Yes
Agent Only: No
Deadline(s): October 20, 2014

Yaddo
Box 395
Saratoga Springs, NY 12866
Phone: (518) 584-0746
Fax: (518) 584-1312
chwait@yaddo.org
www.yaddo.org
Notes: Est. 1900. Residencies of 2 weeks-2 months on 400-acre turn-of-century estate in Saratoga Springs, New York. Free room/board/private studio space. See website for submission materials.
Preferred Genre: All genres
Submission Materials: see website
Submission Fee: Yes
Agent Only: No

Conferences & Festivals

6 Women Playwriting Festival
Lynette Reagan, Festival Coordinator
7413 Stonecrop Court
Colorado Springs, CO 80919
Phone: (719) 201-7554

Lynwalks@hotmail.com
www.sixwomenplayfestival.com
Notes: Author must be a woman. Six plays will have full production each with $100

honorarium, 1 of these will be chosen for workshop and author brought to Colorado.
Preferred Genre: Plays (No Musicals)
Special Interest: Women's Interest
Preferred Length: 10-min./10pgs.
Submission Materials: see website
Submission Fee: No
Agent Only: No
Deadline(s): September 30, 2014

AACT New Play Fest
American Association of Community Theatre (AACT)
Julie Crawford, Executive Director
1300 Gendy St.
Fort Worth, TX 76107
Phone: (817) 732-3177
Fax: (817) 732-3178
info@aact.org
www.aact.org
Notes: AACT is answering a critical need in developing exciting new plays that our audiences will enjoy by launching AACT New Play Fest! AACT is also partnering with the Dramatic Publishing Company, and they are set to print an anthology of the winning plays. They will also include the plays in their catalog and license the performances rights. Please check our website for submission guidelines on the 2014 festival.
Preferred Genre: Plays (No Musicals)
Submission Materials: see website
Submission Fee: No
Agent Only: No

Actors Theatre of Louisville, Humana Festival [KY]
Amy Wegener, Literary Director
316 W. Main St.
Louisville, KY 40202
Phone: (502) 584-1265
Fax: (502) 561-3300
awegener@actorstheatre.org
www.actorstheatre.org/humana-festival-of-new-american-plays
Notes: Est. 1976. Festival of 10-12 fully produced new plays (world premieres) running February-April. Unagented writers may submit a synopsis and 10-page sample from script for consideration. Festival also includes 3-4 ten-minute plays; see website for National Ten-Minute Play Contest guidelines and full Humana Festival guidelines.
Preferred Genre: All genres

Preferred Length: Full-length
Submission Materials: agent-only
Submission Fee: No
Agent Only: Yes

Actors' Playhouse National Children's Theatre Festival
Earl Maulding, Director, TYA
280 Miracle Mile
Coral Gables, FL 33134
Phone: (502) 584-1265
Fax: (502) 561-3300
awcgener@actorstheatre.org
www.actorsplayhouse.org
Notes: Est. 1994. Cast limit up to 8 adults and/or 15 young performers. Prefer all materials be submitted electronically to listed email. No previous production required. Submissions are accepted year-round.
Preferred Genre: Theatre for Young Audiences
Special Interest: Theatre for Young Audiences
Preferred Length: 50-60 min.
Submission Materials: audio CD, full script, vocal score
Submission Fee: Yes
Agent Only: No

Alabama Shakespeare Festival - Southern Writers' Project
Nancy Rominger, Associate Director
1 Festival Dr.
Montgomery, AL 36117
Phone: (334) 271-5300
Fax: (334) 271-5348
swp@asf.net
www.southernwritersproject.net
Notes: Est. 1972. The Southern Writers' Project of the Alabama Shakespeare Festival accepts original scripts and adaptations, not professionally produced, that meet one or more of the following criteria: You are a Southern Writer. Your script is set in the South, or deals specifically with Southern issues, characters, or themes. See website for more information. Submissions are accepted year-round.
Preferred Genre: All genres
Preferred Length: Full-length
Submission Materials: see website
Submission Fee: No
Agent Only: No

Ashland New Plays Festival
Elizabeth von Radics, Marketing Director
Box 3314
Ashland, OR 97520-3314
Phone: (541) 488-7995
Fax: (541) 472-0512
info@ashlandnewplays.org
www.ashlandnewplays.org
Notes: Est. 1992. Four playwrights are
chosen each year. Annual weeklong October
festival with rehearsals, 2 workshops and 8
staged readings (2 of each winning script)
with professional directors and actors.
Production: 8-character limit (no doubling).
$1,000 stipend and lodging. Application Fee
$10 via US Mail; $15 for online submissions.
Preferred Genre: Plays (No Musicals)
Preferred Length: Full-length
Submission Materials: see website
Submission Fee: Yes
Agent Only: No
Deadline(s): December 16, 2014

Baltimore Playwrights Festival
Rodney S. Bonds, Chair
Box 38122
Baltimore, MD 21231
librarian@baltplayfest.org
www.baltplayfest.org
Notes: Est. 1981. Plays chosen for 3-week
summer production and selected public
readings. The submission period is from
April 1 to July 31.
Preferred Genre: All genres
Preferred Length: Full-length
Submission Materials: see website
Submission Fee: Yes
Agent Only: No
Deadline(s): July 31, 2014

**Barter Theatre's Appalachian Festival of
Plays & Playwrights**
Nick Piper, Associate Director - New Play
Development
P.O. Box 867
Abingdon, VA 24212
Phone: (276) 619-3316
Fax: (276) 619-3335
apfestival@bartertheatre.com
www.bartertheatre.com/festival
Notes: Est. 2001. Plays must be either
written by a playwright living in Appalachia
(from New York to Alabama) or the play
must contain Appalachian setting/themes.
Readings of six new plays with cash reward

plus travel and housing for playwright; and
one mini production (full production,
minimal tech, brief run) selected from
previous year's readings, in a two week
festival, judged by panel. Must be
unproduced/unpublished.
Preferred Genre: All genres
Preferred Length: Full-length
Submission Materials: full script
Submission Fee: No
Agent Only: No
Deadline(s): March 1, 2014

Bay Area Playwrights Festival (BAPF)
1616 16th Street
Suite 350
San Francisco, CA 94103
Phone: (415) 626-2176
literary@playwrightsfoundation.org
www.playwrightsfoundation.org
Notes: Est. 1976. 2-week July festival of 5-6
full-length plays by US writers. Submissions
not returned. Response time: 4 months.
Preferred Genre: Comedy
Preferred Length: Any length
Submission Materials: see website
Submission Fee: No
Agent Only: No

Boomerang Theatre Company
Tim Errickson, Artistic Director
P.O. Box 237166, Ansonia Station
New York, NY 10023
info@boomerangtheatre.org
www.boomerangtheatre.org
Notes: Est. 1999. First Flight New Play
Festival takes place in November of each
year. Includes 6-8 presentations of scripts in
development, produced either as staged
readings or workshops. Open submission
period August 15th to September 30th
annually. Plays submitted at other times are
not logged and read until the next open
submission window.
Preferred Genre: Plays (No Musicals)
Preferred Length: Full-length
Submission Materials: 10-pg sample, query
letter, resume, S.A.S.E., synopsis
Submission Fee: No
Agent Only: No
Deadline(s): September 30, 2014

Boston Theater Marathon
Kate Snodgrass, Artistic Director
949 Commonwealth Avenue

Boston, MA 02215
Phone: (617) 353-5899
Fax: (617) 353-6196
newplays@bu.edu
www.bu.edu/btm
Notes: Est. 1999. Fifty 10-minute plays by
fifty New England playwrights by fifty New
England theaters over the course of a single
day. Production: small orchestra, minimal set.
Response time: 4 months. Alternate website:
www.bostonplaywright.org
Preferred Genre: All genres
Preferred Length: 10-min./10pgs.
Submission Materials: see website
Submission Fee: No
Agent Only: No
Deadline(s): November 15, 2014

Centre Stage New Play Festival
Melanie Wiliford, New Play Festival Director
Box 8451
Greenville, SC 29604
Phone: (864) 233-6733
Fax: (864) 233-6733
melanie.wiliford@centrestage.org
www.centrestage.org
Notes: Est. 2002. Submission process is on
the Centre Stage website. Three of the
submitted scripts receive staged-readings at
the Centre Stage New Play Festival.
Playwrights of those scripts receive travel to
and lodging during the festival. Scripts must
be unpublished/unproduced. Cast Limit: 7
actors, doubling not recommended.
Preferred Genre: Plays (No Musicals)
Preferred Length: Full-length
Submission Materials: see website
Submission Fee: No
Agent Only: No
Deadline(s): February 1, 2014

Cincinnati Fringe Festival
1120 Jackson Street
Cincinnati, OH 45202
Phone: (513) 300-5669
Fax: (513) 421-3435
fringesubmissions@knowtheatre.com
www.cincyfringe.com
Notes: Est. 2004. Annual Fringe Festival late
May/early June. Submissions not returned.
Response time: 3 months.
Preferred Genre: Plays or Musicals
Preferred Length: Any length
Submission Materials: application

Submission Fee: Yes
Agent Only: No

City Wrights Playwrights Conference
City Theatre [FL]
Susan Westfall, Literary Director
444 Brickell Ave., #229
Miami, FL 33131
Phone: (305) 755-9401
Fax: (305) 755-9404
10minuteplays@citytheatre.com
www.citytheatre.com
Notes: Save the date: June 19-21, 2014. Be
inspired by new ideas, playwriting
techniques, attend readings of fresh new
work, receive feedback in creative workshop
of your new works, all led by Master
Playwrights. Learn the latest in professional
development sessions all from leading
industry experts. We invite you to join us at
City Wrights where playwrights will have fun
and learn something new, make new friends
and new connections. Please see our website
for additional information.
Submission Materials: see website
Submission Fee: Yes
Agent Only: No

**Cleveland Public Theatre New Plays
Festival**
6415 Detroit Ave.
Cleveland, OH 44102
Phone: (216) 631-2727
Fax: (216) 631-2575
cpt@en.com
www.cptonline.org
Notes: Biennial four-week festival of staged
readings. Assistance: room/board, travel, per
diem. Frequency: biennial. Production: cast
of up to 10, simple set.
Preferred Genre: All genres
Preferred Length: Full-length
Submission Materials: 10-pg sample,
S.A.S.E., synopsis
Submission Fee: No
Agent Only: No

Collaboraction: Sketchbook Festival
Anthony Moseley, Executive Artistic Director
437 N. Wolcott, #201
Attn: SKBK06
Chicago, IL 60622
Phone: (312) 226-9633
Fax: (312) 226-6107
Sketchbook14@collaboraction.org

www.collaboraction.org
Notes: Annual festival of short plays. Email submissions. Check website for details.
Submission Materials: application, full script
Submission Fee: No
Agent Only: No
Deadline(s): October 20, 2014

Cultural Conversations
Susan Russell, Artistic Director
116 Arts Bldg.
Penn State University School of Theatre
University Park, PA 16802
Phone: (814) 863-1451
sbr13@psu.edu
www.culturalconversations.psu.edu
Notes: Est. 2007. Readings of new plays by actors 15 - 35 addressing themes of local and global diversity. We will not be accepting submissions for 2014. Please check website for updates.
Preferred Genre: Plays (No Musicals)
Preferred Length: Full-length
Submission Materials: full script
Submission Fee: No
Agent Only: No

Dayton Playhouse FutureFest
Fran Pesch, FutureFest Program Director
PO Box 3017
Dayton, OH 45401
Phone: (937) 424-8477
dp_futurefest@yahoo.com
www.daytonplayhouse.org
Notes: Est. 1991. Adjudicated July festival of new work. Work must be longer than 75 minutes. Submission Fee: $20 (waived for members of the Dramatists Guild). Check website for updates to submission guidelines. Submissions not returned. Submissions are accepted between August 1 - October 31.
Preferred Genre: Plays (No Musicals)
Preferred Length: Full-length
Submission Materials: full script, synopsis
Submission Fee: Yes
Agent Only: No
Deadline(s): October 31, 2014

Discovery New Musical Theatre Festival
Ball State University
Muncie, IN 47306
Phone: (765) 285-5557
njabbott@bsu.edu
www.bsudiscoveryfestival.com

Notes: Ball State University's Department of Theatre and Dance, in association with the Discovery Group and the Provost Immersive Learning Initiative, is looking for unproduced, emerging musical theatre librettists and composers interested in having their work performed in the first annual Discovery New Musical Theatre Festival of new musicals at BSU during the Summer of 2014. Three musicals will be chosen from the submissions and performed as concert readings in the festival. From the three finalists, one will be selected for inclusion in the BSU theatre season in Strother Theater, and be entered as a participating entry in KCACTF.
Preferred Genre: Musical theatre
Preferred Length: Any length
Submission Materials: see website
Submission Fee: No
Agent Only: No
Deadline(s): January 10, 2014

Edinburgh Festival Fringe Society
180 High St.
Edinburgh EH1 1QS
United Kingdom
Phone: (440) 131-2260 Ext 026
admin@edfringe.com
www.edfringe.com
Notes: Est. 1947. The Edinburgh Festival Fringe is entirely open access and there is no selection process. Performers and companies are responsible for organizing all aspects of their own production.
Preferred Genre: All genres
Preferred Length: Any length
Submission Materials: see website
Submission Fee: Yes
Agent Only: No
Deadline(s): April 10, 2014

Firehouse Theatre Project's Festival of New American Plays
1609 W. Broad St.
Richmond, VA 23220
Phone: (804) 355-2001
Fax: (804) 355-0999
info@firehousetheatre.org
www.firehousetheatre.org
Notes: Est. 2003. Submit script and recommendation (theatre professional) by US mail with author's info on removable cover page. Submissions not returned. Response: 9 months.

Preferred Genre: All genres
Preferred Length: Any length
Submission Materials: see website
Submission Fee: No
Agent Only: No
Deadline(s): September 1, 2014

Fresh Fruit Festival
145 E. 27th St., #1-A
New York, NY 10016
Phone: (212) 857-8701
artisticdirector@freshfruitfestival.com
www.freshfruitfestival.com
Notes: Est. 2003. Work submitted must be
unproduced in NYC and unoptioned.
Response: 2 months.
Preferred Genre: Plays or Musicals
Special Interest: LGBT
Preferred Length: Any length
Submission Materials: see website
Submission Fee: No
Agent Only: No

FusionFest
8500 Euclid Ave.
Cleveland, OH 44106
Phone: (216) 795-7000
Fax: (216) 795-7007
sgordon@clevelandplayhouse.com
www.clevelandplayhouse.com
Notes: Est. 1995. Reading series of
unoptioned/unproduced new plays. Author
must be resident of Ohio. Response: 6
months.
Submission Materials: agent-only
Submission Fee: No
Agent Only: Yes

Indo-American Arts Council Inc. (IACC)
517 East 87th Street, Suite 1B
New York, NY 10128
Phone: (212) 529-2347
Fax: (212) 477-4106
aroon@iaac.us
www.iaac.us
Notes: Est. 1998. Annual film and
playwrights festivals.
Preferred Genre: Plays (No Musicals)
Preferred Length: Any length
Submission Materials: application, full
script, S.A.S.E., synopsis, video
Submission Fee: No
Agent Only: No
Deadline(s): February 1, 2014

Inspirato Festival
Dominik Loncar
124 Broadway Ave.
Ste. 112
Toronto, ON M4P-1V8 Canada
Phone: (416) 483-2222
inspirato@ca.inter.net
www.inspiratofestival.ca
Notes: Canada's largest ten-minute play
festival has a call out for submissions starting
in August. Playwrights are asked to submit a
ten-minute play based on a creative
challenge. Performances are held in the first
two weeks in June. See website for more
information.
Preferred Genre: Plays (No Musicals)
Preferred Length: 10-min./10pgs.
Submission Materials: full script
Submission Fee: No
Agent Only: No
Deadline(s): December 18, 2014

International Mystery Writers' Festival
Donna Conkwright, Program Director
101 Daviess St.
Owensboro, KY 42303
Phone: (270) 687-2770
Fax: (270) 687-2775
dconkwright@riverparkcenter.org
www.newmysteries.org
Notes: Est. 2007. Accepts unproduced plays,
teleplays or short screenplays in
mystery/thriller genre. Submissions not
returned. Response: 3 months.
Preferred Genre: Mystery
Preferred Length: Any length
Submission Materials: see website
Submission Fee: No
Agent Only: No

**Jewish Ensemble Theater Festival of New
Plays**
Christopher Bremer, Managing Director
Jewish Ensemble Theater
6600 W. Maple Rd.
West Bloomfield, MI 48322
Phone: (248) 788-2900
Fax: (248) 788-5160
c.bremer@jettheatre.org
www.jettheatre.org
Notes: Est. 1989. Submit by US mail only.
Preferred Genre: Plays or Musicals
Preferred Length: Any length
Submission Materials: full script, S.A.S.E.

Submission Fee: Yes
Agent Only: No
Deadline(s): August 1, 2014

Juneteenth Legacy Theatre
605 Water St. #21B
New York, NY 10002
Phone: (212) 964-1904
Fax: (212) 964-1904
juneteenthlegacy@aol.com
www.juneteenthlegacytheatre.com
Notes: Est. 1999. Juneteenth Legacy Theatre is now accepting one-act scripts for it's 2nd Annual Juneteenth Festival of New Plays in NYC. JLT accepts open submissions, with running times of less than 45 minutes, from established and emerging playwrights, who write about the African-American experience and its legacy. Preferred themes are: 19th Century experience especially in NY, Harlem Renaissance Era, an images of women. Please mail 4 copies of your script with current contact information. Please include a $15 script reading fee payable by money order to JLT. Electronic submissions and synopses are not accepted. Scripts are not returned.
Preferred Genre: Plays or Musicals
Special Interest: African-American
Preferred Length: One-Act
Submission Materials: full script (4 copies)
Submission Fee: Yes
Agent Only: No
Deadline(s): March 15, 2014

Kennedy Center American College Theater Festival
Gregg Henry, Artistic Director, KCACTF
Kennedy Center
Washington, DC 20566
Phone: (202) 416-8857
Fax: (202) 416-8802
kcactf@kennedy-center.org
www.KCACTF.org
Notes: Est. 1969. KCACTF is a national theater program involving 18,000 students from colleges and universities nationwide which has served as a catalyst in improving the quality of college theater in the United States.
Preferred Genre: All genres
Preferred Length: Any length
Submission Materials: full script, query letter, S.A.S.E., synopsis

Submission Fee: No
Agent Only: No
Deadline(s): December 1, 2014

Kitchen Dog Theater (KDT) New Works Festival
Tina Parker, Co-Artistic Director, Administrative Director
3120 McKinney Ave., #100
Dallas, TX 75204
Phone: (214) 953-1055
Fax: (214) 953-1873
tina@kitchendogtheater.org
www.kitchendogtheater.org
Notes: Est. 1990. Winner receives production, travel stipend, and royalty; 6 finalists receive reading. Submit by US mail only. Submissions recycled, not returned. Response: 8 months.
Preferred Genre: Plays (No Musicals)
Preferred Length: Full-length
Submission Materials: see website
Submission Fee: No
Agent Only: No
Deadline(s): January 1, 2014

Lark Play Development Center: Playwrights' Week
311 West 43rd Street, Suite 406
New York, NY 10036
Phone: (212) 246-2676
Fax: (212) 246-2609
submissions@larktheatre.org
www.larktheatre.org
Notes: Submissions accepted August - November for a fest of development. Public readings the following fall. See website for submission guidelines and deadlines. Response: 9 months.
Preferred Genre: Plays or Musicals
Preferred Length: Full-length
Submission Materials: application, full script
Submission Fee: No
Agent Only: No
Deadline(s): October 15, 2014

Last Frontier Theatre Conference
Dawson Moore, Coordinator
Box 97
Valdez, AK 99686
Phone: (907) 834-1614
Fax: (907) 834-1611
dmoore@pwscc.edu
www.theatreconference.org

Notes: Est. 1993. Application free. See website for conference fees. Work must not have been professionally produced.
Preferred Genre: Plays (No Musicals)
Preferred Length: Any length
Submission Materials: full script
Submission Fee: No
Agent Only: No
Deadline(s): November 15, 2014

Lavender Footlights Festival
P.O. Box 942107
Miami, FL 33194
Phone: (305) 433-8111
Fax: (305) 672-7818
Ryan@Lavenderfootlights.org
Notes: Est. 2000. Festival of readings with gay and lesbian themes.
Preferred Genre: Plays (No Musicals)
Special Interest: LGBT
Preferred Length: Full-length
Submission Materials: full script, S.A.S.E., synopsis
Submission Fee: No
Agent Only: No

Little Festival of the Unexpected
Portland Stage
Box 1458
Portland, ME 04104
Phone: (207) 774-1043
Fax: (207) 774-0576
dburson@portlandstage.com
www.portlandstage.com
Notes: Est. 1989. 1-week fest of new plays (unproduced, unpublished, unoptioned) with writers developing work through staged readings. Production: cast limit 8. US mail submission only. Submissions accepted year-round.
Preferred Genre: Plays (No Musicals)
Preferred Length: Full-length
Submission Materials: 10-pg sample, query letter, synopsis
Submission Fee: No
Agent Only: No

Long Beach Playhouse New Works Festival
5021 East Anaheim Street
Long Beach, CA 90804
Phone: (562) 494-1014 Ext 526
joblack@dslextreme.com
www.lbplayhouse.org

Notes: Est. 1989. Spring fest of 4 new unproduced plays in staged readings. Production: cast limit 10, limited set. Response: 3 months after festival.
Preferred Genre: Plays (No Musicals)
Preferred Length: Full-length
Submission Materials: see website
Submission Fee: Yes
Agent Only: No
Deadline(s): September 30, 2014

Los Angeles Women's Theatre Festival
11411 Cumpston Street
#204
Los Angeles, CA 91601
Phone: (818) 760-0408
Fax: (818) 760-0506
lawtfspotlight@yahoo.com
www.lawtf.com
Notes: The Los Angeles Women's Theatre Festival ("LAWTF") was organized to provide a vehicle for the development of women artists utilizing theatre to educate, enlighten and empower solo artists, audiences and volunteers.
Special Interest: Women's Interest
Submission Materials: see website
Submission Fee: Yes
Agent Only: No

Midtown International Theatre Festival (MITF)
John Chatterton, Exec. Producer
347 W. 36th St., #1204
New York, NY 10018
festival@oobr.com
www.midtownfestival.org
Notes: Every summer (starting in 2000) in midtown Manhattan, the Midtown International Theatre Festival (MITF) celebrates the diversity of theatre in New York City and beyond. We emphasize imaginative, low-tech staging. But putting on a play in a festival burgeoning with many other shows in only a handful of theatres means tight organization, both in the Festival and among the participants. We have sufficient caring, paid staff to keep the trains running on time. We are truly the Festival That Cares. In addition to offering a safe environment to develop innovative theatre, the MITF is devoted to keeping costs for participants down, starting with such benefits as 20 hours' FREE rehearsal space for full-length shows, FREE storage, FREE showcase

insurance, and more. The MITF welcomes submission of any kind of stage play, musical or otherwise, new or revived, mainstream or focused on an ethnic or cultural niche. Please visit our website for updated submissions guidelines.
Preferred Genre: All genres
Preferred Length: Any length
Submission Materials: see website
Submission Fee: Yes
Agent Only: No
Deadline(s): January 21, 2014

Mind the Gap BritBits Short Play Festival
Paula D'Alessandris, Artistic Director
535 W 23rd St.
S11G
New York, NY 10011
Phone: (212) 252-3137
allaboard@mindthegaptheatre.com
www.mindthegaptheatre.com
Notes: Writer must be native British, Scottish, Welsh, Irish. Prefer agent submission or by request from the organization. If neither of those apply, there is a $5 submission fee. Please submit a PDF or Word version of the play and a brief bio or CV. Submissions accepted year-round.
Preferred Genre: Plays (No Musicals)
Preferred Length: 10-min./10pgs.
Submission Materials: E-mail only
Submission Fee: Yes
Agent Only: Yes

Minnesota Shorts Festival of Plays
Greg F. Abbott, Coordinator
805 Garfield Avenue
North Mankato, MN 56003
Phone: (507) 934-8133
mnshorts@yahoo.com
www.mnshorts.com
Notes: The Minnesota Shorts Play Festival will begin accepting submissions starting January 1, 2014 for its sixth annual festival. Scripts can be on any topic but remember that the festival is a community performance (that means excessive foul language and nudity might not make the cut). Short plays must be performed in 15 minutes or less and sent as a PDF or DOC file. Keep all identifying information (Playwright name and contact info) to the title page because the plays are judged blind. Minnesota writers may submit 2 scripts but writers outside of Minnesota may submit 1. Playwrights must

find a director and cast for the play. The MN Shorts staff can help link you to actors and directors from the area. Each night the audience will pick a "Best of the Festival Play" that can win an additional $100. Please visit our website for more information.
Preferred Genre: All genres
Preferred Length: 15 min.
Submission Materials: E-mail only
Submission Fee: No
Agent Only: No
Deadline(s): April 30, 2014

National Alliance for Musical Theatre (NAMT)
Betsy King Militello, Executive Director
520 8th Ave., #301
New York, NY 10018
Phone: (212) 714-6668
Fax: (212) 714-0469
info@namt.org
www.namt.org/festival-submission.aspx
Notes: Est. 1985. Equity Showcase of 8 musicals in 45-minute presentations over 2 days. Participants receive stipend from NAMT. Invitation is industry only. Response: 6 months. Visit our website for specific submission guidelines.
Preferred Genre: Musical theatre
Preferred Length: Full-length
Submission Materials: application, audio CD, full script
Submission Fee: Yes
Agent Only: No
Deadline(s): February 26, 2014

National Black Theatre Festival
610 Coliseum Dr.
Winston-Salem, NC 27106
Phone: (336) 723-2266
nbtf@bellsouth.net
www.nbtf.org
Notes: Est. 1989. Biennial (odd years) festival in August of productions about the Black experience.
Preferred Genre: All genres
Special Interest: African-American
Preferred Length: Full-length
Submission Materials: see website
Submission Fee: No
Agent Only: No

National Music Theater Conference
The Eugene O'Neill Theater Center
Anne G. Morgan, Literary Manager

305 Great Neck Rd.
Waterford, CT 06385
Phone: (860) 443-5378
Fax: (860) 440-3161
litoffice@theoneill.org
www.theoneill.org
Notes: Est. 1978. Artistic Director, Paulette
Haupt. 2-3 week residency (July-August),
with rehearsal and in-hand public readings.
Assistance: stipend, room/board, travel.
Frequency: annual
Preferred Genre: Musical theatre
Preferred Length: Full-length
Submission Materials: see website
Submission Fee: Yes
Agent Only: No

National Playwrights Conference
The Eugene O'Neill Theater Center
Anne G. Morgan, Literary Manager
305 Great Neck Road
Waterford, CT 06385
Phone: (860) 443-5378
Fax: (860) 443-9653
litoffice@theoneill.org
www.oneill.org
Notes: Est. 1964. Artistic Director, Wendy C.
Goldberg Month residency (June-July),
includes 4-day workshop and 2 in-hand
readings with professional actors and
directors. Assistance: stipend, room/board,
travel. Frequency: annual
Preferred Genre: Plays (No Musicals)
Preferred Length: Full-length
Submission Materials: see website
Submission Fee: Yes
Agent Only: No
Deadline(s): October 25, 2014

**New Jersey Playwrights Festival of New
Plays**
Box 1663
Bloomfield, NJ 07003
Phone: (973) 259-9187
Fax: (973) 259-9188
info@12mileswest.org
www.12mileswest.org
Notes: Annual fest of plays by NJ
playwrights. Production: cast of 2-7, unit set.
Response: 1 yr.
Preferred Genre: All genres
Preferred Length: Any length
Submission Materials: see website
Submission Fee: No
Agent Only: No

New Play Festival
Chad Henry, Literary Associate
Denver Center
1101 13th Street
Denver, CO 80204
Phone: (303) 572-4456
Fax: (303) 893-3206
chenry@dcpa.org
www.denvercenter.org
Notes: Est. 2005. Workshop readings of four
to five new plays presented in February at the
Colorado Summit for industry and general
audience. At least two full productions of
previously workshopped plays each season.
New, unproduced plays only. Agent
submissions only for writers outside the
Rocky Mountain states. Response: up to 6
months. Submissions accepted year-round.
Preferred Genre: Plays or Musicals
Preferred Length: Full-length
Submission Materials: full script, S.A.S.E.
Submission Fee: No
Agent Only: No

New Professional Theatre Writers Festival
229 W. 42nd St., #501
New York, NY 10036
Phone: (212) 398-2666
Fax: (212) 398-2924
newprof@aol.com
www.newprofessionaltheatre.org
Notes: Est. 1991. Annual festival of work by
African-Americans, Asians, and Latinos. Also
business seminars, mentoring, and 2-week
residencies.
Preferred Genre: All genres
Preferred Length: Full-length
Submission Materials: see website
Submission Fee: No
Agent Only: No

New York City 15-Minute Play Fest
Elizabeth Keefe, Executive Director
American Globe Turnip Fest
145 W. 46th St., Fl. 3
New York, NY 10036
Phone: (212) 869-9809
Fax: (212) 869-9807
liz@americanglobe.org
www.15minuteplayfestival.org/index.html
Notes: Est. 1993. 2-week festival in May of
4-5 new plays each night. Production: cast of
2-10, no set. Response: 2 months. See
website for submission guidelines. Additional
website: www.americanglobe.org

Preferred Genre: Plays (No Musicals)
Preferred Length: 15 min.
Submission Materials: full script, S.A.S.E.
Submission Fee: No
Agent Only: No
Deadline(s): December 20, 2014

New York Musical Theatre Festival (NYMF)
Mary Kate Burke, Director of Programming
242 W. 49th Street, Suite 601
New York, NY 10019
Phone: (212) 664-0979
Fax: (212) 664-0978
literary@nymf.org
www.nymf.org
Preferred Genre: Musical theatre
Submission Materials: see website
Submission Fee: Yes
Agent Only: No

Northeast Indiana Playwright Festival
Fort Wayne Civic Theatre
Phillip H. Colglazier, Executive/Artistic Director
303 E. Main St.
Fort Wayne, IN 46802
Phone: (260) 422-8641
Fax: (260) 422-6699
pcolglazier@fwcivic.org
www.fwcivic.org
Notes: The Civic Theatre has established a playwright festival encouraging emerging and professional playwrights to submit their unproduced and unpublished plays. When the imagination is free to explore, not knowing any boundaries, and without intimidation, self-esteem and confidence matures in developing one's craft. Being a playwright requires soul searching, risk taking, courage, research, readings, feedback, and lots of rewriting that will hopefully lead to a fully staged production. The Civic Theatre continues to foster the creative potential that is within us as actors, dancers, singers and now as playwrights. 1st Place-$750, 2nd Place-$500, 3rd Place-$250, and possible stage reading and/or production May 30 - June 15, 2014. See website for submission guidelines.
Preferred Genre: All genres
Preferred Length: Any length
Submission Materials: see website

Submission Fee: No
Agent Only: No
Deadline(s): September 1, 2014

Old Opera House Theatre Company New Voice Play Festival
Steven Brewer, Managing and Artistic Director
204 N. George St.
Charles Town, WV 25414
Phone: (304) 752-4420
ooh@oldoperahouse.org
www.oldoperahouse.org
Notes: Est. 2001. Call or email for application and deadlines. One act play festival. Seeking plays 10 to 40 minutes in length.
Preferred Genre: Plays (No Musicals)
Preferred Length: One-Act
Submission Materials: see website
Submission Fee: Yes
Agent Only: No
Deadline(s): March 1, 2014

Penobscot Theatre
131 Main Street
4th Floor
Bangor, ME 04401
Phone: (207) 947-6618
info@penobscottheatre.org
www.penobscottheatre.org
Notes: 2 week New Play Festival featuring readings & workshops.
Preferred Genre: All genres
Preferred Length: Any length
Submission Materials: cover letter
Submission Fee: Yes
Agent Only: No

Play by Play
Stageworks/Hudson [NY]
Laura Margolis, Executive Artistic Director
41-A Cross St.
Hudson, NY 12534
Phone: (518) 828-7843
Fax: (518) 828-4026
literary@stageworkshudson.org
www.stageworkshudson.org/index.html
Notes: Play By Play is our annual festival of new one-act plays. Each season, we invite emerging and established playwrights to submit previously unpublished works to our selection committee. The plays are selected based on specific guidelines, as well as a "mix" that makes for great theatre.

Playwrights interested in this festival should email their contact information with the words "Play by Play playwright inquiry" in the subject line and your request for the guidelines in the body of the message.
Preferred Genre: All genres
Preferred Length: Any length
Submission Materials: E-mail only
Submission Fee: No
Agent Only: No

Playfest - Harriett Lake Festival of New Plays
812 E. Rollins St., #100
Orlando, FL 32803
Phone: (407) 447-1700
Fax: (407) 447-1701
patrickf@orlandoshakes.org
www.orlandoshakes.org
Notes: Est. 1989. 10 new plays receive readings, 2-3 developmental in Festival of new plays.
Preferred Genre: Plays (No Musicals)
Preferred Length: Full-length
Submission Materials: see website
Submission Fee: No
Agent Only: No
Deadline(s): March 15, 2014

Premiere Stages Play Festival
Clare Drobot, Producing Associate
Hutchinson Hall, 1000 Morris Ave.
Union, NJ 07083
Phone: (908) 737-4092
Fax: (908) 737-4636
premiere@kean.edu
www.kean.edu/premierestages
Notes: Est. 2004. Annual festival for playwrights born or living in New Jersey, Connecticut, New York, or Pennsylvania. Four public readings in March, full Equity production of winner in July., and 29 Hour Staged Reading for a second play in June. Frequency: annual. Production: cast limit 8. See website for details.
Preferred Genre: Plays (No Musicals)
Preferred Length: Full-length
Submission Materials: see website
Submission Fee: No
Agent Only: No
Deadline(s): January 15, 2014

Raymond J. Flores Short Play Festival (Around the Block)
5 E. 22nd St., #9-K
New York, NY 10010
Phone: (212) 673-9187
info@aroundtheblock.org
www.aroundtheblock.org
Notes: Est. 2004. Theme: Urban life and dreams. No children's plays. Electronic (e-mail or CD) submissions only. Also include a synopsis please.
Preferred Genre: Plays (No Musicals)
Preferred Length: 10-min./10pgs.
Submission Materials: application, bio, full script
Submission Fee: Yes
Agent Only: No
Deadline(s): November 30, 2014

Samuel French, Inc. Off Off Broadway Short-Play Festival
Billie Davis, Festival Coordinator
45 W. 25 St.
New York, NY 10010
Phone: (212) 206-8990
Fax: (202) 206-1429
oobfestival@samuelfrench.com
http://oob.samuelfrench.com
Notes: Est. 1976. 1-week festival hosted by Samuel French in NYC. 30 plays are selected for production. 6 finalists chosen for publication and representation by Samuel French. Shows must run 30 minutes or less. See website for submission guidelines.
Preferred Genre: Plays or Musicals
Preferred Length: One-Act
Submission Materials: application, full script
Submission Fee: Yes
Agent Only: No

San Francisco Fringe Festival (SFFF)
156 Eddy St.
San Francisco, CA 94102
Phone: (415) 931-1094
Fax: (415) 931-2699
mail@sffringe.org
www.sffringe.org
Notes: For 2013, we celebrate the 22nd annual San Francisco Fringe Festival with 36 companies presenting 158 performances between September 6th and September 21st. The Fringe is open to all artists, with performers selected through a public lottery. This creates diversity with performers

emerging and re-emerging across a range of disciplines and ethnicities. The San Francisco Fringe Festival is the largest grass roots theater festival in the Bay Area .
Preferred Genre: All genres
Preferred Length: Any length
Submission Materials: see website
Submission Fee: No
Agent Only: No

Seven Devils Playwrights Conference
Jeni Mahoney, Artistic Director
343 E. 30th St., #19-J
New York, NY 10016
Phone: (917) 881-9114
jeni@idtheater.org
www.idtheater.org
Notes: Est. 2001. 2-week play development conference in June. 4-6 new plays selected from open submissions for development in McCall, Idaho. Plays are presented to the public as either fully staged or seated readings.
Preferred Genre: Plays (No Musicals)
Preferred Length: Any length
Submission Materials: see website
Submission Fee: Yes
Agent Only: No
Deadline(s): November 15, 2014

Short Attention Span PlayFEST
Atlantis Playmakers
5261 Whitsett Avenue #20
Valley Village, CA 91607
Phone: (978) 667-0550
kdb@atlantisplaymakers.com
www.atlantisplaymakers.com
Notes: Est. 1998. Atlantis Playmakers developed two distinct programs: outstanding professional theater with a focus on highly physical storytelling, and classes to guide and develop the next generation of artists.
Preferred Genre: Plays (No Musicals)
Submission Materials: see website
Submission Fee: No
Agent Only: No

Short Play Festival
Milwaukee Repertory Theater
Leda Hoffmann, Literary Coordinator
108 E. Wells St.
Milwaukee, WI 53202
Phone: (414) 224-1761
Fax: (414) 224-9097
lhoffmann@milwaukeerep.com

www.milwaukeerep.com
Notes: Milwaukee Repertory Theatre's Fourth Annual Rep Lab Short Play Festival features the Rep's artistic intern ensemble in an evening of short plays. As we plan our fourth season of Rep Lab, we welcome submissions of short plays for the 2014 festival. Plays should be thirty seconds to twenty minutes in length with a cast size of one to twelve actors. Plays will be cast from the Rep's multi-ethnic ensemble of intern actors between the ages of 22 and 35, directed by a combination of staff, artistic associates, and directing interns, and produced and designed by the Rep's production interns, all under the guidance of the Rep's professional staff. Playwrights who plays are selected for production will receive commensurate royalty payments. All scripts received will be kept on file for consideration in future Rep Lab festivals. Please e-mail scripts in PDF or Word former with "Rep Lab - "Title of Play" in the subject line. Please include your name, contact information and agent info (if applicable) on the front page of the script. Please label the script file as follows: PLAY TITLE (Playwright's last name).
Submission Materials: see website
Submission Fee: No
Agent Only: No

ShowOff! Ten-Minute Playwriting Festival
Camino Real Playhouse
31776 El Camino Real
San Juan Capistrano, CA 92675
Phone: (949) 248-0808
Fax: (949) 248-0808
box_office@sbcglobal.net
www.caminorealplayhouse.org
Notes: Est. 1993. Material must be unpublished. Response: 3 months.
Preferred Genre: Plays (No Musicals)
Preferred Length: 10-min./10pgs.
Submission Materials: full script
Submission Fee: Yes
Agent Only: No
Deadline(s): October 15, 2014

Southern Appalachian Repertory Theatre (SART) - ScriptFEST
Sharon Christensen, SART Board Member & ScriptFEST Coordinator
Box 1720
Mars Hill, NC 28754

Phone: (828) 689-1384
Fax: (828) 689-1272
scriptfest@mhc.edu
www.sartplays.org
Notes: Est. 1981. Readings & critique of 4-6 plays in 3-day conference in Asheville and Mars Hill, North Carolina. Submissions must abide the specific guidelines. See website. Response: August/September.
Preferred Genre: Plays or Musicals
Preferred Length: Full-length
Submission Materials: see website
Submission Fee: No
Agent Only: No

Stony Point Cental
17 Crickettown Road
Stony Point, NY 10980
Phone: (347) 636-2765
dramaturgycentral@gmail.com
stonypointcenter.org/get-involved/latest-
    news/151-
    callforplaysnov2013#.UkSc5D_ueYk
Notes: You are invited to submit an original 10-minute play to a Playwriting Festival for early November 2014 to be held at Stony Point Center. This festival, Can America Make it? will benefit the Community of Living Traditions, a multifaith residency program that practices hospitality, engages faith and cultivates nonviolence and justice. This will be an opportunity for unproduced writers to have their work presented. The challenge of the Festival is the necessity for social action to heal the problems in our society. Using your skills and imagination, write an original play, drama or comedy that will be presented as staged productions. Our Can America Make It? festival calls for plays that deal with some aspect of nonviolent social action in response to injustice in a community and/or society. We are seeking plays written in any style that reveal fresh plot, interesting character(s), sufficient conflict and a running time of 10 minutes maximum.
Preferred Length: 10-min./10pgs.
Submission Materials: see website
Submission Fee: No
Agent Only: No
Deadline(s): October 13, 2014

Summer Shorts Festival
City Theatre [FL]
Susan Westfall, Literary Director

444 Brickell Ave., #229
Miami, FL 33131
Phone: (305) 755-9401
Fax: (305) 755-9404
10minuteplays@citytheatre.com
www.citytheatre.com
Notes: City Theatre is looking for wonderful short plays (up to ten minutes) for Summer Shorts and other programming. Having produced hundreds of plays, we know what we want; scripts that are lively and timely, hilarious and thought-provoking, poignant and dangerous. We look for plays that span style and genre. We will consider bilingual scripts and ten-minute musicals. We have no restriction on the age range of the characters. In other words, for us to consider a script for production, we are seeking compelling plays that rise above the ordinary. Submissions accepted annually August 30 - September 30.
Preferred Genre: All genres
Preferred Length: 10-min./10pgs.
Submission Materials: see website
Submission Fee: No
Agent Only: No
Deadline(s): September 30, 2014

Teatro del Pueblo
Alberto Justiniano, Artistic Director
209 West Page St.
Ste 208
St. Paul, MN 55107
Phone: (651) 224-8806
Fax: (651) 298-5796
al@teatrodelpueblo.org
www.teatrodelpueblo.org
Notes: Teatro del Pueblo promotes Latino culture through the creation and presentation of performing arts. Teatro develops and supports Latino artists, provides educational opportunities for all to experience Latino culture and promotes cross-cultural dialogue.
Preferred Genre: Plays or Musicals
Special Interest: Latino
Preferred Length: One-Act
Submission Materials: full script, synopsis
Submission Fee: No
Agent Only: No

Tennessee Williams/New Orleans Literary Festival
Jessica Ramakrishnan, Contest Coordinator
938 Lafayette St., #514
New Orleans, LA 70113
Phone: (504) 581-1144

Fax: (504) 581-3270
info@tennesseewilliams.net
www.tennesseewilliams.net
Notes: Each year the festival brings more than 130 authors, actors, and musicians for our five-day event, provides professional writing education to more than 200 area students, supports year-round literary programs in the community, nurtures up-and-coming literary and theatrical talent through our contests and readings, which bring in more than 1,700 poems, short stories, and one-act plays, and creates a total economic impact of 1 million dollars during the five-day event. The Festival's mission is threefold: to serve the community through educational, theatrical, literary, and musical programs; to nurture, support, and showcase regional, national, and international writers, actors, musicians, and other artists; and to honor the creative genius of Tennessee Williams, who considered this city his spiritual home. Please visit our website about our various contest submission guidelines.
Preferred Genre: Plays (No Musicals)
Submission Materials: see website
Submission Fee: Yes
Agent Only: No

The Kentucky Women Writers Conference
Phone: (859) 257-2874
wwk.program@gmail.com
www.kentuckywomenwriters.org
Notes: Will award a national playwriting prize to bring more scripts by women to the stage, especially those featuring majority-female casts. The winner will receive a production by Balagula Theatre in Lexington, Kentucky (www.balagula.com), plus a cash prize of $500. The winning play will be workshopped prior to its world premier for a paying audience in winter. One-act or full-length scripts in English, with a running time between 45 and 90 minutes, that have not been published or commercially produced as of the entry deadline and will not be published or produced before the release of the KWWC production. However, scripts that have been staged in a workshop production or script-in-hand staged readings are eligible.
Special Interest: Women's Interest
Submission Materials: see website
Submission Fee: No
Agent Only: No

Theatre Three [NY] One-Act Play Festival
Jeffrey Sanzel, Executive Artistic Director
Box 512, 412 Main St.
Port Jefferson, NY 11777
Phone: (631) 928-9202
Fax: (631) 928-9120
jeffrey@theatrethree.com
www.theatrethree.com
Notes: Est. 1997. Festival of One-Act Plays. Each season, festival presents 5 to 6 world premieres on the second stage. Non-equity productions. All plays performed 10 times. Preferred length: 35 minute maximum. Frequency: annual. Production: any age, casts up to 10 people, minimal set. Response Time: 3-6 months
Preferred Genre: Plays (No Musicals)
Preferred Length: One-Act
Submission Materials: see website
Submission Fee: No
Agent Only: No
Deadline(s): September 30, 2014

Trustus Playwrights' Festival
Sarah Hammond, Literary Manager
Box 11721
Columbia, SC 29211
Phone: (803) 254-9732
Fax: (803) 771-9153
shammond@trustus.org
www.trustus.org/playwrights.php
Notes: Est. 1984. Trustus Theatre in Columbia, South Carolina produces a new play every August. To apply, please send a 10-page sample, synopsis, bio/resume, and contact information to shammond@trustus.org. Trustus will request full scripts from the semi-finalists. Please see the website for complete guidelines.
Preferred Genre: Plays (No Musicals)
Submission Materials: 10-pg sample, bio, synopsis
Submission Fee: Yes
Agent Only: No
Deadline(s): March 1, 2014

Utah Shakespeare Festival: New American Playwrights Project
Charles Metten, Director, NAPP
351 W. Center St.
Cedar City, UT 84720
Phone: (435) 586-7880
Fax: (435) 865-8003
metten@bard.org
www.bard.org

Notes: August festival of 3 play readings, with writers in residence. Production: cast of 8-10, flexible stage. Unproduced, with single author. Special Interest: Western Themes.
Preferred Genre: Plays (No Musicals)
Preferred Length: Full-length
Submission Materials: full script
Submission Fee: Yes
Agent Only: No
Deadline(s): November 1, 2014

Weathervane Playhouse
Eileen Moushey, Coordinator, 10 Minute Play Contest
1301 Weathervane Lane
Akron, OH 44313
Phone: (330) 836-2323
Fax: (330) 873-2150
10minuteplay@weathervaneplayhouse.com
www.weathervaneplayhouse.com
Notes: Weathervane Community Playhouse produces high-quality live theater with volunteer artists, designers, and technicians under professional direction, provides education and training in theater arts and appreciation, and engages and entertains its audience and constituents to enrich the quality of life in Northeast Ohio.
Preferred Genre: Plays (No Musicals)
Preferred Length: 10-min./10pgs.
Submission Materials: E-mail only
Submission Fee: Yes
Agent Only: No
Deadline(s): May 1, 2014

WildClaw Theatre Deathscribe Festival
WildClaw Theatre
Scott T. Barsotti, Literary Manager
Chicago, IL 60613
deathscribe2014@gmail.com
www.wildclawtheatre.com
Notes: The Annual DEATHSCRIBE Festival of Horror Radio Plays seeks submissions of 10-minute radio plays in the Horror genre, formatted for radio with sound cues included. Limit 2 submissions per author, per year. 5 finalists are selected annually to have their radio plays produced at the December event. A panel of judges selects the winner of the Bloody Axe Award. See website for guidelines.
Preferred Genre: Radio plays
Preferred Length: 10-min./10pgs.
Submission Materials: see website

Submission Fee: No
Agent Only: No
Deadline(s): August 1, 2014

Williamstown Theatre Festival
229 W. 42nd St., #801
New York, NY 10036
Phone: (212) 395-9090
Fax: (212) 395-9099
wtfinfo@wtfestival.org
www.wtfestival.org
Notes: Est. 1955. New Play Staged Reading Series offers 7 works/season. Agent Submission only. Through these 58 years, the Festival's goals remain constant: to attract top talent, cultivate young artists, produce reinterpreted versions of classics and new plays from gifted playwrights and to continue to attract audiences with the quality and ambition of our work.
Preferred Genre: Plays (No Musicals)
Preferred Length: Full-length
Submission Materials: query letter, S.A.S.E.
Submission Fee: No
Agent Only: Yes

Year-End Series (YES) New Play Festival
Sandra Forman, Project Director
Northern Kentucky University
One Nunn Drive, Fine Arts 228
Highland Heights, KY 41099
Phone: (859) 572-6303
Fax: (859) 572-6057
forman@nku.edu
www.nku.edu/~theatre
Notes: Est. 1983. Biennial (odd years) festival in April of 3 new works receive full productions. Playwrights flown in for final week of rehearsals and opening night. Submission deadlines are even number years. Submissions accepted between May 1 - September 30, 2014.
Preferred Genre: Plays or Musicals
Preferred Length: Full-length
Submission Materials: character breakdown, full script, S.A.S.E., synopsis
Submission Fee: No
Agent Only: No
Deadline(s): September 30, 2014

Young Playwrights Festival
Center Stage [MD]
Literary Dept., Dramaturg
700 N. Calvert Street
Baltimore, MD 21202

Phone: (410) 986-4042
Fax: (410) 986-4046
dramaturg@centerstage.org
www.centerstage.org
Notes: Students in grades K-12 throughout the state of Maryland are eligible and may even get to see their play on stage. Numerous plays are honored each year with workshops, in-school performances, and even performances at Center Stage.
Preferred Genre: All genres
Preferred Length: Any length
Submission Materials: see website
Submission Fee: No
Agent Only: No
Deadline(s): February 7, 2014

Contests

Anna Zornio Memorial Children's Theatre Playwriting Award
Michael Wood, Administrative Manager
UNH Theatre/Dance Dept.
PCAC, 30 Academic Way
Durham, NH 03824
Phone: (603) 862-3038
Fax: (603) 862-0298
mike.wood@unh.edu
http://cola.unh.edu/theatre-dance/resource/zornio
Notes: Est. 1979. Quadrennial cash/production award for unproduced, unpublished children's work for residents of U.S. and Canada. Next award will be given in 2016. See website for updated information.
Preferred Genre: All genres
Special Interest: Theatre for Young Audiences
Preferred Length: Full-length
Submission Materials: see website
Submission Fee: No
Agent Only: No

Arts & Letters Prize in Drama
Georgia College
GCSU Campus Box 89
Milledgeville, GA 31061
Phone: (478) 445-1289
Fax: (478) 445-5961
al@gcsu.edu
http://al.gcsu.edu
Notes: Est. 1999. Response Time: 3 months. Our regular reading period for submissions is August 1 to January 31. See website for specific submission guidelines.
Preferred Genre: All genres
Preferred Length: One-Act
Submission Materials: see website
Submission Fee: Yes
Agent Only: No
Deadline(s): January 31, 2014

Aurora Theatre Company: Global Age Project
Matthew Graham Smith, GAP Producer
2081 Addison St.
Berkeley, CA 94704
Phone: (510) 843-4042
Fax: (510) 843-4826
literary@auroratheatre.org
www.auroratheatre.org
Notes: Celebrating fresh forward-looking visions of global significance. Online submissions only. Response time: 5 months. The Global Age Project, a new play program, has an annual submission deadline each summer. Check website for details.
Preferred Genre: Plays or Musicals
Preferred Length: Any length
Submission Materials: full script
Submission Fee: Yes
Agent Only: No

Babes With Blades - Joining Sword and Pen
Morgan Manasa
Babes With Blades
7016 N. Greenview, #2
Chicago, IL 60626
swordandpen@babeswithblades.org
www.babeswithblades.org
Notes: Est. 1997. New play development program and contest. Work must include fighting roles for women!
Preferred Genre: All genres
Special Interest: Women's Interest
Preferred Length: Full-length
Submission Materials: see website
Submission Fee: No
Agent Only: No

Charles M. Getchell Award, SETC
Judi Rossabi, Communications & Marketing Manager
1175 Revolution Mill Drive, Studio 14

Greensboro, NC 27405
Phone: (864) 656-5415
Fax: (864) 656-1013
info@setc.org
www.setc.org
Notes: Submit full script via online
application only. See website for eligibility
guidelines.
Preferred Genre: All genres
Preferred Length: Any length
Submission Materials: application, full
script
Submission Fee: Yes
Agent Only: No
Deadline(s): June 1, 2014

Christopher Brian Wolk Award
Kim T. Sharp, Literary Manager
Abingdon Theatre
312 W. 36th St., 6th floor
New York, NY 10018
Phone: (212) 868-2055
Fax: (212) 868-2056
ksharp@abingdontheatre.org
www.abingdontheatre.org
Notes: Est. 2001. Mail printed copy of
unoptioned script, unproduced in NYC, with
character breakdown, production history, bio.
No Musicals. See website for updated
guidelines. Production: cast limit 8. Response
time: 3-6 months.
Preferred Genre: Plays (No Musicals)
Preferred Length: Full-length
Submission Materials: see website
Submission Fee: No
Agent Only: No
Deadline(s): June 1, 2014

**City Theatre National Award for Short
Playwriting Contest**
City Theatre [FL]
Susan Westfall, Literary Director
444 Brickell Ave., #229
Miami, FL 33131
Phone: (305) 755-9401
Fax: (305) 755-9404
10minuteplays@citytheatre.com
www.citytheatre.com
Notes: The City Theatre National Award for
Short Playwriting furthers the Company's
mission to identify, acknowledge and award
excellence in dramatic writing. With the
mission of developing and producing original
short plays by established talents and
promising new voices, City Theatre will

select up to fifteen playwrights from among
the hundreds who annually submit their ten-
minute plays to the company for special
recognition. The winning play will be
produced in the annual Summer Shorts
festival, for which the playwright will earn
royalties and be invited to Miami for the
festival. Transportation, hotel, the Weekend
and a cash prize will be awarded up to a
value of $2,000.00. Finalists will be
considered for production in the Summer
Shorts festival and other programming, and
submitted to the Samuel French Off-
Broadway Festival. The Summer Shorts
Festival is produced annually in Miami
during the month of June.
Preferred Genre: All genres
Preferred Length: 10-min./10pgs.
Submission Materials: see website
Submission Fee: No
Agent Only: No

**Clauder Competition for New England
Playwrights**
Portland Stage
Box 1458
Portland, ME 04104
Phone: (207) 774-1043
Fax: (207) 774-0576
dburson@portlandstage.org
www.portlandstage.org
Notes: Est. 1981. Competition for
unpublished/unproduced work from New
England writers (current or former resident;
student). Frequency: every 3 years.
Production: cast limit 8. US Mail submission
only.
Preferred Genre: All genres
Preferred Length: Full-length
Submission Materials: full script
Submission Fee: No
Agent Only: No
Deadline(s): March 1, 2015

College of Charleston (CofC)
Marie Oleksiak, Office Manager
Theatre Department
66 George St.
Charleston, SC 29424
Phone: (843) 953-6306
Fax: (843) 953-8210
oleksiakm@cofc.edu
http://theatre.cofc.edu/index.php
Notes: College of Charleston School of the
Arts announces the Todd McNerney 4th

Annual National Playwriting Contest. The winner will be awarded a $400 cash prize, a stage reading at the Piccolo Spoleto Festival, and a travel allowance for the author to attend the reading. The Runner-up will be awarded a $100 cash prize and a stage reading at the Piccolo Spoleto Festival. E-mail a PDF and mail 1 hard copy to the addresses listed. Both items and entry fee must be received to be eligible. Entry fee of $10 is payable to the College of Charleston. Material must be unpublished and unproduced.
Preferred Genre: Plays (No Musicals)
Preferred Length: Full-length
Submission Materials: see website
Submission Fee: Yes
Agent Only: No
Deadline(s): February 3, 2014

Community Theatre Association of Michigan
Vincent Weiler, Playwriting Contest Chair
4026 Lester
Oscoda, MI 48750
Phone: (231) 354-7291
vweiler@ioscoresa.net
www.communitytheatre.org
Notes: Author must be a resident of Michigan. Submit script by e-mail, PDF only.
Preferred Genre: Plays (No Musicals)
Preferred Length: Full-length
Submission Materials: full script
Submission Fee: Yes
Agent Only: No
Deadline(s): May 15, 2014

David C. Horn Prize
Alison MacKeen, Editor
Yale Univ. Press
Box 209040
New Haven, CT 06520
Phone: (203) 432-0975
Fax: (203) 436-1064
info@dchornfoundation.org
www.dchornfoundation.org
Notes: Est. 2006. Submissions not returned. Submissions accepted from June 1 - August 15. See website for specific submission guidelines.
Preferred Genre: Plays (No Musicals)
Preferred Length: Full-length
Submission Materials: see website

Submission Fee: No
Agent Only: No
Deadline(s): August 15, 2014

David Mark Cohen Playwriting Award
Kennedy Center American College Theater Festival
Kennedy Center, Education Div.
Washington, DC 20566
Phone: (202) 416-8857
Fax: (202) 416-8802
skshaffer@kennedy-center.org
www.kcactf.org
Notes: Plays accepted only from college/university participating in KC/ACTF program.
Preferred Genre: Plays (No Musicals)
Preferred Length: Full-length & 10-min.
Submission Materials: application, full script, synopsis
Submission Fee: Yes
Agent Only: No
Deadline(s): November 1, 2014

Dezart Performs
78884 Stansbury Ct
Palm Desert, CA 92211
Phone: (760) 322-0179
playsubmissions@dezartperforms.com
www.dezartperforms.com
Notes: Dezart Performs is a professional non-profit theatre company in Palm Springs dedicated to bringing new and provocative works for the stage to the Coachella Valley. Four to seven plays will be chosen for the Annual Play Reading Series, a two-weekend festival in downtown Palm Springs. All submissions are reviewed by a 12-member committee of entertainment professionals and members of the theatre community.
Preferred Genre: Plays (No Musicals)
Preferred Length: Any length
Submission Materials: see website
Submission Fee: Yes
Agent Only: No
Deadline(s): October 11, 2014

Dubuque Fine Arts Players One Act Play Contest
Thomas Boxleiter, Contest Coordinator
Dubuque Fine Arts Players
P.O. Box 1160
Dubuque, IA 52004
contact@dbqoneacts.com
www.dbqoneacts.org

Notes: Est. 1977. Unproduced/unpublished material can be sent via US Mail or electronically. Production: cast of 2-5, unit set. Response: 6 months. Cash prizes. Winning plays are usually produced. See website for submission guidelines.
Preferred Genre: Plays (No Musicals)
Preferred Length: One-Act
Submission Materials: see website
Submission Fee: Yes
Agent Only: No
Deadline(s): January 31, 2014

Essential Theatre Playwriting Award
Peter Hardy, Producing Artistic Director
1414 Foxhall Lane #10
Atlanta, GA 30316
Phone: (404) 212-0815
pmhardy@aol.com
www.essentialtheatre.com
Notes: Material must be unproduced of at least an hour's length. Writer must be resident of Georgia.
Preferred Genre: Plays or Musicals
Preferred Length: Any length
Submission Materials: full script
Submission Fee: No
Agent Only: No
Deadline(s): April 23, 2014

FirstStage One-Act Play Contest
Box 38280
Los Angeles, CA 90038
Phone: (323) 350-6271
firststagela@aol.com
www.firststagela.org
Notes: Est. 1983. Staged readings of new/unproduced work (30 minutes or less). Submissions not returned. See website for details. Response: 3 weeks.
Preferred Genre: Plays (No Musicals)
Preferred Length: One-Act
Submission Materials: full script
Submission Fee: Yes
Agent Only: No
Deadline(s): October 15, 2014

Fred Ebb Award
Roundabout Theatre
231 W. 39th St., #1200
New York, NY 10018
info@fredebbfoundation.org
www.fredebbfoundation.org
Notes: Est. 2005. Named for lyricist Fred Ebb (1928-2004), award recognizes

excellence by a songwriter or songwriting team that hasn't yet achieved significant commercial success. Frequency: annual. Award: $50,000. Applications are accepted June 3-28. Check website for updated guidelines.
Preferred Genre: Musical theatre
Agent Only: No
Deadline(s): June 28, 2014

FUSION Theatre Company
Dennis Gromelski, Executive Director
700 1st Street NW
Albuquerque, NM 87102
Phone: (505) 766-9412
info@fusionabq.org
www.FUSIONnm.org
Notes: Eighth annual short works fest entitled "The Seven". Works must be unproduced/unpublished. Winner flown to New Mexico for production. $5 fee if you submit via e-mail, fee waved if sent by mail. See website for details.
Preferred Genre: Plays or Musicals
Preferred Length: 10-min./10pgs.
Submission Materials: see website
Submission Fee: Yes
Agent Only: No
Deadline(s): April 11, 2014

Garrard Best Play Competition
1101 Honor Heights Dr.
Muskogee, OK 74401
Phone: (918) 683-1701
Fax: (918) 683-3070
5civilizedtribes@sbcglobal.net
www.fivetribes.org
Notes: Biennial (even years) competition for playwrights of Cherokee, Chickasaw, Choctaw, Creek or Seminole lineage that reflect the history, culture, or traditions of the Five Civilized Tribes.
Preferred Genre: All genres
Special Interest: Native American
Submission Materials: bio, full script (4 copies), proof of heritage
Submission Fee: No
Agent Only: No

Georgia College and State University
Porter Hall CBX 066
Milledgeville, GA 31061
Phone: (478) 445-1980
Fax: (478) 445-1633
kbermanth@aol.com

www.gcsu.edu/theatre
Notes: Work must be unoptioned, unproduced, unpublished and author must be available for a short residency.
Preferred Genre: Plays (No Musicals)
Preferred Length: Full-length
Submission Materials: see website
Submission Fee: Yes
Agent Only: No

Goshen College Peace Playwriting Contest
Douglas Caskey, Director of Theatre
1700 S. Main St.
Goshen, IN 46526
Phone: (574) 535-7393
Fax: (574) 535-7660
douglc@goshen.edu
http://www.goshen.edu/theater/peace-play/
Notes: $500 cash prize
Preferred Genre: Plays (No Musicals)
Preferred Length: One-Act
Submission Materials: full script, resume, synopsis
Submission Fee: No
Agent Only: No
Deadline(s): December 31, 2014

Grawemeyer Award for Music Composition
Marc Satterwhite, Director
Univ. of Louisville School of Music
Louisville, KY 40292
Phone: (502) 852-1787
Fax: (502) 852-0520
GrawemeyerMusic@louisville.edu
www.grawemeyer.org/music
Notes: Est. 1984. The University of Louisville offers an international prize in recognition of outstanding achievement by a living composer in a large musical genre: choral, orchestral, chamber, electronic, song-cycle, dance, opera, musical theater, extended solo work and more.
Preferred Length: Any length
Submission Materials: see website
Submission Fee: Yes
Agent Only: No

Harold & Mimi Steinberg National Student Playwriting Award
Kennedy Center American College Theater Festival
Gregg Henry, Artistic Director, KCACTF
Kennedy Center for the Performing Arts
Washington, DC 20566

Phone: (202) 416-8864
Fax: (202) 416-4892
ghenry@kennedy-center.org
www.kcactf.org
Notes: For the outstanding student-written, full-length play premiering at a college or university participating in KCACTF program.
Preferred Genre: Plays (No Musicals)
Preferred Length: Full-length
Submission Materials: application
Submission Fee: Yes
Agent Only: No
Deadline(s): November 1, 2014

Jackie White Memorial Nat'l. Children's Play Writing Contest
Betsy Phillips, Director
309 Parkade Blvd.
Columbia, MO 65202
Phone: (573) 874-5628
bybetsy@yahoo.com
www.cectheatre.org
Notes: Est. 1988. In memory of Jackie Pettit White (1947-91). All scripts read and receive evaluation. Please also include author's resume with your submission. Production: at least 7 speaking roles, sets appropriate for community theaters.
Preferred Genre: Plays or Musicals
Preferred Length: Full-length
Submission Materials: application, full script, S.A.S.E.
Submission Fee: Yes
Agent Only: No
Deadline(s): June 1, 2014

Jane Chambers Playwriting Award
Dept. of Perf. Arts, Georgetown U.
108 Davis Center, Box 571063
Washington, DC 20057
Phone: (202) 687-1327
mer46@georgetown.edu
www.athe.org/displaycommon.
    cfm?an=1&subarticlenbr=138
Notes: Award for plays and performance texts by females that reflect a feminist perspective and contain a majority of opportunities for women performers. Submissions not returned.
Preferred Genre: All genres
Special Interest: Women's Interest
Preferred Length: Any length
Submission Materials: application, full script (3 copies), resume, synopsis

Submission Fee: No
Agent Only: No
Deadline(s): March 1, 2014

Jane Chambers Student Playwriting Award

230 W. 56th St., #65-A
New York, NY 10019
jenscottmob@gmail.com
Notes: Award for plays and texts by female students that reflect a feminist perspective and contain a majority of opportunities for women performers. Submissions not returned.
Preferred Genre: All genres
Special Interest: Women's Interest
Preferred Length: Full-length
Submission Materials: application, full script (2 copies), resume, synopsis
Submission Fee: No
Agent Only: No
Deadline(s): March 1, 2014

Jean Kennedy Smith Playwriting Award

Kennedy Center American College Theater Festival
Gregg Henry, Artistic Director, KCACTF
Kennedy Center, Education Div.
Washington, DC 20566
Phone: (202) 416-8864
Fax: (202) 416-4892
ghenry@kennedy-center.org
www.kcactf.org
Notes: Award for a student-written play addressing issues of disability (as defined by the ADA). Plays accepted only from college/university participating in KC/ACTF program.
Preferred Genre: Plays (No Musicals)
Special Interest: Disabled
Preferred Length: Any length
Submission Materials: see website
Submission Fee: Yes
Agent Only: No
Deadline(s): November 1, 2014

John Cauble Short Play Awards Program

Kennedy Center American College Theater Festival
Gregg Henry, Artistic Director, KCACTF
Kennedy Center, Education Div.
Washington, DC 20566
Phone: (202) 416-8864
Fax: (202) 416-4892
skshaffer@kennedy-center.org

www.kcactf.org
Notes: Plays accepted only from college/university participating in KC/ACTF program.
Preferred Genre: Plays (No Musicals)
Preferred Length: One-Act
Submission Materials: application, full script, synopsis
Submission Fee: Yes
Agent Only: No
Deadline(s): November 1, 2014

John Gassner Memorial Playwriting Award

Joseph Juliano, Manager, Operations
NETC
215 Knob Hill Dr.
Hamden, CT 06518
Phone: (617) 851-8535
Fax: (203) 288-5938
mail@NETConline.org
www.NETConline.org
Notes: Est. 1967. Honors theater historian John Gassner for his lifetime dedication to all aspects of professional and academic theater. Seeking unproduced/unpublished plays.
Preferred Genre: Plays (No Musicals)
Preferred Length: Full-length
Submission Materials: full script, query letter
Submission Fee: Yes
Agent Only: No
Deadline(s): April 15, 2014

Julie Harris Playwright Awards

Beverly Hills Theatre Guild
Box 148
Beverly Hills, CA 90213
Phone: (310) 273-3390
www.beverlyhillstheatreguild.com
Notes: The Beverly Hills Theatre Guild annually sponsors the Julie Harris Playwright Awards Competition to discover new theatrical works and to encourage established or emerging writers to create quality works for the theatre. Prizes are as follows: FIRST PRIZE: $3,500 -- The Janet and Maxwell Salter Playwright Award. SECOND PRIZE: $2,500 -- The Dr. Henry and Lilian Nesburn Playwright Award. THIRD PRIZE: $1,500 -- The Irma Colen Memorial Award. We accept scripts from August 1st to November 1st for this competition. See website for specific guidelines. There is a $15 submission fee

(check or money order to Beverly Hills Theatre Guild).
Preferred Genre: All genres
Preferred Length: Full-length
Submission Materials: see website
Submission Fee: No
Agent Only: No
Deadline(s): November 1, 2014

Kernodle New Play Award
Robert Ford, Director
619 Kimpel Hall
University of Arkansas
Fayetteville, AR 72701
Phone: (479) 575-2953
Fax: (479) 575-7602
kernodle@uark.edu
http://theatre.uark.edu
Notes: Co-administered by Theatre Squared and the Department of Theatre, University of Arkansas. Playwrights who live or have lived in Arkansas are strongly encouraged, and we give preference to plays and musicals that reflect the rich diversity of mid-America. Award is $500, plus a reading in the Department's "Off the Page" series. Submissions automatically considered for the 2015 Arkansas New Play Festival. Further details at http://theatre2.org/playwright-resources
Preferred Genre: All genres
Preferred Length: Full-length
Submission Materials: full script, query letter
Submission Fee: No
Agent Only: No
Deadline(s): November 1, 2014

Laity Theatre Company
3053 Rancho Vista Blvd. Ste. H336
Palmdale, CA 93551
Phone: (888) 732-6092
Fax: (661) 430-5423
contact@laityarts.org
www.laityarts.org
Notes: Seeking unproduced/unpublished material for readings/workshops thematically linked to women, theatre for young audiences, writers of color and people with disabilities.
Preferred Genre: Plays (No Musicals)
Preferred Length: Any length
Submission Materials: 15-pg sample, query letter, synopsis

Submission Fee: No
Agent Only: No

Lakeshore Players Theatre
Phone: (651) 426-3275
Fax: (651) 426-3275
office@lakeshoreplayers.com
www.lakeshoreplayers.com/13-14PlayContestRULES.html
Notes: Lakeshore Players mission is to provide community enrichment opportunities through the performing arts. Lakeshore serves as the premier performing arts center for the White Bear Lake area and is committed to providing opportunities for our community to participate in and experience live theatre. Lakeshore Players Theatre is accepting submissions for 10-minute plays.
Preferred Genre: Plays (No Musicals)
Preferred Length: 10-min./10pgs.
Submission Materials: see website
Submission Fee: No
Agent Only: No
Deadline(s): November 25, 2014

Latino Playwriting Award
Kennedy Center American College Theater Festival
Kennedy Center, Education Div.
Washington, DC 20566
Phone: (202) 416-8857
Fax: (202) 416-8802
skshaffer@kennedy-center.org
www.kcactf.org
Notes: The award will be presented to the author of the best student-written play by a Latino student playwright attending a college/university participating in KCACTF.
Preferred Genre: Plays (No Musicals)
Special Interest: Latino
Preferred Length: Full-length
Submission Materials: application
Submission Fee: Yes
Agent Only: No
Deadline(s): November 1, 2014

LiveWire Chicago Theatre
Krista D'Agostino, Literary Manager
P.O. Box 11226
Chicago, IL 60611
Phone: (312) 533-4666
livewirechicago@gmail.com
www.livewirechicago.com
Notes: Annual short play festival surrounding a central theme. Work must be previously

unproduced. See website for theme guidelines, submission criteria, deadlines and more info. Submissions are accepted January 15th through April 15th.
Preferred Genre: Plays (No Musicals)
Preferred Length: 10-min./10pgs.
Submission Materials: full script
Submission Fee: No
Agent Only: No
Deadline(s): April 15, 2014

Lorraine Hansberry Playwriting Award
Kennedy Center American College Theater Festival
Gregg Henry, Artistic Director, KCACTF
Kennedy Center, Education Div.
Washington, DC 20566
Phone: (202) 416-8864
Fax: (202) 416-4892
ghenry@kennedy-center.org
www.kcactf.org
Notes: For the outstanding play written by a student of African or Diasporan heritage. Plays accepted only from college/university participating in KC/ACTF program.
Preferred Genre: Plays (No Musicals)
Special Interest: African-American
Preferred Length: Any length
Submission Materials: see website
Submission Fee: Yes
Agent Only: No
Deadline(s): November 1, 2014

Mark Twain Prize for Comic Playwriting
Kennedy Center American College Theater Festival
Gregg Henry, Artistic Director, KCACTF
Kennedy Center, Education Office
Arlington, VA 22210
Phone: (212) 330-6045
Fax: (212) 330-6015
mdambrosi@markspaneth.com
www.kcactf.org
Notes: For the outstanding student-written comedy or play with a significant comic element from college/university participating in KC/ACTF program.
Preferred Genre: Comedy
Preferred Length: Any length
Submission Materials: application
Submission Fee: Yes
Agent Only: No
Deadline(s): November 1, 2014

McLaren Memorial Comedy Playwriting Competition
MaryLou Cassidy, McLaren Chair
Midland MCT
2000 W. Wadley Ave.
Midland, TX 79705
Phone: (432) 682-2544
Fax: (432) 682-6136
tracy@mctmidland.org
www.mctmidland.org
Notes: Est. 1989. Finalists provided with a reader's theatre presentation of script to a live audience and the winner may be produced as part of an upcoming MCT Season. Prize money awarded. Electronic submissions to our website preferred. Fee and Form must be sent by regular post.
Preferred Genre: Comedy
Preferred Length: Full-length
Submission Materials: see website
Submission Fee: Yes
Agent Only: No
Deadline(s): February 28, 2014

MetLife Nuestras Voces National Playwriting Competition
Allison Astor-Vargas, Special Projects Manager & Education Outreach
Repertorio Espanol
138 E. 27th St.
New York, NY 10016
Phone: (212) 225-9950
Fax: (212) 225-9085
nuestrasvoces@repertorio.org
www.repertorio.org/opportunities/
Notes: US, Latino Playwrights and those from Puerto Rico - over 18 years old and/or plays that deal with subjects and themes relating to Hispanics/Latinos living in the US. Electronic submissions only.
Preferred Genre: Plays (No Musicals)
Special Interest: Latino
Preferred Length: Full-length
Submission Materials: E-mail only
Submission Fee: No
Agent Only: No
Deadline(s): June 1, 2014

Mississippi Theatre Association
707 Bardwell Road
Starkville, MS 39759
Phone: (812) 320-3534
tklee1976@gmail.com
www.mta-online.org

Notes: This competition is open to all Mississippi writers either in state or abroad. Submit via online form available on website.
Preferred Genre: All genres
Preferred Length: One-Act
Submission Materials: application, full script, synopsis
Submission Fee: No
Agent Only: No
Deadline(s): October 17, 2014

Musical Theater Award
Kennedy Center American College Theater Festival
Gregg Henry, Artistic Director, KCACTF
Kennedy Center, Education Div.
Washington, DC 20566
Phone: (202) 416-8864
Fax: (202) 416-4892
ghenry@kennedy-center.org
www.kcactf.org
Notes: For the outstanding musical theater or music theater piece written and/or developed at a college or university. At least one member of the Composer/Lyricist/Librettist team must be a student or faculty member at a college/university participating in KC/ACTF program.
Preferred Genre: Musical theatre
Preferred Length: Any length
Submission Materials: application
Submission Fee: Yes
Agent Only: No
Deadline(s): November 1, 2014

Naples Players ETC
701 5th Ave. S.
Naples, FL 34102-6662
Phone: (239) 434-7340
venus46@naples.net
www.naplesplayers.com
Notes: Writer must reside in Collier, Lee, Charlotte, Glades or Hendry counties in Florida and may not be a member of the anonymous judging panel. Please see our website for updated submission guidelines.
Preferred Genre: Plays (No Musicals)
Preferred Length: One-Act
Submission Materials: see website
Submission Fee: No
Agent Only: No

National Latino Playwriting Award
Katherine Monberg, Literary Assistant
Arizona Theatre Company
343 S. Scott Avenue
Tucson, AZ 85701
Phone: (520) 884-8210
Fax: (520) 628-9129
kmonberg@arizonatheatre.org
www.arizonatheatre.org
Notes: Must be resident of US, or Mexico; Latino.
Preferred Genre: All genres
Special Interest: Latino
Preferred Length: Full-length
Submission Materials: see website
Submission Fee: No
Agent Only: No
Deadline(s): December 31, 2014

National One-Act Playwriting Competition
The Little Theatre of Alexandria
600 Wolfe Street
Alexandria, VA 22314
Phone: (703) 683-5778
asklta@thelittletheatre.com
www.thelittletheatre.com
Notes: All submissions must be original, unpublished and un-produced (not staged for a paying audience as of date of entry) one-act plays. Time permitting, the Little Theatre of Alexandria will present a staged-reading or small-scale production of the top three shows. In addition, cash awards of $350 for 1st Place, $250 for 2nd Place and $150 for 3rd Place are presented. Submissions must be postmarked between the dates of January 1 - October 31, 2014. All submissions must include a $20.00 (per play) entry fee. Only two plays per author will be considered. See website for complete guidelines.
Preferred Genre: All genres
Preferred Length: One-Act
Submission Materials: see website
Submission Fee: Yes
Agent Only: No
Deadline(s): October 31, 2014

National Ten-Minute Play Contest
Sarah Lunnie, Literary Manager
Actors Theatre of Louisville
316 W. Main St.
Louisville, KY 40202
Phone: (502) 584-1265
Fax: (502) 561-3300
slunnie@actorstheatre.org
actorstheatre.org/participate/submit-a-play/national-ten-minute-play-contest

Notes: Est. 1989. Characters in submitted plays should be in age range 18-28. See website for full submission guidelines. Submission window is September 1-November 1 (postmark deadlines). Submissions are limited to the first 500 scripts received. No electronic submissions accepted. See website for full guidelines.
Preferred Genre: Plays (No Musicals)
Preferred Length: 10-min./10pgs.
Submission Materials: full script
Submission Fee: No
Agent Only: No
Deadline(s): November 1, 2014

New Voices One-Act Play Competition
YouthPlays
Jonathan C. Dorf, Partner
7119 W. Sunset Blvd. #390
Los Angeles, CA 90046
Phone: (424) 703-5315
info@youthplays.com
www.youthplays.com
Notes: Youth PLAYS New Voices One-Act Play Competition is designed to encourage young writers to create new works for the stage. There will be cash prizes and free software for the winner and runner-up, as well as representation of the winning play through Youth PLAYS, the online publisher of plays for young actors and audiences. The New Voices One-Act Play Competition is open for young playwrights 19 and under. Please visit our website's "Submit a Play" page for guidelines and info on our current needs before submitting.
Preferred Genre: Plays (No Musicals)
Preferred Length: Any length
Submission Materials: see website
Submission Fee: No
Agent Only: No
Deadline(s): May 1, 2014

North Carolina New Play Project
Stephen Hyers, Director
Greensboro Playwrights Forum
Greensboro Cultural Center
200 N. Davie St., Box 2
Greensboro, NC 27401
Phone: (336) 335-6426
Fax: (336) 373-2659
stephen@playwrightsforum.org
www.playwrightsforum.org
Notes: Work must be unpublished/unproduced. Email submission.

Author must be a current resident of North Carolina. Production: small cast, simple set. Response: 6 months.
Preferred Genre: Plays (No Musicals)
Preferred Length: Full-length
Submission Materials: full script
Submission Fee: No
Agent Only: No
Deadline(s): October 15, 2014

Northern Michigan University - Playwriting Competition
1401 Presque Isle Ave
Marquette, MI 49855
newplays@nmu.edu
www.nmu.edu/forestrobertstheatre/node/40
Preferred Length: Full-length
Submission Materials: see website
Submission Fee: No
Agent Only: No

One Act Play Contest
Tennessee Williams/New Orleans Literary Festival
Jessica Ramakrishnan, Contest Coordinator
938 Lafayette St., #514
New Orleans, LA 70113
Phone: (504) 581-1144
Fax: (504) 581-3270
info@tennesseewilliams.net
www.tennesseewilliams.net
Notes: Our Annual One-Act Play Contest accepts submissions by mail and online from June 1st through November 1st each year. The winner will be announced by March 1, 2014. The contest is judged by University of New Orleans' Creative Writing Workshop and the Department of Film, Theatre, and Communication Arts. Grand Prize: $1,500; Staged reading at the next Festival; Full production at the Festival the following year; VIP All-Access Festival pass for two years ($1,000 value); Publication in Bayou. Top Ten Finalists: Names will appear on website. Finalists will also receive a panel pass ($75 value) to attend the next Festival. Please see website for detailed submission guidelines.
Preferred Genre: All genres
Preferred Length: One-Act
Submission Materials: see website
Submission Fee: Yes
Agent Only: No
Deadline(s): November 1, 2014

One-Act Playwriting Competition
Dr. Mick Sokol, Professor
900 N. Benton Ave.
Springfield, MO 65802
Phone: (417) 873-6821
Fax: (417) 873-7572
msokol@drury.edu
www.drury.edu
Notes: Est. 1984.
Preferred Genre: Plays (No Musicals)
Preferred Length: One-Act
Submission Materials: full script, S.A.S.E.
Submission Fee: No
Agent Only: No
Deadline(s): December 1, 2014

Paul Newman/Joan Woodward Drama Award
Bloomington Playwrights Project
107 W. 9th Street
Bloomington, IN 47404
Phone: (812) 334-1188
literarymanager@newplays.org
www.newplays.org
Notes: The Woodward/Newman Drama Award is named after Paul Newman and Joanne Woodward in honor of their many great dramas together. This award offers a cash prize of $3,000, a full production as part of the Bloomington Playwrights Project's Mainstage season, along with travel reimbursement. In addition, the Bloomington Playwrights Project has a partnership with Dramatic Publishing and in most instances is able to offer the option of publication. Entrance fee is waved for Dramatists Guild members. Please see website for complete submission guidelines.
Preferred Genre: Drama
Preferred Length: Full-length
Submission Materials: see website
Submission Fee: Yes
Agent Only: No
Deadline(s): March 1, 2014

Paul Stephen Lim Playwriting Award
Kennedy Center American College Theater Festival
Gregg Henry, Artistic Director, KC/ACTF
Kennedy Center, Education Division
Washington, DC 20566
Phone: (202) 416-8864
Fax: (202) 416-4892
ghenry@kennedy-center.org
www.kcactf.org

Notes: Award for the outstanding student-written play by a student of Asian or Pacific Rim heritage from college/university participating in KCACTF program.
Preferred Genre: Plays (No Musicals)
Special Interest: Asian-American
Preferred Length: Any length
Submission Materials: see website
Submission Fee: Yes
Agent Only: No
Deadline(s): December 1, 2014

Paula Vogel Award for Playwriting
Kennedy Center American College Theater Festival
Gregg Henry, Artistic Director, KCACTF
Kennedy Center
Washington, DC 20566
Phone: (202) 416-8864
Fax: (202) 416-4892
ghenry@kennedy-center.org
www.kcactf.org
Notes: Est. 2003. Award for the outstanding student-written play that explores issues of gender, diversity, sexuality and tolerance. Plays accepted only from college/university participating in KC/ACTF program.
Preferred Genre: All genres
Preferred Length: Any length
Submission Materials: application
Submission Fee: Yes
Agent Only: No
Deadline(s): December 1, 2014

PEN/Laura Pels International Foundation Awards for Drama
Paul Morris, Director
588 Broadway, #303
New York, NY 10012
Phone: (212) 334-1660
Fax: (212) 334-2181
awards@pen.org
www.pen.org
Notes: Est. 1998. Award to US playwright in mid-career writing in English. See website for details and submission deadlines. Send letters of nomination between October 1 - December 16.
Submission Materials: see website
Submission Fee: No
Agent Only: No
Deadline(s): December 16, 2014

Playwrights First
Emily Andren, Director of Public Relations
c/o John E. Donnelly
250 East 73rd Street, Apt. 12G
New York, NY 10021
Phone: (612) 332-7481
Fax: (612) 332-6037
hayleyf@pwcenter.org
Notes: No submissions before August 1
please. No electronic submissions. $1000
grant for winners and professional reading
where appropriate, introductions to actors,
literary managers, directors, etc. No
adaptations or translations. One author per
play- original, full-length, unproduced prior
to submission, in English.
Preferred Genre: Plays (No Musicals)
Preferred Length: Full-length
Submission Materials: full script, resume,
synopsis
Submission Fee: No
Agent Only: No
Deadline(s): October 15, 2014

Public Access Television Corp. (PATC)
Shirley Bruno, Executive Director
1111 Marcus Ave., #LL27
Lake Success, NY 11042
Phone: (516) 629-3710
Fax: (516) 629-3704
info@patv.org
www.patv.org
Notes: Est. 1998. TV opportunity only. One-
act play competition. Fees: $5 Frequency:
annual Production: cast of 2-3 adults,unit set.
Response Time: 2 months. Submissions will
be accepted as of Fall 2014. Limit of 2
entries per playwright. Scripts will not be
returned. Include email, phone, or address for
notification of results of competition. Submit
a typed manuscript to address listed to the
attention of "New Playwrights Competition".
The prizes will be a production of the two
winning plays on PATV, Channel 20 &
Channel 37 inclusive of an interview with
author, and $100 given to each winning
author, plus a one year membership in the
PATC and a copy of the complete program.
Preferred Genre: Comedy
Preferred Length: One-Act
Submission Materials: full script
Submission Fee: Yes
Agent Only: No

**Richard Rodgers Awards for Musical
Theater**
633 W. 155th St.
New York, NY 10032
Phone: (212) 368-5900
Fax: (212) 491-4615
academy@artsandletters.org
www.artsandletters.org
Notes: Est. 1978. Awards for musicals by
writers and composers not already established
in field.
Preferred Genre: Musical theatre
Submission Materials: application, audio
CD, full script, S.A.S.E., synopsis
Submission Fee: No
Agent Only: No
Deadline(s): November 1, 2014

Robert Chesley Award
Victor Bumbalo, President
828 N. Laurel Ave.
Los Angeles, CA 90046
Phone: (323) 658-5981
VictorTom@aol.com
www.chesleyfoundation.org
Notes: Est. 1991. In honor of Robert Chesley
(1943-90) to recognize gay and lesbian
themed work. Nominations open in early fall.
Preferred Genre: Plays (No Musicals)
Special Interest: LGBT
Preferred Length: Full-length
Submission Materials: full script, S.A.S.E.
Submission Fee: No
Agent Only: No
Deadline(s): January 18, 2014

**Robert J. Pickering Award for Playwriting
Excellence**
89 Division St.
Coldwater, MI 49036
Phone: (517) 279-7963
Fax: (517) 279-8095
Notes: Est. 1984. Award for unproduced
plays and musicals.
Preferred Genre: Plays or Musicals
Preferred Length: Full-length
Submission Materials: full script, S.A.S.E.
Submission Fee: No
Agent Only: No
Deadline(s): December 31, 2014

Rosa Parks Playwriting Award
Kennedy Center American College Theater
Festival
Gregg Henry, Artistic Director, KCACTF

Kennedy Center, Education Division
Washington, DC 20566
Phone: (202) 416-8864
Fax: (202) 416-4892
ghenry@kennedy-center.org
www.kcactf.org
Notes: Awarded for the outstanding student
or faculty written play on the theme of civil
rights and social justice from
college/university participating in KC/ACTF
program.
Preferred Genre: Plays (No Musicals)
Preferred Length: Any length
Submission Materials: see website
Submission Fee: Yes
Agent Only: No
Deadline(s): November 1, 2014

Santa Cruz Actors' Theatre Play Contests
1001 Center St., #12
Santa Cruz, CA 95060
Phone: (831) 425-1003
Fax: (831) 425-7560
admin@santacruzactorstheatre.org
www.sccat.org/
Notes: Est. 1985. Contests for full and ten-
minute long plays, as well as for young
playwrights.
Preferred Genre: Plays (No Musicals)
Preferred Length: Any length
Submission Materials: see website
Submission Fee: Yes
Agent Only: No

Scholastic Art & Writing Awards
557 Broadway
New York, NY 10012
Phone: (212) 343-7729
Fax: (212) 389-3939
info@artandwriting.org
www.artandwriting.org
Notes: Est. 1923. National awards in 2
categories (grades 7-8; grades 9-12), selected
from regional contests. Regional deadlines
vary. Regional Gold Key works are
considered for national awards.
Preferred Genre: Plays (No Musicals)
Preferred Length: 10-min./10pgs.
Submission Materials: application, full
script
Submission Fee: No
Agent Only: No

SETC High School New Play Award
Nancy Gall-Clayton, Chair, High School
Playwriting Contest
1175 Revolution Mill Dr., Suite 14
Greensboro, NC 27405
Phone: (336) 272-3645
Fax: (336) 272-8810
nancygallclayton@earthlink.net
www.setc.org/hs-new-play-contest-awards
Notes: Author must be a student & resident
of Alabama, Florida, Georgia, Kentucky,
Mississippi, North Carolina, South Carolina,
Tennessee, Virginia or West Virginia and
work must be unpublished/unproduced.
Submissions accepted October 1 - December
1 of each year.
Preferred Genre: Plays (No Musicals)
Preferred Length: One-Act
Submission Materials: see website
Submission Fee: No
Agent Only: No
Deadline(s): December 1, 2014

Southern Rep's The Ruby Prize
Amiee Hayes, Artistic Director
333 Canal St Box 34
New Orleans, LA 70130
Phone: (504) 523-9857
Fax: (504) 523-9859
theruby@southernrep.com
www.southernrep.com
Notes: Must be a US citizen and self-
identified woman of color. Open to
established or emerging playwrights. No
collaborations, translations, one-acts, or
works previously submitted to Southern Rep.
For musicals, only playwright is eligible. No
plays written as a result of commission or
that have had a previously professional
production (workshop/non-professional OK.)
If selected as prize-winner or finalist,
playwright agrees that their work may be
included in annual Ruby Prize publication
(non-exclusive).
Preferred Genre: Plays or Musicals
Special Interest: Women's Interest
Preferred Length: Full-length
Submission Materials: see website
Submission Fee: No
Agent Only: No
Deadline(s): October 15, 2014

STAGE International Script Competition
Professional Artists Lab
CNSI-MC 6105

3241 Elings Hall Building 266
University of California
Santa Barbara, CA 93106-6105
stage@cnsi.ucsb.edu
www.stage.cnsi.ucsb.edu
Notes: The professional Artists Lab and the
California Nano Systems Institute at UCSB
collaborate on STAGE- Scientists,
Technologists and Artists Generating
Exploration for the best new play about
science and/or technology. See website for
full info: www.stage.cnsi.ucsb.edu. The
STAGE International script Competition is
biennial; guidelines/deadlines may alter with
each cycle.
Preferred Length: Full-length
Submission Materials: see website
Submission Fee: No
Agent Only: No

Stanley Drama Award
Wagner College
One Campus Road
Staten Island, NY 10301
Phone: (718) 420-4338
Fax: (718) 390-3323
todd.price@wagner.edu
www.wagner.edu/theatre/stanley-drama
Notes: Est. 1957. Work must be unoptioned,
unproduced, unpublished. Response: 6
months. See website for details.
Preferred Genre: Plays or Musicals
Preferred Length: Full-length
Submission Materials: audio CD, full script,
S.A.S.E.
Submission Fee: Yes
Agent Only: No
Deadline(s): October 31, 2014

Summerfield G. Roberts Award
Janet Knox, Administrative Assistant
1717 8th St.
Bay City, TX 77414
Phone: (979) 245-6644
Fax: (979) 244-3819
srttexas@srttexas.org
www.srttexas.org/
Notes: Award for creative writing about the
Republic of Texas, to encourage literature &
research about the events and personalities of
1836-46.
Submission Materials: full script, S.A.S.E.
Submission Fee: No
Agent Only: No
Deadline(s): January 15, 2014

Susan Smith Blackburn Prize
3239 Avalon Pl.
Houston, TX 77019
Phone: (713) 308-2842
Fax: (713) 654-8184
play@blackburnprize.com
www.blackburnprize.org
Notes: Est. 1978. Plays accepted only from
specified source theaters in US, UK and
Ireland. Writers should bring their work to
the attention of the theatre companies listed
on website.
Preferred Genre: Comedy
Preferred Length: Any length
Submission Materials: full script, S.A.S.E.
Submission Fee: No
Agent Only: No
Deadline(s): September 15, 2014

**TeCo Theatrical Productions New Play
Competition**
Teresa Coleman Walsh, Executive Artistic
Director
215 South Tyler Street
Dallas, TX 75208
Phone: (214) 948-0716
Fax: (214) 948-3706
teresa@tecotheater.org
www.tecotheater.org
Notes: Est. 1993. Author must be resident of
Dallas. Submit
unoptioned/unpublished/unproduced by US
mail. Production: cast limit 4, minimal set
and costume changes. Response: 2 months.
Preferred Genre: Plays (No Musicals)
Preferred Length: One-Act
Submission Fee: No
Agent Only: No
Deadline(s): December 1, 2014

Ten Minute Musicals Project
Michael Koppy, Producer
Box 461194
West Hollywood, CA 90046
info@TenMinuteMusicals.org
www.TenMinuteMusicals.org
Notes: Est. 1989. Production: cast limit 10.
Preferred Genre: Musical theatre
Preferred Length: 10-min./10pgs.
Submission Materials: audio CD, full script,
S.A.S.E., vocal score
Submission Fee: No
Agent Only: No
Deadline(s): August 31, 2014

Ten-Minute Play Award
Kennedy Center American College Theater Festival
Gregg Henry, Artistic Director, KCACTF
Kennedy Center
Washington, DC 20566
Phone: (202) 416-8864
Fax: (202) 416-4892
ghenry@kennedy-center.org
www.kcactf.org
Notes: Plays accepted only from college/university participating in KC/ACTF program.
Preferred Genre: Plays (No Musicals)
Preferred Length: 10-min./10pgs.
Submission Materials: application, full script, synopsis
Submission Fee: Yes
Agent Only: No
Deadline(s): November 1, 2014

The Reva Shiner Comedy Award
Bloomington Playwrights Project
107 W. 9th Street
Bloomington, IN 47404
Phone: (812) 334-1188
literarymanager@newplays.org
www.newplays.org
Notes: The Reva Shiner Comedy Award offers a $1,000 cash prize, a full production as part of the Bloomington Playwrights Project's Mainstage season, along with travel reimbursement. In addition, the Bloomington Playwrights Project has a partnership with Dramatic Publishing and in most instances is able to offer the option of publication. The submission fee is waved for Dramatists Guild members. Please see website for complete submission guidelines.
Preferred Genre: Comedy
Preferred Length: Full-length
Submission Materials: see website
Submission Fee: Yes
Agent Only: No
Deadline(s): October 31, 2014

Theater for Youth Playwriting Award
Kennedy Center American College Theater Festival
Kennedy Center
Washington, DC 20566
Phone: (202) 416-8857
Fax: (202) 416-8802
skshaffer@kennedy-center.org
www.kcactf.org

Notes: Award for student-written play appealing to young people in grades K-12. Plays accepted only from college/univ. participating in KC/ACTF program.
Preferred Genre: Plays (No Musicals)
Special Interest: Theatre for Young Audiences
Preferred Length: Any length
Submission Materials: application
Submission Fee: Yes
Agent Only: No
Deadline(s): November 1, 2014

Theatre Conspiracy
10091 McGregor Blvd
Fort Myers, FL 33919
Phone: (239) 936-3239
info@theatreconspiracy.ord
www.theatreconspiracy.org/npcontest.html
Notes: Theatre Conspiracy will be accepting submissions for its Fourteenth Annual New Play Contest between November 2013 and March 30, 2014. All works submitted will be read and judged by a panel of qualified theatre teachers, directors and performers. Script Parameters: Work submitted to the contest must be a full length play with eight characters or less and have simple to moderate technical demands. Plays having up to three previous productions are welcome. No musicals. Remuneration: First place: $700.00 and full production. However, it is our goal to produce more than one entry each year. Entry fee waived for members of the Dramatists Guild.
Preferred Genre: All genres
Preferred Length: Full-length
Submission Materials: see website
Submission Fee: No
Agent Only: No

Theatre in the Raw Biennial One-Act Play Writing Contest
Jay Hamburger, Artistic Director
3521 Marshall St.
Vancouver, BC V5N 4S2 Canada
Phone: (604) 708-5448
Fax: (604) 708-1454
theatreintheraw@telus.net
www.theatreintheraw.ca
Notes: Est. 1994. Submission fee: $25 for one play/$45 for two plays. Cast limit: 6. Minimal sets ideal, 3-6 scenes max. Please submit original,

unoptioned/unpublished/unproduced scripts via ground mail.
Preferred Genre: All genres
Preferred Length: One-Act
Submission Materials: full script, S.A.S.E.
Submission Fee: Yes
Agent Only: No
Deadline(s): December 31, 2014

Theatre Oxford 10-Minute Play Contest
Alice Walker, Contest Director
PO Box 1394
Oxford, MS 38655
10minuteplays@gmail.com
www.10minuteplays.com
Notes: Est. 1998. Production: casts 2-4, minimal set, props. Only winners & finalists will be contacted. Work must be unoptioned, unproduced, unpublished. Submissions not returned.
Preferred Genre: Plays (No Musicals)
Preferred Length: 10-min./10pgs.
Submission Materials: full script
Submission Fee: Yes
Agent Only: No
Deadline(s): February 15, 2014

University of Central Missouri Competition
Theater Dept., Martin 113
Warrensburg, MO 64093
Phone: (660) 543-4020
Fax: (660) 543-8006
wilson@ucmo.edu
www.ucmo.edu/theatre/about/write.cfm
Notes: Est. 2001. Has produced children's plays for over 25 years. Now focused on world-premiere originals, through national competition.
Special Interest: Theatre for Young Audiences
Submission Materials: see website
Submission Fee: Yes
Agent Only: No
Deadline(s): October 28, 2014

University of Wyoming Amy & Eric Burger Essays on Theatre
Jim Volz, President, Consultant for the Arts
Univ. of Wyoming c/o Dr. Jim Volz
Theatre & Dance, PO Box 6850
Fullerton, CA 92834
jvolz@fullerton.edu
Notes: Seek unpublished essays (between 1800 & 7500 words) on Theatre/Drama for

award. Email Dr. Volz (jvolz@fullerton.edu) for submission requirements. Winner notified by June 2014. $2,500 prize. A Dramatists Guild Member won the award last year!
Preferred Genre: All genres
Submission Materials: 2 copies of essay
Submission Fee: No
Agent Only: No
Deadline(s): March 7, 2014

Urban Stages Emerging Playwright Award
555 8th Ave.
Suite #1800
New York, NY 10018
Phone: (212) 421-1380
Fax: (212) 421-1387
urbanstage@aol.com
www.urbanstages.org
Notes: Est. 1986. Material must be unoptioned/unproduced/unpublished. Production: cast limit 6. Response: 6 months. Submissions accepted year-round.
Preferred Genre: Plays (No Musicals)
Preferred Length: Full-length
Submission Materials: full script
Submission Fee: No
Agent Only: No

Vermont Playwrights Award
Sharon Kellermann, Coordinator
Valley Players
P.O. Box 441
Waitsfield, VT 05673
Phone: (802) 583-6767
valleyplayers@madriver.com
www.valleyplayers.com
Notes: Est. 1982. Must be resident of Maine, New Hampshire, Vermont. Work must be unoptioned, unpublished, unproduced.
Preferred Genre: Plays (No Musicals)
Preferred Length: Full-length
Submission Materials: application, full script, S.A.S.E.
Submission Fee: No
Agent Only: No
Deadline(s): February 1, 2014

Write a Play! NYC Contest
Nick Gandiello, Literary Manager
Young Playwrights Inc
Post Office Box 5134
New York, NY 10185
Phone: (212) 594-5440
Fax: (212) 594-5443
literary@youngplaywrights.org

www.youngplaywrights.org
Notes: Contest open to all NYC students in 3 categories: elementary, middle and high school. All receive certificate of achievement, written evaluation, and invitation to awards ceremony.
Preferred Genre: Plays (No Musicals)
Preferred Length: Full-length
Submission Materials: full script
Submission Fee: No
Agent Only: No
Deadline(s): March 1, 2014

Young Playwrights Inc. National Playwriting Competition
Nick Gandiello, Literary Manager
Young Playwrights, Inc.
Post Office Box 5134
New York, NY 10185
Phone: (212) 594-5440
Fax: (212) 594-5443
literary@youngplaywrights.org
www.youngplaywrights.org
Notes: Est. 1981. Young Playwrights Inc. identifies and develops young (18 and younger) US playwrights by involving them as active participants in the highest quality professional productions of their plays. See website for competition guideline.
Preferred Genre: No musicals or adaptations

Preferred Length: Any length
Submission Materials: full script, S.A.S.E.
Submission Fee: No
Agent Only: No
Deadline(s): January 2, 2014

Youth Theatre Marilyn Hall Award
Beverly Hills Theatre Guild
Box 148
Beverly Hills, CA 90213
Phone: (310) 273-3390
www.beverlyhillstheatreguild.com
Notes: The Beverly Hills Theatre Guild annually sponsors the Competition for Youth Theatre to discover new theatrical works and to encourage established or emerging writers to create quality works for youth theatre. The Play Competition for Youth Theatre represents grades 6-8 and grades 9-12 and offers two prizes: FIRST PRIZE: $1,200. SECOND PRIZE: $600. Submissions are accepted from January 15th to February 28th. Please visit our website for complete submission guidelines.
Preferred Genre: Plays (No Musicals)
Preferred Length: Full-length
Submission Materials: see website
Submission Fee: No
Agent Only: No
Deadline(s): February 28, 2014

Grants & Fellowships

Alabama State Council on the Arts
201 Monroe St.
Montgomery, AL 36130
Phone: (334) 242-4076
Fax: (334) 240-3269
randy.shoults@arts.alabama.gov
www.arts.alabama.gov
Notes: Artist Fellowships and Artist in Education Residency in performing artists, literature, and visual artists. Must be a 2-year resident of Alabama.
Submission Fee: No
Agent Only: No
Deadline(s): March 1, 2014

Alaska State Council on the Arts (ASCA)
411 W. 4th Ave., #1-E
Anchorage, AK 99501
Phone: (888) 278-7424
Fax: (907) 269-6601

aksca_info@eed.state.ak.us
www.eed.state.ak.us/aksca
Notes: Est. 1966. See website for specific deadlines and submission guidelines.
Preferred Genre: All genres
Preferred Length: Full-length
Submission Materials: see website
Submission Fee: No
Agent Only: No

Alavi Foundation
500 Fifth Ave, Suite 2320
New York, NY 10110
Phone: (212) 944-8333
Fax: (212) 921-0325
www.alavifoundation.org
Notes: The Foundation's mission is to promote charitable and philanthropic causes through educational, religious, and cultural programs. It supports organizations that

sustain interfaith harmony and promote Islamic culture and Persian language, literature, and civilization. Grants are awarded in the areas of colleges and universities, Persian schools, Islamic organizations, disaster relief, support for the arts, and scholarly research. It also has established a book distribution program for those unable to purchase books related to Islamic/Persian culture on their own.
Submission Materials: see website
Submission Fee: No
Agent Only: No

American-Scandinavian Foundation (ASF)
58 Park Ave.
New York, NY 10016
Phone: (212) 879-9779
Fax: (212) 249-3444
grants@amscan.org
www.amscan.org
Notes: Grants for short visits and fellowships for full year of study or research in Denmark, Finland, Iceland, Norway or Sweden by U.S. citizens/residents. Proficient in host language preferred.
Submission Materials: see website
Submission Fee: Yes
Agent Only: No
Deadline(s): November 1, 2014

Arch & Bruce Brown Foundation
Arch Brown, President
502 West Pico Road
Palm Springs, CA 92262
Phone: (760) 202-1125
jwillis@aabbfoundation.org
www.aabbfoundation.org
Notes: The Foundation holds annual writing competitions for full-length works for the stage [comedies, dramas, musicals, operas, song cycles] that are based on, or inspired by, History. $1,000 first prize (not limited to a single winner). The Foundation also offers $1,000 Production Grants to Producing Organization to aid in producing historic works. For more information see www.aabbfoundation.org.
Special Interest: LGBT
Submission Materials: see website
Submission Fee: No
Agent Only: No
Deadline(s): June 30, 2014

Arthur Foundation
Thomas A. Hett, Director of Programs
19 Riverside Drive
Suite 6
Riverside, IL 60546
Phone: (708) 443-5710
Fax: (708) 443-5717
www.arthurfdn.org/index.php
Notes: The Foundation's grant making is focused on improving the health of the population. Funding is awarded to organizations that provide accessible, affordable, and appropriate health services to vulnerable populations. Funding is awarded to projects that provide academic resources for schools, curricular enhancements in the visual and performing arts, educational opportunities to the disabled, programs that encourage college attendance, and those that train and educate doctors, nurses, teachers, and charitable organization managers. Education grants fall under the Foundation's Initiative for Educational Excellence program targeted at schools located in the City of Berwyn, the town of Cicero, and the western suburbs of Chicago. The Foundation asks potential applicants to send a two- or three-page letter outlining briefly the project, the amount of funding sought, and time frame in which the funds are needed.
Submission Materials: see website
Submission Fee: No
Agent Only: No

Artist Trust
Miguel Guillien, Program Manager
1835 12th Ave.
Seattle, WA 98122
Phone: (206) 467-8734
Fax: (206) 467-9633
miguel@artisttrust.org
www.artisttrust.org
Notes: Artist Trust provides Washington State artists of all creative disciplines the necessary support to launch and sustain successful careers, through financial grants, career training and professional resources. See website for specific submission guidelines.
Preferred Genre: All genres
Submission Materials: see website
Submission Fee: No
Agent Only: No

Baird Foundation
P.O Box 0672
Milwaukee, WI 53201
Phone: 1 (800) 792-2473
www.rwbaird.com/about-baird/culture/baird-
foundation.aspx
Notes: The Foundation is the philanthropic
arm of Robert W. Baird & Co., a financial
services firm. The Foundation provides direct
support to health, education, the arts, and
other quality of life causes, often with a
focus on diversity and helping individuals
achieve their full potential. The Foundation
has offices in 100 locations across the United
States, and in Europe and Asia. Grants are
awarded to organizations in Hamburg,
Germany, Hong Kong, London, and China,
as well as the United States.
Submission Fee: No
Agent Only: No

Chaim Schwartz Foundation
www.chaimschwartz.org
Notes: The Foundation is dedicated to
preserving and enriching Yiddishkeit, the
Yiddish language, culture, theater, and art.
Named after Chaim Schwartz, a poet,
Yiddishist, and social activist, the Foundation
was created by his daughter, to carry on his
life's work. Proposals may be project specific
or for general support. The Foundation is
particularly interested in projects that
continue on the social justice heritage of
Yiddishkeit.
Special Interest: Jewish
Submission Materials: query letter
Submission Fee: No
Agent Only: No
Deadline(s): April 1, 2014

Charles Lafitte Foundation
Jennifer Vertetis, President and Executive
Director
818 Linden Lane
Brielle, NJ 08730
Jennifer@charleslafitte.org
http://charleslafitte.org
Notes: Founded in 1999 to help people help
themselves and the others around them lead
healthy, satisfying, and enriched lives. The
Foundation believes that exposure to the arts
is vital to fostering and sustaining healthy
communities. Goals for arts funding include:
cultivating new talent; supporting established
artists; providing educational programs that

encourage children's creativity; furthering
equal access to the arts; and establishing
therapeutic arts programs. The Foundation
accepts letters of inquiry throughout the year.
It prefers to underwrite specific projects with
distinct goals, and targets grants that will
have notable impact and make a material
difference. The Foundation looks for
creativity, innovation, and initiative when
awarding funds. Grant making should
promote inclusiveness and diversity. The
Foundation likes projects that remove barriers
to full economic and/or social participation in
society.
Submission Materials: see website
Submission Fee: No
Agent Only: No

Children's Theater Foundation Grants
www.childrenstheatrefoundation.org
Notes: The Children's Theater Foundation
offers grants to small and mid-sized theater
companies that produce children's plays. The
grants offset cost of children's theater
productions, enable theater's to purchase
scripts and royalties, and provide better
rehearsal facilities for their young
performers. If you belong to a community
theater and would like more information
about obtaining a grant from the Foundation,
please visit our website.
Preferred Genre: Theatre for Young
Audiences
Special Interest: Theatre for Young
Audiences
Submission Materials: see website
Submission Fee: No
Agent Only: No

**Children's Theatre Foundation: Aurand
Harris Fellowship**
Mina H. Casmir, CTFA VP - Grants
c/o 8950 Koch Field Road at Silver Saddle
Flagstaff, AZ 86004
info@childrenstheatrefoundation.org
www.childrenstheatrefoundation.org
Notes: Est. 1958. The Children's Theatre
Foundation of America (CTFA) issues the
Aurand Harris Fellowship award for
individuals with specific projects or with
specific plans for developing excellence in
children's theater.
Preferred Genre: All genres
Special Interest: Theatre for Young
Audiences

Submission Materials: see website
Submission Fee: No
Agent Only: No
Deadline(s): April 9, 2014

Connecticut Office of the Arts (DECD)
Tamara Dimitri, Program Specialist
One Constitution Plaza
2nd Fl.
Hartford, CT 06103
Phone: (860) 256-2800
Fax: (860) 256-2811
tamara.dimitri@ct.gov
www.cultureandtourism.org
Notes: Artistic fellowship for resident of
Connecticut.
Submission Materials: see website
Submission Fee: No
Agent Only: No

Delaware Division of the Arts
820 N. French St.
Wilmington, DE 19801
Phone: (302) 577-8278
Fax: (302) 577-6561
kristin.pleasanton@state.de.us
www.artsdel.org
Notes: Invidual artists fellowships. Must be
18+ and resident of Delaware.
Submission Materials: 10-pg sample,
application, S.A.S.E.
Submission Fee: No
Agent Only: No

Don and Gee Nicholl Fellowships
Joan Wai, Program Manager
1313 Vine St.
Hollywood, CA 90028
Phone: (310) 247-3010
Fax: (310) 247-3794
nicholl@oscars.org
www.oscars.org/nicholl
Notes: Est. 1986. Film competition for
screenwriters who haven't earned more than
$5K in film or TV. Up to five $35K
fellowships each year.
Preferred Genre: Screenplays
Preferred Length: Full-length
Submission Materials: application, full
script
Submission Fee: Yes
Agent Only: No
Deadline(s): May 1, 2014

Foundation Center
New York, NY 10003
www.foundationcenter.org
Notes: Grant Source for Individuals provides
online access to accurate, up-to-date
information on foundations that fund:
Educational support - scholarships,
fellowships, loans, and internships, Students
and graduates of specific schools, Arts and
cultural support, Awards, prizes, and grants
by nomination.
Submission Materials: see website
Submission Fee: No
Agent Only: No

Fulbright Program for US Scholars
3007 Tilden St. NW, #5-L
Washington, DC 20008
Phone: (202) 686-7859
Fax: (202) 362-3442
info@cies.iie.org
www.cies.org
Notes: Est. 1947. Grants for US faculty or
professionals to research or lecture abroad for
2-12 months in 140 countries.
Submission Materials: see website
Submission Fee: No
Agent Only: No

**Helen McCloy / MWA Scholarship for
Mystery Writing**
mccloy.MWA@gmail.com
www.mysterywriters.org/about-mwa/helen-
mccloy-scholarship/
Notes: The Helen McCloy/MWA Scholarship
for Mystery Writing seeks to nurture talent in
mystery writing-in fiction, nonfiction,
playwriting, and screenwriting. The
scholarship is open to U.S. citizens or
permanent residents only. Membership in
Mystery Writers of America is not required to
apply. Because the McCloy Scholarship is
intended for serious aspiring mystery writers
who wish to improve their writing skills, we
expect that most applicants will be college
students or adult learners.
Preferred Genre: Mystery
Preferred Length: Full-length
Submission Materials: see website
Submission Fee: No
Agent Only: No
Deadline(s): February 28, 2014

Hodder Fellowship

Mary O'Connor, Assistant to the Chair
185 Nassau Street
Princeton, NJ 08542
Phone: (609) 258-4840
Fax: (609) 258-2230
oconnorm@princeton.edu
www.princeton.edu/arts/fellows/
Notes: One-year fellowships will be given to writers and non-literary artists of exceptional promise to pursue independent projects at Princeton University during the 2015-2016 academic year. Potential Hodder Fellows are writers, composers, choreographers, visual artists, performance artists, or other kinds of artists or humanists who have "much more than ordinary intellectual or literary gifts,". They are selected more "for promise than for performance." No formal teaching is involved and a stipend is provided. Complete information and application guidelines are available online through the Princeton Jobs website at http://jobs.princeton.edu. Search for open positions and enter key word "Hodder Fellow".
Submission Materials: see website
Submission Fee: No
Agent Only: No
Deadline(s): October 1, 2014

Iowa Arts Council

600 E. Locust
Des Moines, IA 50319
Phone: (515) 242-6194
Fax: (515) 242-6498
Linda.lee@iowa.gov
www.iowaartscouncil.org
Notes: Application must be downloaded from website. Applicant must be a resident of Iowa. Response: Approximately 4-6 weeks.
Submission Materials: see website
Submission Fee: No
Agent Only: No

Jerome Playwright-in-Residence Fellowships

Amanda Robbins-Butcher, Artistic Administrator
2301 Franklin Ave E
Minneapolis, MN 55406
Phone: (612) 332-7481
info@pwcenter.org
www.pwcenter.org
Notes: Fellowships to emerging playwrights for one year residency (July-June) in Minnesota using Center services. Apply online.
Submission Materials: see website
Submission Fee: No
Agent Only: No
Deadline(s): November 1, 2014

John Simon Guggenheim Memorial Foundation

Keith B. Lewis, Program Officer
90 Park Ave.
New York, NY 10016
Phone: (212) 687-4470
Fax: (212) 697-3248
fellowships@gf.org
www.gf.org
Notes: Est. 1925. Fellowship to scholars and artists for research or creation.
Submission Materials: see website
Submission Fee: No
Agent Only: No
Deadline(s): September 19, 2014

Jonathan Larson Performing Arts Foundation

Box 672, Prince St. Sta.
New York, NY 10012
Phone: (212) 529-0814
Fax: (212) 253-7604
jlpaf@aol.com
www.americantheatrewing.org/larsongrants/
Notes: Est. 1996. Annual grants to theater composers, lyricists, book writers and to theaters developing new musicals by former Larson award recipients. Response: 4 months.
Preferred Genre: Musical theatre
Preferred Length: Full-length
Submission Materials: application, S.A.S.E.
Submission Fee: No
Agent Only: No
Deadline(s): September 30, 2014

Kleban Award

424 W. 44th St.
New York, NY 10036
Phone: (212) 757-6960
Fax: (212) 265-4738
newdramatists@newdramatists.org
www.newdramatists.org/kleban_award.htm
Notes: Award to lyricists and librettists working in the American musical theater.
Preferred Genre: Musical theatre
Preferred Length: Full-length

Submission Materials: application
Submission Fee: No
Agent Only: No
Deadline(s): September 15, 2014

Laidlaw Foundation
Anna Skinner, Program Manager, Youth
Organizing
300 Bloor Street East
Suite 2000
Toronto, ON M4W 3L4 Canada
Phone: (416) 964-3614 Ext 307
Fax: (416) 975-1428
www.laidlawfdn.org
Notes: The Canadian Foundation promotes
positive youth development through inclusive
youth engagement in the arts, environment,
and in the community. It recognizes that all
young people need the unconditional support
of significant adults in their lives and need
multiple opportunities to locate an individual
talent and the resources necessary to develop
that talent. The Foundation invests in
innovative ideas, convenes interested parties,
shares its learning and advocates for change
in support of young people becoming healthy,
creative, and fully engaged citizens. The
Foundation's core values include youth
engagement, diversity, social inclusion, and
civic engagement.
Submission Materials: see website
Submission Fee: No
Agent Only: No

**Laura Jane Musser Fund: Intercultural
Harmony Program**
www.musserfund.org/index.asp?page_seq=25
Notes: The Intercultural Harmony Program,
an initiative of the Laura Jane Musser Fund,
promotes mutual understanding and
cooperation between groups and citizens of
different cultural backgrounds within defined
geographical areas through collaborative,
cross-cultural projects. Support is provided to
nonprofit organizations in Colorado, Hawaii,
Michigan, Minnesota, Ohio, and Wyoming
that include members of various cultural
communities working together on projects
with common goals. These projects must be
intercultural, rather than focused on just one
culture, and must demonstrate tangible
benefits in the larger community. Funded
projects can be carried out in a number of
areas, including the arts, community service,
and youth activities. Planning or

implementation grants of up to $20,000 are
provided for new projects within their first
three years of operation.
Submission Materials: see website
Submission Fee: No
Agent Only: No

Lincoln & Therese Filene Foundation
Alane Harrington Wallis, Charitable
Foundations Manager
World Trade Center West
155 Seaport Blvd.
Boston, MA 02210
Phone: (617) 439-2498
www.filenefoundation.org
Notes: The Foundation makes grants
primarily to Massachusetts organizations with
some consideration given to other New
England-based programs. Funding is targeted
toward programs and projects that enable
those who are disadvantaged in various ways
to help themselves and others; that reduce
social conflicts and create harmonious
communities; that encourage informed civic
participation on local, state, and regional
levels; and that promote participation in the
performing arts. Grants are awarded in the
following areas: civic education; human
development and self-sufficiency; music
education and performing arts; and public
education and broadcasting.
Submission Materials: see website
Submission Fee: No
Agent Only: No
Deadline(s): September 1, 2014

Louisiana Cultural Economy Foundation
Lisa Picone, Economic Opportunity Fund
Director
1540 Canal Street, Suite 201
New Orleans, LA 70112
Phone: (504) 895-2800
Fax: (504) 910-3001
lisa@culturaleconomy.org
www.culturaleconomy.org
Notes: Grants are made to individuals,
businesses and organizations based in
Louisiana. Grants are not available for
projects or productions. Grants are awarded
for unique ideas to earn a new stream of
income that is not part of regular
programming. See guidelines on website for
more information.
Submission Materials: see website

Submission Fee: No
Agent Only: No
Deadline(s): September 1, 2014

Louisiana Division of the Arts
Box 44247
Baton Rouge, LA 70804
Phone: (225) 342-8180
Fax: (225) 342-8173
dbelanger@crt.state.la.us
www.crt.state.la.us/arts
Notes: Louisiana Division of the Arts in cooperation with the Louisiana State Arts Council is the catalyst for participation, education, development and promotion of excellence in the arts. It is the responsibility of the Division to support established arts institutions, nurture both emerging arts organizations and our overall cultural economy, assist individual artists, encourage the expansion of audiences and stimulate public participation in the arts in Louisiana.
Preferred Genre: Plays or Musicals
Preferred Length: Any length
Submission Materials: see website
Submission Fee: No
Agent Only: No
Deadline(s): March 7, 2014

Marin Arts Council Fund for Artists
555 Northgate Dr., #270
San Rafael, CA 94903
Phone: (415) 388-5200
Fax: (415) 388-1217
literarymanager@marintheatre.org
www.marinarts.org
Notes: Est. 1985. Career Development Grants to individual artists for professional development.
Preferred Genre: All genres
Preferred Length: Any length
Submission Materials: application
Submission Fee: No
Agent Only: No

Massachusetts Cultural Council (MCC)
Dan Blask, Program Coordinator
10 St. James Ave., Fl. 3
Boston, MA 02116
Phone: (212) 971-4862
Fax: (212) 971-4862
info@ma-yitheatre.org
www.massculturalcouncil.org
Notes: Grants for Massachusetts residents alternating between dance, drawing, prose, painting, poetry, traditional arts (even years) and crafts, dramatic writing, film/video, music, photography, sculpture (odd years).
Submission Materials: application
Submission Fee: No
Agent Only: No

McKnight Advancement Grants
www.pwcenter.org/fellows_advancement.php
Notes: The McKnight Advancement Grants recognize playwrights whose work demonstrates exceptional artistic merit and excellence in the field, and whose primary residence is in the state of Minnesota. Two grants of $25,000 each will be awarded in 2013-14, funded by the Minneapolis-based McKnight Foundation as part of its Arts Program. The grants are intended to significantly advance recipients' playwriting development and their careers. Additional funds of $2,000 can be used to support a play development workshop and other professional expenses.
Submission Materials: see website
Submission Fee: No
Agent Only: No
Deadline(s): January 9, 2014

McKnight Theater Artist Fellowship
Amanda Robbins-Butcher, Artistic Administrator
2301 Franklin Ave. E.
Minneapolis, MN 55406
Phone: (612) 332-7481
Fax: (612) 332-6037
info@pwcenter.org
www.pwcenter.org
Notes: Fellowships to theater artists in Minnesota other than writers whose work demonstrates exceptional artistic merit and potential. Please include a work sample and a letter of intent with your application.
Submission Materials: application
Submission Fee: No
Agent Only: No
Deadline(s): April 17, 2014

Meyer Memorial Trust
425 NW 10th Aveneu
Suite 400
Portland, OR 97209
Phone: (503) 228-5512
mmt@mmt.org
www.mmt.org/program/responsive-grants

Notes: The Trust's Responsive Grant program supports nonprofits that deliver significant social benefit throughout the state of Oregon and in Clark County, Wash. Grants are awarded for a wide array of activities in the areas of human services, health, affordable housing, community development, conservation and environment, public affairs, arts and culture, and education. Responsive grants are awarded for project support, expansions, organizational capacity building, and capital construction projects. Letters of inquiry may be submitted throughout the year.
Submission Materials: see website
Submission Fee: No
Agent Only: No

Michener Center for Writers
702 E. Dean Keeton St.
Austin, TX 78705
Phone: (512) 471-1601
Fax: (512) 471-9997
mcw@www.utexas.edu
www.utexas.edu/academic/mcw
Notes: Est. 1993. Financial assistance for full-time students in MFA program. Author must have BA. Playwrights submit 1 full length or 2 one act plays.
Preferred Genre: All genres
Preferred Length: Any length
Submission Materials: application
Submission Fee: Yes
Agent Only: No
Deadline(s): December 15, 2014

Mid Atlantic Arts Foundation
201 N. Charles St., #401
Baltimore, MD 21201
Phone: (410) 539-6656
Fax: (410) 837-5517
info@midatlanticarts.org
www.midatlanticarts.org
Notes: Est. 1999. Artists & Communities program offers matching support for partnerships between artists in New Jersey, New York, Pennsylvania with nonprofit orgs in Washington D.C., Delaware, Maryland, New Jersey, New York, Pennsylvania, Virginia, US Virgin Islands, and West Virginia.
Submission Materials: see website
Submission Fee: No
Agent Only: No

Missouri Arts Council
815 Olive Street
Suite 16
St. Louis, MO 63101
Phone: (314) 340-6845
Fax: (314) 340-7215
moarts@ded.mo.gov
www.missouriartscouncil.org
Submission Materials: application
Submission Fee: No
Agent Only: No
Deadline(s): February 24, 2014

NEH Division for Research Program/Collaborative Research
1100 Pennsylvania Ave NW
Washington, DC 20506
Phone: (202) 606-8461
Fax: (202) 606-8204
mhall@neh.gov
www.neh.gov/grants/guidelines/collaborative.html
Notes: Collaborative Research Grants support interpretive humanities research undertaken by a team of two or more scholars, for full-time or part-time activities for periods of a minimum of one year up to a maximum of three years. Support is available for various combinations of scholars, consultants, and research assistants; project-related travel; field work; applications of information technology; and technical support and services. All grantees are expected to communicate the results of their work to the appropriate scholarly and public audiences. See website for submission guidelines.
Submission Materials: see website
Submission Fee: No
Agent Only: No
Deadline(s): December 5, 2014

New York Coalition of Professional Women in the Arts & Media
Box 2537, Times Sq. Sta.
New York, NY 10108
Phone: (212) 592-4511
collaboration@nycwam.org
www.wamcoalition.org/
Notes: Est. 1990. NYCWAM Collaboration Award is to encourage professional women in the arts and media to work collaboratively with other women on the creation of new works.
Preferred Genre: Plays or Musicals
Special Interest: Women's Interest

Preferred Length: Any length
Submission Materials: 15-20 pg sample
Submission Fee: No
Agent Only: No

New York State Council on the Arts (NYSCA)
175 Varick St., Fl. 3
New York, NY 10014
Phone: (212) 627-4455
Fax: (212) 620-5911
mwhite@nysca.org
www.nysca.org
Notes: The New York State Council on the Arts is dedicated to preserving and expanding the rich and diverse cultural resources that are and will become the heritage of New York's citizens. The Council believes in supporting the artistic excellence and the creative freedom of artists without censure, and the rights of all New Yorkers to access and experience the power of the arts and culture, and the vital contribution the arts make to the quality of life in New York communities. NYSCA strives to achieve its mission through its core grant-making activity and by convening field leaders, providing information and advisory support, and working with partners on special initiatives to achieve mutual goals. See website for various deadlines and submission guidelines.
Submission Materials: see website
Submission Fee: No
Agent Only: No

New York Theatre Workshop (NYTW) Playwriting Fellowship
Aaron Malkin, Literary Associate
83 E. 4th St.
New York, NY 10003
Phone: (212) 780-9037
Fax: (212) 460-8996
aaronm@nytw.org
www.nytw.org
Submission Materials: see website
Submission Fee: No
Agent Only: Yes

Norfolk Southern Foundation
www.nscorp.com/nscportal/nscorp/
  Community/NS%20Foundation/
Notes: The Norfolk Southern Foundation supports nonprofit organizations that focus on educational, cultural, environmental, social

safety net, and economic development opportunities within the region served by Norfolk Southern, primarily in the Eastern, Midwestern, and Southern United States. The Foundation offers grants in the following principal areas: educational programs, primarily at the post-secondary level; community enrichment focusing on cultural and artistic organizations; human services that support basic needs; and environmental programs. Submissions accepted between July 15 and September 30 annually.
Submission Fee: No
Agent Only: No
Deadline(s): September 30, 2014

North Carolina Arts Council
Department of Cultural Resources
Raleigh, NC 27699
Phone: (919) 807-6500
Fax: (919) 807-6532
ncarts@ncmail.net
www.ncarts.org
Submission Materials: see website
Submission Fee: No
Agent Only: No
Deadline(s): March 3, 2014

North Dakota Council on the Arts
Jan Webb, Executive Director
1600 E. Century Ave., Suite 6
Bismarck, ND 58503
Phone: (701) 328-7590
Fax: (701) 328-7595
comserv@nd.gov
www.nd.gov/arts
Notes: Est. 1984. Fellowships for Traditional Arts, Dance, and Theatre (2014); and Visual Art and Media Arts (2015). See website for more information. Deadlines vary.
Submission Materials: see website
Submission Fee: No
Agent Only: No

Page 73 Productions
Liz Jones, Executive Director
138 S. Oxford St. #4E
Brooklyn, NY 11217
Phone: (718) 398-2099
Fax: (718) 398-2794
info@page73.org
www.page73.org
Notes: Est. 1997. Committed to developing and producing the work of emerging playwrights, specifically those who have yet

to receive a professional production in New York City. Page 73 offers five primary programs each year: one or two NYC or world premiere productions of a new play that marks the professional premiere of that playwright in NYC; the P73 Playwriting Fellowship, which provides a $10,000 grant plus a year of developmental support to one early-career playwright; a weeklong summer residency on the campus of Yale University for four playwrights; Interstate 73, a yearlong writers group consisting of six to eight playwrights who meet bimonthly; and Page 2, an extensive workshop offering a lengthy rehearsal process and design support to one play in development. See website for submission and eligibility requirements.
Preferred Genre: All genres
Preferred Length: Any length
Submission Materials: see website
Submission Fee: No
Agent Only: No
Deadline(s): May 1, 2014

Pew Fellowships in the Arts (PFA)
Pew Center for Arts & Heritage
1608 Walnut St., 18th Floor
Philadelphia, PA 19103
Phone: (267) 350-4920
Fax: (267) 350-4997
pfa@pcah.us
www.pcah.us/fellowships
Notes: Est. 1991. As of 2010, a nomination process determines who is invited to apply. All disciplines are considered each year. For more info, see website.
Submission Materials: application
Submission Fee: No
Agent Only: No

Playwrights' Center Many Voices Playwriting Residency
Amanda Robbins-Butcher, Artistic Administrator
The Playwrights' Center
2301 Franklin Ave. E.
Minneapolis, MN 55406
Phone: (212) 595-4597
playwrightsgallery@gmail.com
www.pwcenter.org
Notes: Mentorships available to beginning playwrights of color from Minnesota. Fellowships available to emerging playwrights of color from Minnesota and

nationally. See website for details/award amounts and submission guidelines.
Preferred Genre: Plays or Musicals
Preferred Length: Full-length
Submission Materials: see website
Submission Fee: No
Agent Only: No
Deadline(s): February 13, 2014

Playwrights' Center McKnight Advancement Grants
Amanda Robbins-Butcher, Artistic Administrator
2301 Franklin Ave E
Minneapolis, MN 55406
Phone: (416) 703-0201
Fax: (416) 703-0059
info@playwrightsguild.ca
www.pwcenter.org
Notes: Grants to advance a writer's art and career. Please include a work sample along with your application.
Submission Materials: application
Submission Fee: No
Agent Only: No
Deadline(s): January 9, 2014

Princess Grace Foundation USA Playwriting Fellowship
150 E. 58th St., Fl.25
New York, NY 10155
Phone: (212) 317-1470
Fax: (212) 317-1473
grants@pgfusa.org
www.pgfusa.org
Notes: Est. 1982. 10-week residency with New Dramatists; stipend; and publication/representation by Samuel French for 1 winning playwright.
Preferred Genre: Comedy
Preferred Length: Full-length
Submission Materials: application
Submission Fee: No
Agent Only: No

Princeton Fellowships in the Creative and Performing Arts
Mary O'Connor, Assitant to the Chair
185 Nassau Street
Princeton, NJ 08542
Phone: (609) 258-4840
Fax: (609) 258-2230
www.princeton.edu/arts/fellows
Notes: Princeton Fellowships in the Creative and Performing Arts, funded in part by The

Andrew W. Mellon Foundation, will be awarded to artists whose achievements have been recognized as demonstrating extraordinary promise in any area of artistic practice and teaching. Applicants should be early career poets, novelists, choreographers, playwrights, designers, performers, directors, and performance artists — this list is not meant to be exhaustive — who would find it beneficial to spend two years working in an artistically vibrant university community. Applicants must apply online at http://jobs.princeton.edu by searching for Open Positions and enter key word "Princeton Fellowships".
Submission Materials: see website
Submission Fee: No
Deadline(s): October 1, 2014

Public Theater - Emerging Writers Group
425 Lafayette Street
New York, NY 10003
EWGquestions@publictheater.org
www.publictheater.org
Notes: Targets playwrights at the earliest stages in their careers. Please submit a completed application form (available online), 2 references, a resume, a one-page artistic statement and one full-length play or book of a musical. See website for full details.
Preferred Genre: All genres
Preferred Length: Full-length
Submission Materials: see website
Submission Fee: No
Agent Only: No
Deadline(s): August 30, 2014

Radcliffe Institute Fellowships
8 Garden Street
Cambridge, MA 02138
Phone: (617) 496-1324
Fax: (617) 495-8136
fellowships@radcliffe.edu
www.radcliffe.edu/fellowships
Notes: To support scholars, scientists, artists, and writers of exceptional promise and demonstrated accomplishments to pursue work in academic and professional fields and in the creative arts.
Submission Materials: see website
Submission Fee: Yes
Agent Only: No
Deadline(s): October 1, 2014

Rhode Island State Council on the Arts
Cristina DiChiera, Director, Individual Artists Program
1 Capitol Hill, Fl. 3
Providence, RI 02908
Phone: (401) 222-3880
Fax: (401) 422-3018
cristina.dichiera@arts.ri.gov
www.arts.ri.gov
Notes: Applicants MUST be Rhode Island residents. Annual fellowship in play/screenwriting.
Submission Materials: application
Submission Fee: No
Agent Only: No

Richard H. Driehaus Foundation
Contact: Peter Handler
333 N. Michigan Ave.
Suite 510
Chicago, IL 60601
Phone: (312) 641-5772
Fax: (312) 641-5736
www.driehausfoundation.org
Notes: The Foundation's program for small Chicago theater and dance companies is designed specifically to address the needs of small professional companies. Proposals will only be accepted from companies that emphasize professional presentation instead of education or community outreach. To qualify, companies must have annual operating budgets of less than $150,000, must be based in the Chicago area, and must have produced at least one show in the Chicago area.
Submission Fee: No
Agent Only: No

Seventh Generation Fund for Indian Development
www.7genfund.org
Notes: The Seventh Generation Fund for Indian Development is dedicated to promoting and maintaining the uniqueness of Native peoples and the sovereignty of tribal Nations throughout the Americas. The Fund's primary grant making program areas include the following: Arts and Cultural Expression, Environmental Health and Justice, Human Rights, Sustainable Communities, Intergenerational Leadership, and Women's Leadership.
Submission Materials: see website for application

Submission Fee: No
Agent Only: No

South Dakota Arts Council
711 E. Wells Ave.
Pierre, SD 57501
Phone: (605) 773-3301
Fax: (605) 773-5657
sdac@state.sd.us
www.artscouncil.sd.gov
Notes: Est. 1966. Must be a resident of South Dakota. Submit application and sample online only. Response: 3 months.
Submission Materials: 10-pg sample, application
Submission Fee: No
Agent Only: No

Surdna Foundation
330 Madison Ave
30th Floor
New York, NY 10017
Phone: (212) 557-0010
www.surdna.org/what-we-fund/thriving-
    cultures/80.html
Notes: Under the Foundation's Thriving Cultures priority area, the Teens Artistic Advancement Initiative seeks to address the isolation and lack of opportunities for artistic advancement for young people from disadvantaged communities. Of particular interest are programs that offer unwavering institutional commitment to teens as evidenced by the consistent availability of resources and staff. Programs that offer increasingly complex and long-term opportunities to create art with accomplished artists, those with high quality, experienced faculty and guest artists and professional artistic development opportunities for staff are a priority.
Submission Fee: No
Agent Only: No

Ted Arison Family Foundation USA
Madelon Rosenberg
10800 Biscayne Blvd.
Room 950
Miami, FL 33161
Phone: (305) 891-0017
www.arison.co.il/group/en/
    Content.aspx?PageName=
    The+Ted+Arison+Family+Foundation+
Notes: The Foundation's worldview is rooted in three Jewish values: charity, acts of loving

kindness, and *Tikkun olam* (transformation of the world). The Foundation believes in acting as a role model, creating a better human environment based on fundamental human values, investing in improving the quality of life, and developing public infrastructures and programs based on the commitment to excellence. The Foundation contributes to various projects and to hundreds of nonprofits that operate in seven key spheres: health; education; children and youth; culture, art and sports; populations in distress; disabilities; and scholarships and research.
Submission Materials: see website
Submission Fee: No
Agent Only: No

The Moody's Foundation
Manager Philanthropy Programs
7 World Trade Center
250 Greenwich Street
New York, NY 10007
Phone: (212) 553-3667
www.moodys.com/cust/default.asp
Notes: The Foundation is the philanthropic arm of Moody's Corporation, the parent company of Moody's Investors Services. The Corporation provides credit ratings and research covering debt instruments and securities. The Corporation believes it's important to contribute to the communities in which it operates. It focuses its grant making on four areas: education, health and human services, arts and culture, and civic programs. Arts, culture, and civic grants are aimed at enriching the quality of life in communities where employees live and work. Grants are made to organizations in New York City, San Francisco, and London.
Submission Materials: query letter
Submission Fee: No
Agent Only: No

U.S. Bancorp Foundation
www.usbank.com/cgi_w/cfm/about/
    community_relations/grant_guidelines.cfm
Notes: The U.S. Bancorp Foundation supports nonprofit organizations that improve the quality of life for the residents of the communities served by the bank in Arizona, Arkansas, California, Colorado, Idaho, Illinois, Indiana, Iowa, Kansas, Kentucky, Minnesota, Missouri, Montana, Nebraska, Nevada, North Dakota, Ohio, Oregon, South

Dakota, Tennessee, Utah, Washington, Wisconsin, and Wyoming. The Foundation's areas of interest include affordable housing, self-sufficiency, economic development, education, and artistic and cultural enrichment.

Submission Materials: see website
Submission Fee: No
Agent Only: No

U.S. Dept. of State Fulbright Program for US Students

809 United Nations Plaza
New York, NY 10017
Phone: (212) 984-5525
wjackson@iie.org
www.us.fulbrightonline.org
Notes: Est. 1946. Funds for graduate study, research, or teaching. Students in US colleges must apply thru campus Fulbright Advisers. Those not enrolled in US may apply directly to IIE.
Submission Materials: see website
Submission Fee: No
Agent Only: No
Deadline(s): October 1, 2014

Undiscovered Voices Scholarship

Laura Spencer
The Writer's Center
4508 Walsh Street
Bethesda, MD 20815
Notes: The Writer's Center seeks promising writers earning less than $25,000 annually to apply. This scholarship program will provide complimentary writing workshops to the selected applicant for a period of one year, but not to exceed 8 workshops in that year (and not to include independent studies). The Writer's Center believes writers of all backgrounds and experiences should have an opportunity to devote time and energy toward the perfection of their craft. The recipient will be able to attend writing workshops offered by The Writer's Center free of charge. In addition, he or she will give a reading from his or her work at the close of the scholarship period (June 2014) and will be invited to speak with local high school students on the craft of writing. Please submit: a cover letter signed by the candidate that contains the statement: "I understand and confirm I meet all eligibility requirements of the Undiscovered Voices Scholarship." The cover letter should include information on the impact this scholarship would have on the candidate, contact information for two references who can speak to the candidate's creative work and promise, a work sample in a single genre (Eight pages of poetry, no more than one poem per page, 10 pages of fiction, double-spaced, no more than one work or excerpt, 10 pages of nonfiction (essay, memoir, etc), double-spaced, no more than one work or excerpt, 15 pages of a script or screenplay).

Submission Fee: No
Agent Only: No

Vermont Arts Council

Sonia Rae, Director of Artist & Community Programs
136 State St., Drawer 33
Montpelier, VT 05633
Phone: (802) 828-3293
Fax: (802) 828-3363
srae@vermontartscouncil.org
www.vermontartscouncil.org
Notes: Est. 1994. Grants for artists and organizations. Application submission is online only. Must be a Vermont resident. Response: 2 months.
Submission Materials: see website
Submission Fee: No
Agent Only: No

Verve Grants for Spoken Word Poets - Minnesota

www.intermediaarts.org/
  verve-grants-program-overview
Notes: Intermedia Arts' VERVE grant program provides funding for emerging Minnesota spoken word poets who are interested in artistic advancement and leadership in their communities. Through financial assistance, professional encouragement, and recognition within a culturally and socio-economically diverse group of literary artists, this program strengthens and supports Minnesota's literary community.
Submission Materials: see website
Submission Fee: No
Agent Only: No

William Penn Foundation

Feather Houston, President
Square, 11th Floor
100 North 18th Street
Philadelphia, PA 19103

Phone: (215) 988-1830
moreinfo@williampennfoundation.org
www.williampennfoundation.org
Notes: The Foundation's grant making
focuses on improving the quality of life in
the greater Philadelphia region through
efforts that foster rich cultural expression,
strengthen children's futures, and deepen
connections to nature and community. Grants
are awarded in the following topic areas:
children, youth, and families; environment
and communities; and arts and culture.
Funding priorities for arts and culture grants
include growing a robust cultural community
and leveraging strategic opportunities.

Virtually all of the Foundation's grant
making takes place in the counties of Bucks,
Camden, Chester, Delaware, Montgomery,
and Philadelphia. The Foundation will also
consider requests for projects that, although
administered by an organization located
outside of the region, are expressly for the
benefit of the region and its constituents. The
Foundation occasionally makes grants to
national organizations for work performed by
local affiliates.
Submission Materials: see website
Submission Fee: No
Agent Only: No

Theaters

12 Miles West Theatre Company
Robert Cox, Artistic Director
62 Park Avenue
Rutherford, NJ 07070
Phone: (201) 636-2127
info@12mileswest.com
www.12mileswest.org
Notes: Est. 1992. See website (under FAQ
section) for submission guidelines.
Submissions accepted year-round.
Preferred Genre: All genres
Preferred Length: Any length
Submission Materials: see website
Submission Fee: No
Agent Only: No

16th Street Theater
Ann Filmer, Artistic Director
1619 Wesley Ave
Berwyn, IL 60402
info@16thstreettheater.org
www.16thstreettheater.org/
    scriptsubmissionpolicy.html
Notes: Preference for Illinois resident writers
able to commit to being "playwright-in-
residence." We look for diverse voices, and
we produce at least one "Latino" play per
year. No Musicals. No romantic comedies.
No Theatre for Young Audiences.
Submissions accepted year-round.
Preferred Genre: Plays (No Musicals)
Special Interest: American
Preferred Length: Full-length
Submission Materials: see website
Submission Fee: No
Agent Only: No

24th Street Theatre
Allegra Padilla, Arts Administrator
1117 West 24th St
Los Angeles, CA 90007-1725
Phone: (213) 745-6516
theatre@24thstreet.org
www.24thstreet.org
Notes: The 24th Street Theatre envisions
both a first class Arts Organization and a
Public Benefit service provider, which uses
art as a tool with which to positively impact
our world. We envision a new breed of Arts
Organization in which the term MAIN
STAGE does not exist... where all artistic
programming is of equal value; our
acclaimed season theatrical productions for
adult audiences and family audiences, our
FREE after school arts enrichment programs,
our Teatro Nuevo Latino Initiative projects,
our music series, our outreach programs for
at-risk teens, our free community events, our
teacher training programs, as well as our
Gallery exhibits. 24th Street envisions
building artistic bridges with theatres across
the nation, and internationally. And as we
grow, we shall continue to serve a variety of
diverse audiences with our art in the forms of
performance, outreach, and educational
programming of the highest possible caliber!
Special Interest: Theatre for Young
Audiences
Submission Fee: No
Agent Only: No

52nd Street Project
Lisa Kerner, General Managment Associate
789 10th Ave
New York, NY 10019
Phone: (212) 333-5252
Fax: (212) 333-5598
kerner@52project.org
www.52project.org
Notes: Est. 1981. The 52nd Street Project is
dedicated to the creation and production of
new plays for, and often by, kids between the
ages of nine and eighteen that reside in the
Hell's Kitchen neighborhood in New York
City. The Project does this through a series of
unique mentoring programs that match kids
with professional theater artists. The Project
is about making children proud of
themselves. The Project is not about teaching
children to act, although they will learn to. It
is not about teaching them to write plays,
although they will learn that as well. What it
is about is giving a kid an experience of
success. It is about giving a kid an
opportunity to prove that he or she has
something of value to offer, something that
comes from within that he or she alone
possesses, something that cannot be taken
away.
Submission Fee: No
Agent Only: No

A. D. Players
Lee Walker, Literary Manager
2710 W. Alabama St.
Houston, TX 77098
Phone: (713) 526-2721
Fax: (713) 439-0905
lee@adplayers.org
www.adplayers.org
Notes: Est. 1967. Production cast limit 10
(mainstage)/8 (children's), piano only, limited
sets. Response Time: 3-6 months. Email
professional recommendation. Submissions
accepted year-round.
Preferred Genre: Plays or Musicals
Preferred Length: Full-length
Submission Materials: 10-pg sample, query
letter, synopsis
Submission Fee: No
Agent Only: No

Abingdon Theatre Company
Kim T. Sharp, Literary Manager
312 W. 36th St., Fl. 6
New York, NY 10018
Phone: (212) 868-2055
Fax: (212) 868-2056
ksharp@abingdontheatre.org
www.abingdontheatre.org
Notes: Est. 1993. Production: cast limit 8.
Response Time: 3 - 6 months. Deadline is
ongoing. No musicals. Work must be
unproduced/unoptioned in NYC.
Preferred Genre: Plays (No Musicals)
Preferred Length: Full-length
Submission Materials: see website
Submission Fee: No
Agent Only: No
Deadline(s): June 1, 2014

About Face Theatre
Bonnie Metzgar, Artistic Director
1222 W. Wilson Ave., Fl. 2
Chicago, IL 60640
Phone: (773) 784-8565
Fax: (773) 784-8557
literary@aboutfacetheatre.com
www.aboutfacetheatre.com
Notes: About Face Theatre creates
exceptional, innovative, and adventurous
plays to advance the national dialogue on
gender and sexual identity, and to challenge
and entertain audiences in Chicago, across
the country, and around the world.
Preferred Genre: All genres
Special Interest: Women's Interest
Preferred Length: Any length
Submission Materials: see website
Submission Fee: No
Agent Only: No

Absinthe-Minded Theatre Company
Ralph Scarpato, Producing Artistic Director
1484 Stadium Ave.
Bronx, NY 10465
Phone: (212) 714-4696
rscarp@aol.com
www.absinthe-minded.wix.com/theatre
Notes: Seeking edgy material. All plays
presented in Manhattan. Submissions are
accepted year-round.
Preferred Genre: All genres
Submission Materials: see website
Submission Fee: No
Agent Only: No

Act II Playhouse
Tony Braithwaite, Producing Artistic Director
56 E. Butler Pike
Ambler, PA 19002

Phone: (215) 654-1011
Fax: (215) 654-9050
tony@act2.org
www.act2.org
Notes: Est. 1998. 130-seat SPT. Act II
Playhouse, a non-profit 501(c)(3)
organization in Ambler, Pennsylvania, is
committed to creating and programming
world-class theatre in a venue whose
intimacy draws audiences and actors into
dynamic interaction. Act II produces new,
classic, and contemporary plays and musicals
that reflect the highest artistic standards.
Preferred Genre: Comedy
Submission Fee: No
Agent Only: No

ACT Theater (A Contemporary Theatre)
700 Union St.
Seattle, WA 98101
Phone: (206) 292-7660
Fax: (206) 292-7670
amontgomery@acttheatre.org
www.acttheatre.org
Notes: Est. 1965. Authors from Washington,
Oregon, Alaska, Idaho and Montana only.
Response Time: 6 months. See website for
submission guidelines.
Preferred Genre: All genres
Preferred Length: Full-length
Submission Materials: 15-pg sample, query
letter, synopsis
Submission Fee: No
Agent Only: No

Acting Company
Box 898, Times Square Station
New York, NY 10108
Phone: (212) 258-3111
Fax: (212) 258-3299
mail@theactingcompany.org
www.theactingcompany.org
Notes: Est. 1972. Prefer solo one-acts on US
historical figures for high school tours and
full-length adaptations of classic novels.
Production: Cast limit 13.
Preferred Genre: Educational
Special Interest: Theatre for Young
Audiences
Preferred Length: Any length
Submission Materials: agent-only
Submission Fee: No
Agent Only: Yes

Actor's Express
Freddie Ashley, Artistic Director
887 W. Marietta St. NW, #J-107
Atlanta, GA 30318
Phone: (323) 969-4953
script@actorsart.com
www.actors-express.com
Notes: Est. 1988. Readings, workshops,
production. Assistance: room/board, travel.
Response Time: 6 months. Submissions are
accepted year-round.
Preferred Genre: All genres
Preferred Length: Any length
Submission Materials: full script
Submission Fee: No
Agent Only: Yes

Actors Art Theatre (AAT)
Jolene Adams, Artistic Director
6128 Wilshire Blvd., #110
Los Angeles, CA 90048
Phone: (212) 445-1016
Fax: (212) 445-1015
postarvis@aol.com
www.actorsart.com
Notes: Est. 1994. 32-seat theater developing
plays thru workshops and labs. Produces 1
original play each year, plus one-acts and
solos under Equity 99-seat. Production: no
orchestra, no fly or wing space. Cast size
should not exceed 10. Response Time: 1 year.
Preferred Genre: Plays (No Musicals)
Preferred Length: Any length
Submission Materials: query letter, synopsis
Submission Fee: No
Agent Only: No

Actors Collective
Catherine Russell, Managing Director
447 W. 48th St., Ste. 1W
NEW YORK, NY 10036
Phone: (404) 875-1606
Fax: (404) 875-2791
freddie@actorsexpress.com
www.snappletheater.com
Notes: Est. 1981. Production: cast limit 8.
Response time: 1 month.
Preferred Genre: All genres
Preferred Length: Full-length
Submission Materials: query letter,
S.A.S.E., synopsis
Submission Fee: No
Agent Only: No
Deadline(s): September 12, 2014

Actors Theatre of Louisville [KY]
Amy Wegener, Literary Director
316 W. Main St.
Louisville, KY 40202
Phone: (305) 444-9293 Ext 615
Fax: (305) 444-4181
emaulding@actorsplayhouse.org
www.actorstheatre.org
Notes: Est. 1964. Best time to submit: April-July for full-length scripts, September 1-November 1 postmark window for the National Ten-Minute Play Contest (entries capped at the first 500 ten-minute plays received). See website for full guidelines.
Response Time: 12 months.
Preferred Length: Full-length & 10-min.
Submission Materials: agent-only
Submission Fee: No
Agent Only: Yes

Adventure Stage Chicago (ASC)
Tom Arvetis, Producing Artistic Director
1012 N. Noble St.
Chicago, IL 60642
Phone: (773) 342-4141
Fax: (773) 278-2621
tom@adventurestage.org
www.adventurestage.org
Notes: Est. 1998. Production: ages 18 and older, cast limit 10. Response Time: 1 month. Hard copies only. See website for updates.
Preferred Genre: Theatre for Young Audiences
Special Interest: Theatre for Young Audiences
Preferred Length: Any length
Submission Materials: see website
Submission Fee: No
Agent Only: No

Airmid Theatre Company
Tricia McDermott, Artistic Director
844 Bay Shore Ave
West Islip, NY 11795
Phone: (631) 704-2888
info@airmidtheatre.org
www.airmidtheatre.org
Notes: The Airmid Theatre Company recovers, collects, and produces classic works by women. With these plays at the heart of its mission, the company creates a safe home for women theatre artists, and ignites broad public recognition of the essential contribution women have made to the worlds

of theatre, dramatic literature and society. We are not accepting unsolicited material at this time.
Special Interest: Women's Interest
Submission Materials: see website
Submission Fee: No
Agent Only: Yes

Allenberry Playhouse
1559 Boiling Springs Road
Boiling Springs, PA 17007
Phone: (717) 960-3211
Fax: (717) 960-5280
Aberry@allenberry.com
www.allenberry.com
Notes: Production: age 20-60, cast of 6-10, orchestra limit 5.
Preferred Genre: Musical theatre
Preferred Length: Any length
Submission Materials: 20-pg sample, query letter
Submission Fee: No
Agent Only: No

Alley Theatre
Melissa Flower, Literary Assistant
615 Texas Ave. 18th Floor
Houston, TX 77002
Phone: (713) 228-9341
Fax: (713) 222-6542
melissaf@alleytheatre.org
www.alleytheatre.org
Notes: Est. 1947. The Alley Theatre is unable to accept any unsolicited scripts at this time. See website for updates.
Preferred Genre: All genres
Preferred Length: Full-length
Submission Materials: see website
Submission Fee: No
Agent Only: No

Alliance Theatre
Celise Kalke, Director of New Projects
1280 Peachtree St. NE
Atlanta, GA 30309
Phone: (404) 733-4650
Fax: (404) 733-4625
allianceinfo@woodruffcenter.org
www.alliancetheatre.org
Notes: Est. 1968. Produces world premiere musical and plays, and productions of national significance including theatre for youth and families. No unsolicited scripts except for residents of Georgia.
Preferred Genre: All genres

Special Interest: Theatre for Young
Audiences
Preferred Length: Full-length
Submission Materials: agent-only
Submission Fee: No
Agent Only: Yes

American Folklore Theatre (AFT)
Box 273
Fish Creek, WI 54212
Phone: (920) 854-6117
Fax: (920) 854-9106
dmaier@folkloretheatre.com
www.folkloretheatre.com
Notes: Est. 1990. Original musical works for
families. Production: cast of 3-10. Must have
professional recommendation.
Preferred Genre: Musical theatre
Preferred Length: One-Act
Submission Materials: 10-pg sample,
character breakdown, S.A.S.E., synopsis
Submission Fee: No
Agent Only: No

**American Music Theater Festival/Prince
Music Theater**
Marjorie Samoff, Producing Director
1412 Chestnut Street
Philadelphia, PA 19102
Phone: (215) 972-1000
Fax: (215) 569-3231
info@princemusictheater.org
www.princemusictheater.org
Notes: Submissions are accepted year-round.
Preferred Genre: Musical theatre
Submission Fee: No
Agent Only: No

And Toto Too Theatre Company
P.O. Box 12192
Denver, CO 80212
Phone: (720) 280-7058
submissions@andtototoo.org
www.andtototoo.org
Notes: A theatre company that strives to
challenge assumptions and generalizations by
playwrights in any genre except musicals and
children's plays. Plays must never have been
produced in Colorado and must have 6
characters or fewer and minimal set
requirements. Submissions are accepted year-
round.
Special Interest: Women's Interest
Submission Materials: see website

Submission Fee: No
Agent Only: No

Animated Theaterworks Inc.
Elysabeth Kleinhans, President
240 Central Park S., #13-B
New York, NY 10019
Phone: (212) 757-5085
Fax: (212) 247-3826
info@animatedtheaterworks.org
www.animatedtheaterworks.org
Notes: Est. 1999. Readings and showcase
productions of unpublished/unproduced, new
and developing works. Production: cast limit
6, unit set. Response Time: 6 months.
Preferred Genre: Plays (No Musicals)
Preferred Length: Any length
Submission Materials: 10-pg sample, query
letter, synopsis
Submission Fee: No
Agent Only: No

Arden Theatre Company
40 N. 2nd St.
Philadelphia, PA 19106
Phone: (215) 922-8900
Fax: (215) 922-7011
scripts@ardentheatre.org
www.ardentheatre.org
Notes: Est. 1988. 7 shows/yr in 2 houses.
Response Time: 4-6 months.
Preferred Genre: Adaptation
Preferred Length: Full-length
Submission Materials: see website
Submission Fee: No
Agent Only: Yes

Arena Players Repertory Theatre
Fred De Feis, Producer
269 West 18th Street
Deer Park, NY 11729
Phone: (516) 293-0674
arena109@aol.com
www.arenaplayers.org
Notes: Est. 1950. Award. Production: cast of
2-10. Response time: 6 months.
Unproduced/unpublished.
Preferred Genre: Plays (No Musicals)
Preferred Length: Full-length
Submission Materials: full script, query
letter, S.A.S.E., synopsis
Submission Fee: No
Agent Only: No

Arena Stage
1101 6th St. SW
Washington, DC 20024
Phone: (202) 554-9066
Fax: (202) 488-4056
info@arenastage.org
www.arenastage.org
Notes: Est. 1950. Arena Stage is currently
not accepting script submissions at this time.
See website for changes.
Preferred Genre: All genres
Preferred Length: Full-length
Submission Materials: agent-only
Submission Fee: No
Agent Only: Yes

Arizona Theatre Company
Katherine Monberg, Literary Assistant
343 S. Scott Avenue
Tucson, AZ 85701
Phone: (520) 884-8210
Fax: (520) 628-9129
kmonberg@arizonatheatre.org
www.arizonatheatre.org
Notes: Est. 1966. National Latino
Playwriting Award. Details on website.
Preferred Genre: Plays or Musicals
Preferred Length: Full-length
Submission Materials: see website
Submission Fee: No
Agent Only: Yes
Deadline(s): December 31, 2014

Arizona Women's Theatre Company
6501 E, Greebway Parkway
Suite 103, PMB 338
Scottsdale, AZ 85254
Phone: (480) 422-5386
info@azwtc.org
www.azwtc.org
Notes: Produces contemporary, provocative,
thought provoking plays written by women
and with women from the community.
Provide an innovative, intimate, progressive
forum for women's voices with plays not
previous produced in the Phoenix Metro area.
Preferred Genre: Plays (No Musicals)
Special Interest: Women's Interest
Submission Materials: see website
Submission Fee: No
Agent Only: No

Arkansas Repertory Theatre
Box 110
Little Rock, AR 72201

Phone: (866) 6TH-EREP
Fax: (501) 378-0012
bhupp@therep.org
www.therep.org
Notes: Production: small cast. Response
Time: 3 months query, 6 months script.
Preferred Genre: All genres
Preferred Length: Full-length
Submission Materials: query letter, synopsis
Submission Fee: No
Agent Only: No

Ars Nova
511 W. 54th St.
New York, NY 10019
Phone: (212) 489-9800
Fax: (212) 489-1908
artistic@arsnovanyc.com
www.arsnovanyc.com
Notes: Ars Nova, founded in memory of
Gabe Weiner, is committed to developing and
producing theatre, comedy, music artists in
the early stages of their professional careers.
Submissions are accepted year-round.
Preferred Genre: All genres
Preferred Length: Any length
Submission Materials: see website
Submission Fee: No
Agent Only: No

ART Station
Jon Goldstein, Literary Manager
P.O. Box 1998
Stone Mountain, GA 30086
Phone: (770) 469-1105
Fax: (770) 469-0355
jon@artstation.org
www.artstation.org
Notes: Est. 1986. Work about Southern
experience for Southern, suburban, senior
audience. Production: cast limit 6. Response
time: 1 year. Regular mail submission only.
No email submissions, please.
Preferred Genre: Comedy
Preferred Length: Full-length
Submission Materials: 10-pg sample,
S.A.S.E., synopsis
Submission Fee: No
Agent Only: No

Artists Repertory Theatre
Stephanie Mulligan, Literary Manager
1515 SW Morrison Street
Portland, OR 97205
Phone: (503) 241-9807 Ext 110

Fax: (503) 241-8268
info@artistsrep.org
www.artistsrep.org
Notes: Est. 1981. We are currently not
accepting any submissions at this time.
Preferred Genre: Plays (No Musicals)
Preferred Length: Full-length
Submission Materials: query letter,
S.A.S.E., synopsis
Submission Fee: No
Agent Only: No

ArtsPower National Touring Theatre
271 Grove Ave. Bldg. A
Verona, NJ 07044
Phone: (973) 239-0100
Fax: (973) 239-0165
gblackman@artspower.org
www.artspower.org
Notes: Tourable theater presenting
unpublished one-act plays and musicals for
young and family audiences. Production: cast
limit 4.
Preferred Genre: Plays or Musicals
Special Interest: Theatre for Young
Audiences
Preferred Length: One-Act
Submission Materials: audio CD, S.A.S.E.,
synopsis
Submission Fee: No
Agent Only: No

Asolo Repertory Theatre
5555 N. Tamiami Tr.
Sarasota, FL 34243
Phone: (941) 351-9010
Fax: (941) 351-5796
playsubmissions@asolo.org
www.asolo.org
Notes: Est. 1960. Email preferred. The best
time to submit your materials is between July
to November in order to be considered for
the following season.
Preferred Genre: All genres
Preferred Length: Any length
Submission Materials: see website
Submission Fee: No
Agent Only: No

Atlantic Theater Company
76 9th Ave., #537
New York, NY 10011
Phone: (212) 691-5919
Fax: (212) 645-8755
literary@atlantictheater.org

www.atlantictheater.org
Notes: Est. 1985. 4-show mainstage season,
2-show second stage season. Response time:
6 months. Submit through professional
recommendation, agent or inquiry.
Preferred Genre: Plays or Musicals
Preferred Length: Full-length
Submission Materials: 20-pg sample, audio
CD, full script, query letter, S.A.S.E.
Submission Fee: No
Agent Only: Yes

Attic Ensemble
The Barrow Mansion
83 Wayne St.
Jersey City, NJ 07302
Phone: (201) 413-9200
info@atticensemble.org
www.atticensemble.org
Notes: Est. 1970. Production: cast 4-8,
character ages 15-65, unit set or conceptual.
Preferred Genre: Plays (No Musicals)
Preferred Length: Full-length
Submission Materials: full script, S.A.S.E.
Submission Fee: Yes
Agent Only: No

Axis Theatre Company
Brian Barnhart, Producing Director
1 Sheridan Sq.
New York, NY 10014
Phone: (212) 807-9300
Fax: (212) 807-9039
info@axiscompany.org
www.axiscompany.org
Notes: Est. 1997.
Submission Materials: see website
Submission Fee: No
Agent Only: No

Bailiwick Chicago
Melissa Young, Director of New Works
PO Box 13468
Chicago, IL 60613
Phone: (773) 969-6201
Fax: (773) 883-2017
melissa@bailiwickchicago.com
www.bailiwickchicago.com
Notes: We host a monthly reading series. We
are interested in shows featuring diverse
casts. We produce musicals, plays and one
new work a season. Please check our website
to see the kinds of shows we produce.

Submissions only accepted by personal referral. Submissions are accepted year-round.
Preferred Genre: Plays or Musicals
Special Interest: Multi-Ethnic
Preferred Length: Full-length
Submission Materials: professional referral only
Submission Fee: No
Agent Only: No

Barrington Stage Company
30 Union Street
Pittsfield, MA 01201
Phone: (413) 499-5446
Fax: (413) 499-5447
mdieterle@barringtonstageco.org
http://www.barringtonstageco.org
Notes: Est. 1995. Production: cast of 4-8 (plays) or 10-12 (musicals), modest set. Response Time: 1 month query, 6 months script. Barrington Stage Company welcomes submissions from playwrights, literary agents and theatre colleagues with whom we have an existing professional relationship. Unfortunately, we are not able to accept any unsolicited scripts or queries at this time. Unsolicited scripts will be returned via SASE, or recycled.
Submission Materials: professional referral only
Agent Only: Yes

Barrow Group
Becca Worthington, Literary Manager
312 W. 36th St., #6B
New York, NY 10018
Phone: (212) 760-2615
Fax: (212) 760-2962
lit@barrowgroup.org
www.barrowgroup.org
Notes: Est. 1986. Offers 1-2 mainstage shows/year, plus readings and workshops. Response: 1 month query, 4 months script.
Submission Materials: see website
Submission Fee: No
Agent Only: No

Bay Street Theatre
Box 810
Sag Harbor, NY 11963
Phone: (631) 725-0818 Ext 108
Fax: (631) 725-0906
mail@baystreet.org
www.baystreet.org

Notes: Est. 1991. Mainstage season and play reading series. Production: cast limit 9, unit set, no fly/wing space. Response time: 6 months.
Preferred Genre: Plays (No Musicals)
Preferred Length: Full-length
Submission Materials: agent-only
Submission Fee: No
Agent Only: Yes

Berkeley Repertory Theatre
Julie McCormick, Literary Associate
999 Harrison Street
Berkeley, CA 94710
Phone: (510) 647-2900
Fax: (510) 647-2976
JMcCormick@berkeleyrep.org
www.berkeleyrep.org
Notes: Est. 1968. Response time: 6-9 months. Only accepts scripts from agents and Bay Area playwrights. Prefer to accept scripts during the producing months of September - May. See website for specific guidelines.
Preferred Genre: All genres
Preferred Length: Full-length
Submission Materials: full script
Submission Fee: No
Agent Only: No

Berkshire Theatre Festival
P.O. Box 797
Stockbridge, MA 01262
Phone: (413) 448-8084
Fax: (413) 448-8772
info@berkshiretheatregroup.org
www.berkshiretheatregroup.org
Notes: Est. 1928. New works, small musicals. Production: cast of up to 8. Will respond only if interested. Submissions not returned. Submissions are accepted year-round.
Preferred Genre: Plays or Musicals
Preferred Length: Any length
Submission Materials: E-mail only
Submission Fee: No
Agent Only: No

Black Dahlia Theatre Los Angeles
Ruth McKee, Literary Manager
5453 W. Pico Blvd.
Los Angeles, CA 90019
Phone: (323) 525-0085
DahliaLiterary@gmail.com
www.thedahlia.com

Notes: The Black Dahlia Theatre is dedicated to the development and production of new plays by both established and emerging writers. We seek theatrical, story-driven work, preferably world premieres (or west coast premieres in need of further development). We accept submissions of full-length plays from theatrical literary agents/managers only.
Preferred Genre: All genres
Preferred Length: Any length
Submission Materials: see website
Submission Fee: No
Agent Only: Yes

Black Rep
1717 Olive St., Fl. 4
St. Louis, MO 63103
Phone: (314) 534-3807
Fax: (314) 534-4035
ameerch@theblackrep.org
www.theblackrep.org
Notes: Est. 1976. The Black Rep is the nation's largest, professional African-American theatre company. The mission of The Black Rep is to provide platforms for theatre, dance and other creative expressions from the African-American perspective that heighten the social and cultural awareness of its audiences.
Preferred Genre: Plays (No Musicals)
Special Interest: African-American
Preferred Length: Full-length
Submission Materials: 5-pg sample, query letter, resume, synopsis
Submission Fee: No
Agent Only: No

Black Spectrum Theatre
119-07 Merrick Boulevard
Jamaica, NY 11434
Phone: (718) 723-1800
Fax: (718) 723-1806
info@blackspectrum.com
www.blackspectrum.com
Notes: Est. 1970. The Black Spectrum Theatre aims To stimulate social and cultural consciousness through the production and presentation of message-oriented theatre and films, and to help children and youth develop into responsible citizens through affordable theatre arts. Black Spectrum's primary programs goals are: To create theatre and film productions targeting issues in the African-American community, particularly topics relevant to youth; To provide children, youth, and adults with life skills and artistic experience through training in theatre and film; To bring theatre, film, and performing arts to southeastern Queens and to underserved communities nationwide; and to highlight emerging African-American directors, playwrights, performers, and designers.
Preferred Genre: All genres
Preferred Length: Full-length
Submission Materials: full script
Submission Fee: No
Agent Only: No

Black Swan Theater
109 Roberts Street
Asheville, NC 28801
Phone: (828) 254-6057
Fax: (828) 251-6603
swanthtre@aol.com
www.blackswan.org
Notes: Est. 1988. Develops new scripts & revisits classics. Production: modest cast, simple set. Response time: 3 months. Material must be unpublished. E-mail submissions only.
Preferred Genre: All genres
Preferred Length: Any length
Submission Materials: full script
Submission Fee: No
Agent Only: No

Bloomington Playwrights Project
107 W. 9th St.
Bloomington, IN 47404
Phone: (812) 334-1188
literarymanager@newplays.org
www.newplays.org
Notes: The Bloomington Playwrights Project (BPP) is the only professional theatre in the entire state of Indiana dedicated solely to new plays. In operation for 32 years, we serve both the Bloomington and national theatre community by working with talented playwrights, actors, and artists to develop high-level productions for our patrons as well as the many audiences attending subsequent productions of scripts that originated here at the BPP. We are an advocate for playwrights and new plays and believe firmly that they are not only important but absolutely vital to the future of our art form. Submissions are accepted year-round.
Preferred Length: Full-length

Submission Materials: see website
Submission Fee: No
Agent Only: No

Bond Street Theatre
Joanna Sherman, Artistic Director
2 Bond St.
New York, NY 10012
Phone: (212) 254-4614
Fax: (212) 460-9378
info@bondst.org
www.bondst.org
Notes: Response time: 1 month. We look for scripts with minimal dialogue that can be expressed through the gestural arts.
Preferred Genre: Movement-based
Special Interest: Women's Interest
Preferred Length: Any length
Submission Materials: query letter, S.A.S.E., synopsis
Submission Fee: No
Agent Only: No

Brat Productions
Jess Conda, Artistic Director
2040 Christian Street
Philadelphia, PA 19146
Phone: (267) 586-9093
brat@bratproductions.org
www.bratproductions.org
Notes: Est. 1996. New work, experimental/immersive theatre ideas considered by query; invite to follow if interested. Production: cast limit 7, unit set. Response time: 1 month query, 6 months script. Submissions are accepted year-round.
Preferred Genre: Plays or Musicals
Preferred Length: Full-length
Submission Materials: query letter
Submission Fee: No
Agent Only: No

Brava! for Women in the Arts
2781 24th St.
San Francisco, CA 94110
Phone: (415) 641-7657
Fax: (415) 641-7684
info@brava.org
www.brava.org
Notes: Committed to the artistic expression of women, people of color, and youth. Specializes in creation of new work, especially by lesbians and women of color. Brava is currently not accepting scripts at this time. Please check website for updates.

Special Interest: Women's Interest
Submission Materials: see website
Submission Fee: No
Agent Only: No

Break A Leg Productions
Box 20503, Hammarskjold Ctr.
New York, NY 10017
Phone: (212) 330-0406
Fax: (212) 750-8341
breakalegproductionsnyc@yahoo.com
www.breakalegproductions.com
Notes: Break a Leg Productions believes that comedy, through the use of satire and social criticism, emphasizes what all races and cultures have in common. Through humor, theatre can bridge the gaps which separate people by enabling audiences to recognize and even laugh at the obstacles which divide them. BAL encourages "non-traditional" casting. We are not accepting any submissions until AFTER January 2014. Check our website for updates.
Preferred Genre: Comedy
Preferred Length: Any length
Submission Materials: see website
Submission Fee: No
Agent Only: No

Bridge Theatre Company
Esther Barlow, Co-Artistic Producer
244 W. 54th St.
12th Fl.
New York, NY 10019
esther@thebridgetheatrecompany.com
www.thebridgetheatrecompany.com
Notes: Development through reading, workshops, moving towards off-off Broadway production. The Bridge has produced three successful NY Fringe Festival premieres as well as multiple off-off Broadway productions since 2004. Playwright must be Canadian or the work about Canada in some way. Submissions are accepted year-round.
Preferred Genre: Plays (No Musicals)
Preferred Length: Any length
Submission Materials: 10-pg sample, query letter, synopsis
Submission Fee: No
Agent Only: No

Burning Coal Theatre Company
Jerome Davis, Artistic Director
224 Polk Street
Raleigh, NC 27604

Phone: (919) 834-4001
Fax: (919) 834-4002
coalartisticdir@ncrrbiz.com
www.burningcoal.org
Notes: Est. 1995. 3-4 staged readings/year,
Response time: 6 months. Author must be
resident or connected to North Carolina.
Submit via mail only.
Preferred Genre: Plays or Musicals
Preferred Length: One-Act
Submission Materials: see website
Submission Fee: No
Agent Only: No
Deadline(s): December 16, 2014

Capital Repertory Theatre
111 N. Pearl St.
Albany, NY 12207
Phone: (518) 462-4531
Fax: (518) 465-0213
info@capitalrep.org
www.capitalrep.org
Notes: Est. 1981. Next Act: New Play
Summit. After a call for new work that
resulted in close to 300 submissions the
works presented will be candidates for future
full production. Last year's audience favorite,
The God Game, is being produced as part of
theREP's 2013-2014 season. In addition to
the readings, the three-day Summit will
include other events intended to highlight the
process of new play development, including
discussions with the featured artists. Please
check our website for deadlines and
submission guidelines.
Submission Materials: see website
Submission Fee: No
Agent Only: No

Celebration Theatre
Charls Hall, Literary Manager
7985 Santa Monica Blvd., #109-1
Los Angeles, CA 90046
Phone: (323) 957-1884
Fax: (888) 898-9374
admin@celebrationtheatre.com
www.celebrationtheatre.com
Notes: Est. 1982. Deadline rolling. See
website for guidelines. Production: cast limit
12. Response if interested.
Preferred Genre: Plays or Musicals
Special Interest: LGBT
Preferred Length: Any length
Submission Materials: bio, full script,
synopsis

Submission Fee: No
Agent Only: No

Center Stage [MD]
Literary Dept., Literary Department
700 N. Calvert St.
Baltimore, MD 21202
Phone: (410) 986-4042
Fax: (410) 986-4046
dramaturg@centerstage.org
www.centerstage.org
Notes: Est. 1963. Center Stage is an
artistically driven institution committed to
engaging, educating, and expanding the
horizons of diverse audiences through
challenging, bold, thought-provoking
classical and contemporary theater. Our
professional, nonprofit theater company is
dedicated to the creation and presentation of
a dynamic and diverse array of new and
classic work, and each year hosts an audience
of more than 100,000 in its historic home in
Baltimore's Mount Vernon neighborhood.
With its signature focus on civic and
community engagement, Center Stage, The
State Theater of Maryland, enters its second
50 years with a commitment to exploring
how art and entertainment communicate in
the 21st century, and to igniting conversation
in Baltimore and beyond.
Preferred Genre: Plays (No Musicals)
Preferred Length: Full-length
Submission Materials: 10-pg sample,
character breakdown, S.A.S.E., synopsis
Submission Fee: No
Agent Only: Yes

Center Stage Community Playhouse
Box 138
Westchester Square Station
Bronx, NY 10461
Phone: (212) 823-6434
info@centerstageplayhouse.org
www.centerstageplayhouse.org
Notes: Est. 1969. Nonprofit community
theater seeks unoptioned, unpublished,
unproduced work. Response time: 2 months.
Preferred Genre: Adaptation
Preferred Length: Any length
Submission Materials: query letter, S.A.S.E.
Submission Fee: No
Agent Only: No

Center Theatre Group (CTG)
Mike Sablone, Literary Manager/Resident
Dramaturg
601 W. Temple St.
Los Angeles, CA 90012
Phone: (213) 972-8033
Fax: (213) 972-0746
scripts@ctgla.org
www.centertheatregroup.org
Notes: Est. 1967. Includes Ahmanson
Theatre and Mark Taper Forum at Music
Center in L.A. and Kirk Douglas Theatre in
Culver City. Response time: 6 weeks.
Preferred Genre: All genres
Preferred Length: Any length
Submission Materials: 10-pg sample, query
letter, S.A.S.E., synopsis
Submission Fee: No
Agent Only: No

Charleston Stage
Julian Wiles, Producing Artistic Director
Box 356
Charleston, SC 29402
Phone: (843) 577-5967
Fax: (843) 577-5422
jwiles@charlestonstage.com
www.charlestonstage.com
Notes: Est. 1977. In residence at the Historic
Dock Street Theater. Not accepting new work
at this time.
Preferred Genre: All genres
Preferred Length: Full-length
Submission Materials: see website
Submission Fee: No
Agent Only: No

Cherry Lane Theatre
38 Commerce St.
New York, NY 10014
Phone: (212) 989-2020
Fax: (212) 989-2867
company@cherrylanetheatre.org
www.cherrylanetheatre.org
Notes: Currently not accepting unsolicited
material.
Submission Materials: see website
Submission Fee: No
Agent Only: Yes

Children's Theatre Company (CTC)
2400 3rd Ave. S.
Minneapolis, MN 55404
Phone: (612) 874-0500 Ext 134
Fax: (612) 874-8119

eadams@childrenstheatre.org
www.childrenstheatre.org
Notes: Est. 1965. Children's Theatre
Company creates extraordinary theatre
experiences that educate, challenge and
inspire young people and their communities.
Preferred Genre: Plays or Musicals
Special Interest: Theatre for Young
Audiences
Preferred Length: Full-length
Submission Materials: agent-only
Submission Fee: No
Agent Only: Yes

Children's Theatre of Cincinnati [OH]
Angela Powell Walker, Artistic Director
5020 Oaklawn Drive
Cincinnati, OH 45227
Phone: (513) 569-8080
Fax: (513) 569-8084
angela.powellwalker@thechildrenstheatre.com
www.thechildrenstheatre.com
Notes: Today, the Children's Theatre of
Cincinnati brings art to life for children and
the young-at-heart through three key
programs: MainStage at the Taft, ArtReach
(including WorkShops), and Learning the
Craft. Each season we strive to reach 200,000
people in the Greater Cincinnati/Northern
Kentucky region.
Preferred Genre: Theatre for Young
Audiences
Preferred Length: 50-60 min.
Submission Materials: audio CD, full script
Submission Fee: No
Agent Only: No

Childsplay, Inc
David Saar, Artistic Director
900 S. Mitchell Dr.
Tempe, AZ 85281
Phone: (480) 921-5700
Fax: (480) 921-5777
info@childsplayaz.org
www.childsplayaz.org
Notes: Est. 1977. 6 mainstage and 3 touring
productions/year. Opportunities include
Whiteman New Plays Program. Production:
cast of 2-12.
Preferred Genre: Plays or Musicals
Special Interest: Theatre for Young
Audiences
Preferred Length: Any length
Submission Materials: 10-pg sample,
S.A.S.E., synopsis

Submission Fee: No
Agent Only: No

Cider Mill Playhouse
2 S. Nanticoke Ave.
Endicott, NY 13760
Phone: (607) 748-7363
cmpartdir@gmail.com
www.cidermillplayhouse.com
Notes: Est. 1976. Production: small cast, unit set, no fly space. Response time: 6 months.
Preferred Genre: Adaptation
Submission Materials: agent-only
Submission Fee: No
Agent Only: Yes

Cincinnati Playhouse in the Park
PO Box 6537
Cincinnati, OH 45206
Phone: (513) 345-2242
Fax: (513) 345-2254
www.cincyplay.com
Notes: Est. 1960. Equity LORT B+ and D. Tony Award winner 2004 & 2007. Agent submission of full script. Non-agent submission- please see website for guidelines. Response: 8 months.
Preferred Genre: Plays or Musicals
Preferred Length: Full-length
Submission Materials: see website
Submission Fee: No
Agent Only: No

Cinnabar Theater
3333 Petaluma Blvd. N.
Petaluma, CA 94952
Phone: (707) 763-8920
Fax: (707) 763-8929
elly@cinnabartheater.org
www.cinnabartheater.org
Notes: Est. 1970. Will consider operas.
Submission Materials: see website
Submission Fee: No
Agent Only: No

Circle Theatre [TX]
Rose Pearson, Executive Director
230 W. Fourth St.
Ft. Worth, TX 76102
Phone: (817) 877-3040
Fax: (817) 877-3536
rosepearson@circletheatre.com
www.circletheatre.com
Notes: Est. 1981. Professional contemporary theater in an intimate setting. Unsolicited

scripts from anyone other than agents will not be read or returned. Special interest in plays that would work in a small black box theatre environment. Multiple sets and casts over 9 characters are not appropriate for our space. Submissions are accepted year-round.
Preferred Genre: Plays or Musicals
Preferred Length: Full-length
Submission Materials: E-mail only
Submission Fee: No
Agent Only: Yes

Circle Theatre of Forest Park [IL]
7300 W. Madison St.
Forest Park, IL 60130
Phone: (708) 771-0700
Fax: (708) 771-1826
circletheatre@gmail.com
www.circle-theatre.org
Notes: Est. 1985. Opportunities include new play festival of shorts and full-lengths. We are currently not accepting any scripts at this time.
Preferred Genre: All genres
Preferred Length: Any length
Submission Materials: see website
Submission Fee: No
Agent Only: No

City Garage
Charles Duncombe, Producing Director
2525 Michigan Avenue, Building T1
Santa Monica, CA 90404
Phone: (310) 319-9939
Fax: (310) 396-1040
citygarage@citygarage.org
www.citygarage.org
Notes: Est. 1987. Material should be nonrealistic, experimental, social and political work. Production: Simple, nonrealistic sets. Response time: 2 weeks letter, 6 weeks script.
Preferred Genre: Experimental
Preferred Length: Full-length
Submission Materials: query letter, synopsis
Submission Fee: No
Agent Only: No

City Theatre [FL]
Susan Westfall, Literary Director
444 Brickell Ave., #229
Miami, FL 33131
Phone: (305) 755-9401
Fax: (305) 755-9404
10minuteplays@citytheatre.com

www.citytheatre.com
Notes: Est. 1996. City Theatre is a not-for-profit professional theatre company founded in Miami with the mission to encourage the development and production of original work, specifically the short play, by the nation's established and emerging playwrights. Since its inception, the company has received over 6,000 script submissions, produced over 350 original short plays, and annually brought together an ensemble of talented artists with exciting new material to present Summer Shorts-America's Short Play Festival.
Submission Materials: see website
Submission Fee: No
Agent Only: No

City Theatre Company [PA]
Carlyn Aquiline, Literary Manager/Dramaturg
1300 Bingham St.
Pittsburgh, PA 15203
Phone: (412) 431-4400
Fax: (412) 431-5535
caquiline@citytheatrecompany.org
www.citytheatrecompany.org
Notes: Est. 1974. Produces and develops new and contemporary full-length original plays, musicals, solo work, translations, and adaptations. Production: cast limit 6, prefer 4 or fewer. See website for full guidelines and link for electronic submissions. NO E-mail submissions.
Preferred Genre: Plays or Musicals
Preferred Length: Full-length
Submission Materials: see website
Submission Fee: No
Agent Only: No

Cleveland Play House
Laura Kepley, Associate Artistic Director
8500 Euclid Ave.
Cleveland, OH 44106
Phone: (216) 795-7000
Fax: (216) 795-7005
sgordon@clevelandplayhouse.com
www.clevelandplayhouse.com
Notes: Est. 1916. Response time: 2 months query, 6 months script. Cleveland Play House regrets that it can no longer accept unsolicited manuscripts or 10-page samples unless the writer resides in Ohio.
Preferred Genre: Plays (No Musicals)
Preferred Length: Full-length
Submission Materials: see website

Submission Fee: No
Agent Only: No

Cleveland Public Theatre
Raymond Bobgan, Executive Artistic Director
6415 Detroit Ave.
Cleveland, OH 44102
Phone: (216) 631-2727
Fax: (216) 631-2575
rbobgan@cptonline.org
www.cptonline.org
Notes: Est. 1983. Looking for experimental, poetic, political, intellectually/spiritually challenging work. Response time: 9 months. See website for submission guidelines.
Preferred Genre: Experimental
Preferred Length: Any length
Submission Materials: see website
Submission Fee: No
Agent Only: No

Clubbed Thumb
Clubbed Thumb Info
141 E. 3rd Street
#11H
New York, NY 10009
Phone: (212) 802-8007
Fax: (212) 533-9286
info@clubbedthumb.org
www.clubbedthumb.org
Notes: Accepts submissions of plays that are funny, strange, and provocative, with a running time of an hour to an hour and a half with no intermission. Plays must be unproduced in New York City and must have a reasonable representation of women, both in quantity and quality of roles. We prefer medium sized ensemble casts; at least 3 character. The director of the piece will be chosen by mutual consent of playwright and Clubbed Thumb. We are committed to play development, and therefore produce only plays that are actively being worked on with the expectation that the rehearsal process will prove beneficial to the playwright's writing process. Submit unbound scripts. NOTE: No e-mail submissions. Submissions are accepted year-round.
Special Interest: Women's Interest
Preferred Length: 90 min./no intermission
Submission Materials: see website
Submission Fee: No
Agent Only: No

Colony Theatre Company
555 N. Third St.
Burbank, CA 91502
Phone: (818) 558-7000
Fax: (818) 558-7110
barbarabeckley@colonytheatre.org
www.colonytheatre.org
Notes: Est. 1975. Production: cast limit 4,
simple set, minimal production requirements.
Preferred Genre: Plays or Musicals
Preferred Length: Full-length
Submission Materials: agent-only
Submission Fee: No
Agent Only: Yes

Congo Square Theatre Company
2936 N. Southport #210
Chicago, IL 60657
Phone: (773) 296-0968
tpatton@congosquaretheatre.org
www.congosquaretheatre.org
Notes: Congo Square Theatre Company is an
ensemble dedicated to artistic excellence. By
producing definitive and transformative
theatre, spawned from the African Diaspora
as well as other world cultures, Congo
Square Theatre Company seeks to establish
itself as an institution of multicultural theatre.
Congo Square Theatre's vision is to develop
and produce theater that has the power to
entertain, educate and transform our
community and the world. Submissions for
the August Wilson New Play Initiative are
accepted June 1 - August 1. See website for
guidelines.
Submission Materials: see website
Submission Fee: No
Agent Only: No
Deadline(s): August 1, 2014

**Contemporary American Theatre
Company (CATCO) - Phoenix, Inc**
55 East State Street
Columbus, OH 43215
Phone: (614) 645-7558
jputnam@catco.org
www.catco.org
Notes: Est. 1984. 5-6 plays/season. Merged
with Phoenix Theatre for Children
www.phoenix4kids.org. Production: cast limit
10, set limit 2. Response: 6 months.
Submissions accepted year-round.
Preferred Genre: Plays or Musicals
Special Interest: Theatre for Young
Audiences

Preferred Length: Any length
Submission Materials: 10-pg sample,
synopsis
Submission Fee: No
Agent Only: No

Cornerstone Theater Company
Laurie Woolery, Associate Artistic Director
708 Traction Ave.
Los Angeles, CA 90013
Phone: (213) 613-1700
Fax: (213) 613-1714
lwoolery@cornerstonetheater.org
www.cornerstonetheater.org
Notes: Est. 1986. Collaborating with
playwrights to develop new works with
community. Our development process is
focused on playwrights engaged in a deep
collaboration with community over a 18-24
month process. So PLEASE go to our
website first before submitting plays. Read
our Mission Statement and see examples of
our work. Response 8 months.
Preferred Length: Any length
Submission Materials: 5-pg sample, query
letter
Submission Fee: No
Agent Only: No

Crossroads Theatre Company [NJ]
Marshall Jones, Producing Artistic Director
P.O. Box 238
7 Livingston Ave.
New Brunswick, NJ 08901
Phone: (732) 545-8100
Fax: (732) 907-1864
membership@crossroadstheatrecompany.org
www.crossroadstheatrecompany.org
Notes: Est. 1978. Crossroads Theatre
Company continues to lead the nation with
its commitment to literary works that
examine the African American experience so
that it may be understood and appreciated by
all people. Crossroads is the nation's
premiere African American theater and
recipient of the 1999 Tony Award for
Outstanding Regional Theatre in the United
States.
Preferred Genre: Plays or Musicals
Submission Materials: see website
Submission Fee: No
Agent Only: No

Dad's Garage Theatre Co.
Kevin Gillese, Artistic Director
1105 Euclid Avenue NE
Atlanta, GA 30307
Phone: (404) 523-3141
Fax: (404) 688-6644
kevin@dadsgarage.com
www.dadsgarage.com
Notes: Est. 1995. Dad's Garage engages, cultivates and inspires artists and audiences alike by producing innovative, scripted and improvised works that are recognized locally, nationally and internationally for being undeniably awesome.
Preferred Genre: Comedy
Preferred Length: Any length
Submission Materials: 10-pg sample, query letter, synopsis
Submission Fee: No
Agent Only: No

Dallas Children's Theater
Artie Olaisen, Artistic Associate
5938 Skillman St.
Dallas, TX 75231
Phone: (214) 978-0110
Fax: (214) 978-0118
artie.olaisen@dct.org
www.dct.org
Notes: Est. 1984. Professional Theatre performed for a youth and family audience. Submissions are accepted year-round.
Preferred Genre: Plays or Musicals
Special Interest: Theatre for Young Audiences
Preferred Length: Full-length
Submission Materials: character breakdown, query letter, synopsis
Submission Fee: No
Agent Only: No

Dallas Theater Center
Kevin Moriarty, Artistic Director
2400 Flora Street
Dallas, TX 75201
Phone: (214) 526-8210
Fax: (214) 521-7666
mel.lopez@dallastheatercenter.org
www.dallastheatercenter.org
Notes: Est. 1959. Response: 1 year. If you live in the Dallas/Ft. Worth area, then email a one-page synopsis. Otherwise, Dallas Theatre Center only accepts materials from agents, writers, or artists with whom we have an existing relationship.

Preferred Genre: All genres
Preferred Length: Any length
Submission Materials: 10-pg sample, synopsis
Submission Fee: No
Agent Only: Yes

Danisarte
Alicia Kaplan, Producing Artistic Director
1 Union Square South, Suite 17M
New York, NY 10003
Phone: (212) 561-0191
Danisarte@aol.com
www.danisarte.org
Notes: Est. 1992. Seeking unpublished/unproduced works. Production: cast limit 4. Submissions are accepted year-round.
Preferred Genre: All genres
Special Interest: Theatre for Young Audiences
Preferred Length: 50-60 min.
Submission Materials: query letter, S.A.S.E.
Submission Fee: No
Agent Only: No

Deaf West Theatre (DWT)
DJ Kurs, Artistic Director
5114 Lankershim Blvd.
North Hollywood, CA 91601
Phone: (818) 762-2998
Fax: (818) 762-2981
info@deafwest.org
www.deafwest.org
Notes: Est. 1991.
Submission Fee: No
Agent Only: No

Delaware Theatre Company
200 Water St.
Wilmington, DE 19801
Phone: (302) 594-1104
Fax: (302) 594-1107
literary@delawaretheatre.org
www.delawaretheatre.org
Notes: Est. 1978. Season usually 5-6 readings/productions. Production: cast limit 10, small orchestra, unit set. Response: 6 months.
Preferred Genre: All genres
Preferred Length: Full-length
Submission Materials: agent-only
Submission Fee: No
Agent Only: Yes

Detroit Repertory Theatre
Barbara Busby, Literary Manager
13103 Woodrow Wilson St.
Detroit, MI 48238
Phone: (313) 868-1347
Fax: (313) 868-1705
bbdetrepth@aol.com
www.detroitreptheatre.com
Notes: Est. 1957. Production: age 18-65,
casts no larger than 5-7 characters, non-
traditional casting. We do not double cast.
We prefer "diversity centered" rather than
non-traditional. Response: 6 months.
Submissions are accepted year-round.
Preferred Genre: Plays (No Musicals)
Preferred Length: Full-length
Submission Materials: full script, S.A.S.E.
Submission Fee: No
Agent Only: No

Dicapo Opera Theatre
Michael Capasso, General Director
184 E. 76th St.
New York, NY 10021
Phone: (212) 288-9438
Fax: (212) 744-1082
michael.capasso@dicapo.com
www.dicapo.com
Notes: Limited run performances.
Preferred Genre: Opera
Submission Materials: see website
Submission Fee: No
Agent Only: No

Directors Company
Leah Michalos, Managing Director
311 W. 43rd St., #409
New York, NY 10036
Phone: (212) 246-5877
directorscompany@gmail.com
www.directorscompany.org
Notes: Submissions are accepted year-round.
Submission Materials: E-mail only
Submission Fee: No
Agent Only: No

Diversionary Theatre
John E. Alexander, Executive Director
4545 Park Blvd., #101
San Diego, CA 92116
Phone: (619) 220-6830
Fax: (619) 220-0148
submissions@diversionary.org
www.diversionary.org

Notes: Est. 1986. 3rd oldest LGBT theater in
US. 6-show season and new-work readings in
106-seat space. Apply online. Response: 6
months.
Preferred Genre: All genres
Special Interest: LGBT
Preferred Length: Any length
Submission Materials: synopsis
Submission Fee: No
Agent Only: No

Dixon Place
Ellie Covan, Founding Director
161A Christie Street
New York, NY 10002
Phone: (212) 219-0736
Fax: (212) 219-0761
submissions@dixonplace.org
www.dixonplace.org
Notes: Est. 1986. Nonprofit laboratoty theater
for New York- based performing and literary
artists to create and develop new works in
front of a live audience. Rolling deadline.
Preferred Genre: Experimental
Preferred Length: Any length
Submission Materials: see website
Submission Fee: No
Agent Only: No

Do Gooder Productions
233 East 86th Street, Suite 2A
New York, NY 10023
Phone: (212) 581-8852
dgp@dogooder.org
www.dogooder.org
Notes: Not accepting unsolicited scripts at
this time.
Submission Fee: No
Agent Only: Yes

Dorset Theatre Festival
Box 510
Dorset, VT 05251
Phone: (802) 867-2223
Fax: (802) 867-0144
dina@dorsettheatrefestival.org
www.dorsettheatrefestival.org
Notes: Dorset only accepts scripts of writers
in residence or by invitation. Check out our
website for information on the Jean E. Miller
Young Playwrights Competition and School
Residency Programs.
Submission Materials: see website
Submission Fee: No
Agent Only: No

Dramatic Women
111 Skylie Circle
Santa Barbara, CA 93109
Phone: (805) 965-5826
ellena@silcom.com
http://dramaticwomen.org
Notes: Founded in 1993 to explore and
promote the participation of women in all
areas of theatre & to produce original scripts
by locally-based writers. In the many years
that followed we have produced the work of
30 playwrights, 21 of them women, and 31
directors, 22 of them women. Preference
given to residents of Santa Barbara County.
Special Interest: Women's Interest
Submission Materials: see website
Submission Fee: No
Agent Only: No

Dream Theatre
Andrea Leigh, Artistic Director
484 W. 43rd St., #14-Q
New York, NY 10036
Phone: (212) 564-2628
andrealeigh88@hotmail.com
Notes: Est. 2001. New works, especially
by/for women, that have not been optioned or
produced in NYC. Mailed submissions not
returned. Email preferred. Response: 6
months. Submissions accepted year-round.
Preferred Genre: Plays (No Musicals)
Preferred Length: Any length
Submission Materials: full script, synopsis
Submission Fee: No
Agent Only: No

Drilling Company
Hamilton Clancy, Artistic Director
236 W. 78th Street
3rd floor
New York, NY 10024
Phone: (212) 873-9050
Fax: (917) 330-4234
DrillingCompany@aol.com
www.drillingcompany.org
Notes: Est. 1999. Commissions and
workshops new work. Response: 3 months.
Preferred Genre: Plays (No Musicals)
Preferred Length: Any length
Submission Materials: see website
Submission Fee: No
Agent Only: No

DUO Multicultural Arts Center
Michelangelo Alasa, Artistic Director
62 East 4th Street
New York, NY 10003
Phone: (212) 598-4320
duotheater@gmail.com
www.duotheater.org
Notes: DMAC produces theater works by
Latino playwrights or by non-Latino
playwrights which can be cast with Latino
actors. Prefer small casts of under 7 actors.
Submit full scripts via email only.
Submissions are accepted year-round.
Special Interest: Latino
Submission Materials: E-mail only
Submission Fee: No
Agent Only: No

East West Players
Jeff Liu, Literary Manager
120 N. Judge John Aiso St.
Los Angeles, CA 90012
Phone: (213) 625-7000
Fax: (213) 625-7111
jliu@eastwestplayers.org
www.eastwestplayers.org
Notes: Est. 1965. 4 mainstage
productions/season in addition to readings.
Submissions by US mail only. Response:
12-18 months. Submissions are accepted
year-round.
Preferred Genre: Plays or Musicals
Special Interest: Asian-American
Preferred Length: Full-length
Submission Materials: full script, resume,
S.A.S.E., synopsis
Submission Fee: No
Agent Only: No

Emelin Theatre for the Performing Arts
153 Library Lane
Mamaroneck, NY 10543
Phone: (914) 698-3045
Fax: (914) 698-1404
info@emelin.org
www.emelin.org
Notes: Est. 1972. Production: small cast, no
fly. Response: 6 months.
Preferred Genre: All genres
Preferred Length: Any length
Submission Materials: professional referral
only
Submission Fee: No
Agent Only: Yes

Emerging Artists Theatre (EAT)
Paul Adams, Artistic Director
15 West 28th St., 3rd Floor
New York, NY 10001
Phone: (212) 247-2429
eattheatre@gmail.com
www.emergingartiststheatre.org
Notes: Develop and produce new work.
Submit by email. Production: age 20-70, cast
2-10. Response: 3-6 months.
Preferred Genre: All genres
Special Interest: LGBT
Preferred Length: One-Act
Submission Materials: see website
Submission Fee: No
Agent Only: No
Deadline(s): July 31, 2014

Enrichment Works
5605 Woodman Ave., # 207
Valley Glen, CA 91401
Phone: (818) 780-1400
Fax: (818) 780-0300
dwbabcock@enrichmentworks.org
www.enrichmentworks.org
Notes: Est. 1999. Tours in L.A. schools,
libraries, museums and community venues.
Production: cast limit 3, touring set.
Response: 6 months.
Preferred Genre: Musical theatre
Special Interest: Theatre for Young
Audiences
Preferred Length: One-Act
Submission Materials: full script, S.A.S.E.
Submission Fee: No
Agent Only: No

Ensemble Studio Theatre (EST)
549 W. 52nd St.
New York, NY 10019
Phone: (212) 247-4982
Fax: (212) 664-0041
info@ensemblestudiotheatre.org
www.ensemblestudiotheatre.org
Notes: Est. 1972. The Ensemble Studio
Theatre was founded in the belief that
extraordinary support yields extraordinary
work. We are a dynamic and expanding
family of member artists committed to the
discovery and nurturing of new voices and
the continued support and growth of artists
throughout their creative lives. Through our
unique collaborative process we develop and
produce original, provocative, and authentic

new plays that engage and challenge our
audience and audiences across the country.
Preferred Genre: All genres
Preferred Length: Any length
Submission Materials: see website
Submission Fee: No
Agent Only: No

Ensemble Theatre [TX]
3535 Main St.
Houston, TX 77002
Phone: (713) 807-4316
Fax: (713) 520-1269
ejmorris@ensemblehouston.com
www.ensemblehouston.com
Notes: Est. 1976. Produces contemporary and
classical works devoted to the portrayal of
the African-American experience. Production:
cast limit 5, touring set. Response: 3 months.
Preferred Genre: Plays or Musicals
Special Interest: African-American
Preferred Length: Any length
Submission Materials: 10-pg sample, audio
CD, query letter, S.A.S.E., synopsis
Submission Fee: No
Agent Only: No

First Stage Children's Theater
325 W. Walnut St.
Milwaukee, WI 53212
Phone: (414) 267-2929
Fax: (414) 267-2930
jfrank@firststage.org
www.firststage.org
Notes: Est. 1987. Response : 3 months query,
9 months script.
Preferred Genre: All genres
Special Interest: Theatre for Young
Audiences
Preferred Length: Any length
Submission Materials: query letter, resume,
synopsis
Submission Fee: No
Agent Only: No

Flat Rock Playhouse
Box 310
Flat Rock, NC 28731
Phone: (828) 693-0403
Fax: (828) 693-6795
tom@flatrockplayhouse.org
www.flatrockplayhouse.com
Preferred Genre: Plays or Musicals
Preferred Length: Full-length
Submission Materials: full script

Submission Fee: No
Agent Only: No

Florida Repertory Theatre
2267 1st St.
Fort Myers, FL 33901
Phone: (239) 332-4665
Fax: (239) 332-1808
jasonparrish@floridarep.org
www.floridarep.org
Notes: Est. 1989. 8 mainstage plays
September-June. Production: cast limit 10,
orchestra 4-5, sets limit 2. Response: 1 year.
Preferred Genre: All genres
Preferred Length: Full-length
Submission Materials: agent-only
Submission Fee: No
Agent Only: Yes

Folger Theatre
201 E. Capitol St., SE
Washington, DC 20003
Phone: (202) 675-0344
Fax: (202) 608-1719
tswoape@folger.edu
www.folger.edu/whatsontype.cfm?wotypeid=2
Notes: Est. 1986.
Submission Materials: see website
Submission Fee: No
Agent Only: No

Ford's Theatre Society
511 10th St., NW
Washington, DC 20004
Phone: (202) 638-2941
Fax: (202) 638-6269
literary@fords.org
www.fordstheatre.org
Notes: Est. 1968. 4-5 shows/year, including
perhaps 1 original play or musical. Prefer
plays and musicals that explore the American
Experience and celebrate Abraham Lincoln's
ideals and leadership principles. Production:
orchestra limit 8. Response: 1 year.
Preferred Genre: All genres
Preferred Length: Full-length
Submission Materials: see website
Submission Fee: No
Agent Only: Yes

Fort Wayne Civic Theatre
Phillip H. Colglazier, Executive/Artistic
Director
303 E. Main St.
Fort Wayne, IN 46802

Phone: (260) 422-8641
Fax: (260) 422-6699
pcolglazier@fwcivic.org
www.fwcivic.org
Notes: Fort Wayne Civic Theatre entertains,
enlightens, inspires, educates and enriches the
community through quality live theatre. We
do not accept regular season submissions.
Please see our website for how to get
involved in our annual Festival.
Submission Fee: No
Agent Only: No

Fountain Theatre
Simon Levy, Producing Director
5060 Fountain Ave.
Los Angeles, CA 90029
Phone: (323) 663-2235
Fax: (323) 663-1629
fountaintheatre1@aol.com
www.fountaintheatre.com
Notes: Submit work with professional
recommendation. Production: cast limit 12,
unit set, no fly space. Response: 3 months.
Submissions accepted year-round.
Preferred Genre: Plays (No Musicals)
Preferred Length: Any length
Submission Materials: query letter, synopsis
Submission Fee: No
Agent Only: No

Freed-Hardeman University
Theater Dept., 158 E. Main St.
Henderson, TN 38340
Phone: (731) 989-6780
Fax: (731) 989-6938
cthompson@fhu.edu
www.fhu.edu
Preferred Genre: Plays (No Musicals)
Preferred Length: Any length
Submission Materials: 30-pg sample,
S.A.S.E., synopsis
Submission Fee: No
Agent Only: No

GableStage
Joseph Adler, Producing Artistic Director
1200 Anastasia Ave.
Coral Gables, FL 33134
Phone: (305) 446-1116
Fax: (305) 445-8645
jadler@gablestage.org
www.gablestage.org

Notes: Est. 1979. 6 productions/year. Please submit a query letter by E-mail. Submissions accepted year-round.
Preferred Genre: Plays (No Musicals)
Preferred Length: Full-length
Submission Materials: query letter
Submission Fee: No
Agent Only: No

Galli Theatre for Personal Growth
Tricia Patrick, Executive Director at Galli Theater
230 West 150th Street, #6D
New York, NY 10039
Phone: (212) 731-0668
newyork@galli-group.com
www.gallitheaterny.com
Notes: Performance Address: 347 West 36th Street, New York, NY 10018. Submissions accepted year-round.
Submission Fee: No
Agent Only: No

Geffen Playhouse
10886 LeConte Ave
Los Angeles, CA 90024
Phone: (310) 208-6500
Fax: (310) 208-0341
amy@geffenplayhouse.com
www.geffenplayhouse.com
Notes: Est. 1995. Response Time: 6 months
Submission Materials: agent-only
Submission Fee: No
Agent Only: Yes

George Street Playhouse
9 Livingston Ave.
New Brunswick, NJ 08901
Phone: (732) 846-2895
Fax: (732) 247-9151
sgoldman@georgestplayhouse.org
www.georgestplayhouse.org
Notes: No longer accepting unsolicited scripts or material.
Preferred Genre: No translation or adaptation
Preferred Length: Any length
Submission Fee: No
Agent Only: Yes

Geva Theatre Center
75 Woodbury Blvd.
Rochester, NY 14607
Phone: (585) 232-1366
Fax: (585) 232-4031

www.gevatheatre.org
Notes: Est. 1972. Productions, readings, workshops of classics, musicals, new works. Response: 3 months query; 6 months script.
Preferred Genre: Plays or Musicals
Preferred Length: Any length
Submission Materials: see website
Submission Fee: No
Agent Only: No

Goodman Theatre
170 N. Dearborn St.
Chicago, IL 60601
Phone: (312) 443-3811
Fax: (312) 443-3821
PlaySubmissions@GoodmanTheatre.org
www.goodmantheatre.org
Notes: Est. 1925. Response: 6 - 8 weeks.
Preferred Genre: All genres
Preferred Length: Full-length
Submission Materials: agent-only
Submission Fee: No
Agent Only: Yes

Goodspeed Musicals
Donna Lynn Cooper Hilton, Line Producer
6 Main St
P.O. Box A
East Haddam, CT 06423-0281
Phone: (860) 873-8664
Fax: (860) 873-2329
info@goodspeed.org
www.goodspeed.org
Notes: Est. 1959.
Preferred Genre: Musical theatre
Preferred Length: Full-length
Submission Materials: agent-only
Submission Fee: No
Agent Only: Yes

Gorilla Theatre
Sandra L. Locher, President of the Board
PO Box 152225
Tampa, FL 33684
Phone: (813) 879-2914
info@gorillatheatre.com
www.gorillatheatre.com
Notes: Submissions accepted year-round.
Agent Only: No

Great Lakes Theater Festival
1501 Euclid Ave., # 300
Cleveland, OH 44115
Phone: (216) 241-5490
Fax: (216) 241-6315

mail@greatlakestheater.org
www.greatlakestheater.org
Notes: Est. 1961. Response: 3 months.
Preferred Genre: Plays (No Musicals)
Preferred Length: Full-length
Submission Materials: professional referral only
Submission Fee: No
Agent Only: No

Green Light Arts
1819 JFK BLVD
#400
Philadelphia, PA 19103
Phone: (215) 681-0211
alex@greenlightarts.org
www.greenlightarts.org
Notes: Green Light Arts is a member-based nonprofit organization that supports and unites women artists of all disciplines to create art that enriches our society.
Special Interest: Women's Interest
Submission Materials: see website
Submission Fee: No
Agent Only: No

Greenbrier Valley Theatre
Cathey Sawyer, Artistic Director
113 E. Washington St.
Lewisburg, WV 24901
Phone: (304) 645-3838
Fax: (304) 645-3818
cathey@gvtheatre.org
www.gvtheatre.org
Notes: Est. 1967. Production: age 7 and older, cast of 6-10, orchestra of 1-4, set limit 1-2. Submit character descriptions, scenic requirements, synopsis, and first ten pages. Submissions not returned. Response: 6 months.
Preferred Genre: Plays or Musicals
Preferred Length: Full-length
Submission Fee: No
Agent Only: No

Growing Stage - The Children's Theatre of New Jersey
P.O. Box 36
Netcong, NJ 07857
Phone: (973) 347-4946
Fax: (973) 691-7069
exdir@growingstage.com
www.growingstage.com

Notes: Est. 1982. We review submissions between May through August only. Response Time: 4 months
Special Interest: Theatre for Young Audiences
Submission Fee: No
Agent Only: No
Deadline(s): August 31, 2014

Guthrie Theater
Jo Holcomb, Literary Specialist
818 S. 2nd St.
Minneapolis, MN 55415
Phone: (612) 225-6000
Fax: (612) 225-6004
JoH@GuthrieTheater.org
www.guthrietheater.org
Notes: Est. 1963. New 3-theater complex opened 2006, includes 1,100-seat thrust, 700-seat proscenium and 199-seat studio. The Guthrie Theatre does not accept unsolicited scripts from any source and does not request scripts based on reading synopses or sample dialogue. Any unsolicited scripts received will be recycled.
Submission Fee: No
Agent Only: Yes

Harlequin Productions of Cayuga Community College
Robert Frame, Director of Theater
197 Franklin St.
Auburn, NY 13021
Phone: (315) 255-1743
Fax: (315) 255-2117
framer@cayuga-cc.edu
www.cayuga-cc.edu
Notes: Est. 1958. 6 performances over 2 weekends (fall and spring) with college students in high-quality extracurricular program. Production: age 16-35, cast of 7-14. Response: 1 year. Submissions accepted year-round.
Preferred Genre: Plays (No Musicals)
Preferred Length: Any length
Submission Materials: full script, S.A.S.E.
Submission Fee: No
Agent Only: No

Hartford Stage
50 Church St.
Hartford, CT 06103
Phone: (860) 525-5601
Fax: (860) 224-0183
litman@hartfordstage.org

www.hartfordstage.org
Notes: Est. 1963. Author must be a
Connecticut resident.
Preferred Genre: All genres
Preferred Length: Full-length
Submission Materials: agent-only
Submission Fee: No
Agent Only: Yes

**Harwich Junior Theatre (HJT; Harwich
Winter Theatre)**
105 Division St.
West Harwich, MA 02671
Phone: (508) 432-2002
Fax: (508) 432-0726
hjt@capecod.net
www.hjtcapecod.org
Notes: Est. 1951 New plays for
intergenerational casts and audiences.
Production: intergenerational, no fly.
Response: 6 months.
Preferred Genre: All genres
Special Interest: Theatre for Young
Audiences
Preferred Length: Any length
Submission Materials: S.A.S.E., synopsis
Submission Fee: No
Agent Only: No

Hedgerow Theatre
64 Rose Valley Rd.
Media, PA 19063
Phone: (610) 565-4211
Fax: (610) 565-1672
preed@hedgerowtheatre.org
www.hedgerowtheatre.org
Notes: Est. 1923. Readings of new plays by
Delaware Valley writers in readings and
workshops. Production: cast of 2-8.
Response: 2 months query, 4 months script.
Preferred Genre: All genres
Preferred Length: Any length
Submission Materials: query letter, synopsis
Submission Fee: No
Agent Only: No

Hip Pocket Theatre
Box 136758
Ft. Worth, TX 76136
Phone: (817) 246-9775
Fax: (817) 246-5651
hippockettheatre@aol.com
www.hippocket.org
Notes: Est. 1977. Production: simple set,
outdoor amphitheater. Response: 2 months.

Preferred Genre: Plays or Musicals
Preferred Length: Full-length
Submission Materials: audio CD, synopsis
Submission Fee: No
Agent Only: No

Hobo Junction Productions
2526 West Argyle Avenue
Apt 2
Chicago, IL 60625
Phone: (773) 820-2732
hobojunction@sbcglobal.net
www.hobojunctionproductions.com
Notes: Established in 2008. Focus on
innovative, imaginative and original
approaches to comedy. See website for
details. Rolling deadline.
Preferred Genre: Comedy
Preferred Length: Full-length
Submission Materials: full script, query
letter, S.A.S.E., synopsis
Submission Fee: No
Agent Only: No

Honolulu Theatre for Youth
Eric Johnson, Artistic Director
1129 Bethel Street, Suite 700
Honolulu, HI 96813
Phone: (808) 839-9885
Fax: (808) 839-7018
artistic@htyweb.org
www.htyweb.org
Notes: Est. 1955. Commissioning and
producing new plays, September-May.
Production: cast limit 5. Submissions
accepted year-round.
Preferred Genre: Theatre for Young
Audiences
Special Interest: Theatre for Young
Audiences
Preferred Length: 50-60 min.
Submission Materials: query letter
Submission Fee: No
Agent Only: No

Horizon Theatre Rep [NY]
Rafael De Mussa, Artistic Director
117 East 37th Street, Suite 4C
New York, NY 10016
info@htronline.org
www.htronline.org
Notes: Est. 2000. Unproduced/unoptioned
only. Submissions not returned. Production:
ages 16-75, cast size 4-15. Response: 1
month. Submissions accepted year-round.

Preferred Genre: Plays (No Musicals)
Preferred Length: Any length
Submission Materials: synopsis
Submission Fee: No
Agent Only: No

Hubris Productions

Lorraine Freund
2257 N Lincoln Ave
Chicago, IL 60614
Phone: (773) 398-3273
lorraine@hubrisproductions.com
www.hubrisproductions.com
Notes: Looking for new work; unoptioned, unproduced, unpublished. Email submissions only. Play submissions should be sent with a money order made out to: Hubris Productions. Submissions accepted year-round.
Preferred Genre: Plays (No Musicals)
Special Interest: LGBT
Preferred Length: Full-length
Submission Materials: full script, query letter, synopsis
Submission Fee: Yes
Agent Only: No

Hudson Theatres

Elizabeth Reilly, Artistic Director
6539 Santa Monica Blvd.
Los Angeles, CA 90038
Phone: (323) 856-4252
Fax: (323) 856-4316
ereilly@hudsontheatre.com
www.hudsontheatre.com
Notes: Est. 1991. Response: 6 months query, 1 year script.
Preferred Genre: All genres
Preferred Length: Full-length
Submission Materials: 10-pg sample, query letter, synopsis
Submission Fee: No
Agent Only: No

Huntington Theatre Company

264 Huntington Ave.
Boston, MA 02115
Phone: (617) 273-1503
Fax: (617) 353-8300
chaugland@huntingtontheatre.bu.edu
www.huntingtontheatre.org
Notes: Est. 1981. Massachusetts or Rhode Island writers send unsolicited. Others, must have agent submit. Response: 1 year.
Preferred Genre: All genres

Preferred Length: Any length
Submission Materials: full script, S.A.S.E.
Submission Fee: No
Agent Only: No

Hypothetical Theatre Company

P.O. Box 944
New York, NY 10009
Phone: (212) 780-0800
Fax: (212) 780-0859
htc@hypotheticaltheatre.org
www.hypotheticaltheatre.org
Notes: Est. 1986. Work must be unproduced in NYC. Response: 6 months.
Preferred Genre: Plays (No Musicals)
Preferred Length: Full-length
Submission Materials: agent-only
Submission Fee: No
Agent Only: Yes

IATI Theatre (Instituto Arte Teatral Internacional)

Haydn Diaz, Literary Associate
59-61 East 4th Street, 2nd Floor
New York, NY 10003
Phone: (212) 505-6757
info@iatitheater.org
www.iatitheater.org
Notes: Established in 1968, IATI Theater is dedicated to addressing contemporary issues of broad human interest. Our mission is to perform and promote our contemporary Latino heritage through programming that displays vibrant texts and explore the avant-garde, sometimes incorporating dance and music. Staged readings and workshops are also part of our creative output, thus serving as a bridge between artists and underserved communities nationwide from our New York home in the East Village.
Special Interest: Latino
Preferred Length: Full-length
Submission Materials: online only
Submission Fee: No
Agent Only: No
Deadline(s): June 30, 2014

Idaho Repertory Theatre (IRT)

University of Idaho - Box 442008
Moscow, ID 83844
Phone: (208) 885-6465
Fax: (208) 885-2558
theatre@uidaho.edu
www.idahorep.org

Notes: Seeking work from new/emerging unpublished writer. Submit via email only. Production: ages 13-35, cast of 2-10. Response: 4 months.
Preferred Genre: All genres
Preferred Length: Any length
Submission Materials: query letter
Submission Fee: No
Agent Only: No

Illusion Theater
Michael Robins, Executive Producing Director
528 Hennepin Ave., #704
Minneapolis, MN 55403
Phone: (612) 339-4944
Fax: (612) 337-8042
info@illusiontheater.org
www.illusiontheater.org
Notes: Est. 1974. Submit via email. Response: 1 year.
Preferred Genre: All genres
Preferred Length: Any length
Submission Materials: professional referral only
Submission Fee: No
Agent Only: No

Imagination Stage
4908 Auburn Ave.
Bethesda, MD 20814
Phone: (301) 961-6060
Fax: (301) 718-9526
kbryer@imaginationstage.org
www.imaginationstage.org
Notes: Est. 1979. Production: cast of 4-10.
Preferred Genre: All genres
Preferred Length: Any length
Submission Materials: 10-pg sample, outline, query letter
Submission Fee: No
Agent Only: No

Indiana Repertory Theatre
Richard J. Roberts, Resident Dramaturg
140 W. Washington St.
Indianapolis, IN 46204
Phone: (317) 635-5277
Fax: (317) 236-0767
rroberts@irtlive.com
www.irtlive.com
Notes: Est. 1972. Please submit your script through a literary agent, or by e-mail accompanied by a letter of recommendation from a theatre-professional (an artistic director or literary manager at a professional or university theatre). The IRT employs a playwright-in-residence from whom the majority of our new work is commissioned. We occasionally place other subject-specific commissions. Special interest in adaptations of classic literature; plays that explore cultural/ethnic issues with a Midwestern voice. Response time: 6 months. Submissions accepted year-round but season is selected in February. See website for more information.
Preferred Genre: Plays (No Musicals)
Preferred Length: Any length
Submission Materials: see website
Submission Fee: No
Agent Only: No

INTAR (International Arts Relations) Theatre
Louis Moreno, Artistic Director
500 West 52nd Street, 4th Floor
New York, NY 10019
Phone: (212) 695-6134
lmoreno@intartheatre.org
www.intartheatre.org
Notes: Nurture the professional development of Latino theater artists, produce bold, innovative, artistically significant plays that reflect diverse perspectives. We are looking for full length plays, solo shows, musicals, adaptations, or translations that fit INTAR's mission. Please include full script, brief cover letter, a short bio, development history of the play, and current contact information.
Special Interest: Latino
Submission Fee: No
Agent Only: No

InterAct Story Theatre
Ali Oliver-Krueger, General Artistic Director
32 Pennydog Court
Wheaton, MD 20902
Phone: (301) 879-9305
Fax: (240) 491-9884
info@interactstory.com
www.interactstory.com
Notes: InterAct Story Theatre is a touring theatre for young audiences that performs for a variety of age groups. We are interested in scripts to be performed by professional adult actors for early childhood audiences (ages 3-5), elementary school audiences (ages 4-11), or middle school audiences (ages 11-14). Elementary age scripts must be suitable for 2-3 actors with doubling, or be able to be

adapted for 2-3 actors. Early childhood and middle school scripts must be suitable for 1-2 actors with double or be able to be adapted as such. In all InterAct performances, the audiences becomes part of the action from their seats, becoming group characters, providing sounds, etc. Scripts must include meaningful audience interaction. In reviewing scripts, we prioritize original works over adaptations. We do not produce adaptations of popular fairy tales and children's books. Please do not send us adaptations of Cinderella, Little Red Riding Hood, etc. Submissions include a treatment and up to five pages. Submissions accepted year-round.
Special Interest: Theatre for Young Audiences
Preferred Length: One-Act
Submission Materials: 5-pg sample, query letter
Submission Fee: No
Agent Only: No

InterAct Theatre Company [PA]
2030 Sansom St.
Philadelphia, PA 19103
Phone: (215) 568-8077
Fax: (215) 568-8095
bwright@interacttheatre.org
www.interacttheatre.org
Notes: Est. 1988. Looking for work that explores specific social/political themes/issues. Production: 1-8. Response: 6-12 months.
Preferred Genre: Plays (No Musicals)
Preferred Length: Full-length
Submission Materials: see website
Submission Fee: No
Agent Only: No

Irish Arts Center
553 W. 51st St.
New York, NY 10019
Phone: (212) 757-3318
Fax: (212) 247-0930
info@irishartscenter.org
www.irishartscenter.org
Notes: Est. 1972. Response time: 6-12 months for unsolicited material. Submissions accepted year-round.
Submission Materials: see website
Submission Fee: No
Agent Only: No

Irish Repertory Theatre
Kara Manning, Literary Manager
132 W. 22nd St.
New York, NY 10011
Phone: (212) 255-0270
Fax: (212) 255-0281
kara@irishrep.org
www.irishrep.org
Notes: Ongoing new works reading series reflecting the Irish and Irish American experience. Female playwrights and writers of color encouraged.
Preferred Genre: All genres
Preferred Length: Any length
Submission Materials: see website
Submission Fee: No
Agent Only: No

Itheatrics
Lindsay Weiner
628 W 52 St. Suite 1F
New York, NY 10019
Phone: (646) 467-8090
Fax: (646) 467-8096
info@itheatrics.com
www.itheatrics.com
Notes: Our mission is to ensure kids everywhere experience the transformative power of musical theater: By adapting Broadway musicals for performance by elementary, middle and high school students; By building intuitive teaching resources that guarantee educators have a successful experience producing one of our shows; By creating study guides and innovative educational programs for Broadway shows; By creating new musicals for family audiences like: The Musical Adventures of Flat Stanley, Roald Dahl's Willy Wonka, The Ant and the Elephant and Jim Henson's Emmet Otter; By constantly researching and developing the absolute best practices that allow educators to create successful, cost-effective and sustainable musical theater programs. With programs like the Junior Teaching Intensives and Junior Theater Academy, we help students and teachers develop their skills as musical theater artists.
Submission Fee: No
Agent Only: No

Jewish Theater of New York
Box 845, Times Sq. Sta.
New York, NY 10108
Phone: (212) 494-0050

Fax: (212) 494-0050
thejtny@aol.com
www.jewishtheater.org
Notes: Est. 1994. Seeking
unproduced/unpublished/unoptioned work.
Submissions not returned. Response: 3
months.
Preferred Genre: Musical theatre
Preferred Length: Full-length
Submission Materials: synopsis
Submission Fee: No
Agent Only: No

Jewish Women's Theatre
Ronda Spinak, Artistic Director
521 Latimer Road
Santa Monica, CA 90402
Phone: (310) 704-7154
Fax: (310) 454-1858
ronda@jewishwomenstheatre.org
www.jewishwomenstheatre.org
Notes: Jewish Women's Theatre produces
three themed Salons a year, which include
short plays, poems, monologues, memoirs
and songs. Please check the website for
themes this season and submit accordingly.
There are three submission deadlines.
Special Interest: Jewish
Preferred Length: 10-min./10pgs.
Submission Materials: see website
Submission Fee: No
Agent Only: No

Josiah Theatre Works
Nickolas L. Long, Playwright-at-large,
Artistic Director
345 Lenox Ave
New York, NY 10027
Phone: (347) 291-6289
joshiahtheatre@gmail.com
Notes: Josiah Theatre Works welcomes
playwrights and lyricists seeking productions
in Manhattan and touring shows. We
specialize in period drama and musicals.
Preferred Genre: Plays or Musicals
Preferred Length: Any length
Submission Fee: Yes
Agent Only: No

Judith Shakespeare Company NYC
Joanne Zipay, Artistic Director/Producer
367 Windsor Hwy., #409
New Windsor, NY 12553
judithshakes@gmail.com
www.judithshakespeare.org

Notes: Est. 1995. Offers "Resurgence"
concert reading series and full productions of
new plays with heightened language and
significant roles for women. Submit by US
mail only. Submissions accepted year-round.
Preferred Genre: Plays (No Musicals)
Preferred Length: Any length
Submission Materials: 10-pg sample,
synopsis
Submission Fee: No
Agent Only: No

Kairos Italy Theater (KIT)
Laura Caparrotti, Artistic Director
60 E. 8th Street, #12B
New York, NY 10003
Phone: (212) 254-4025
Fax: (801) 749-6727
info@kitheater.com
www.kitheater.com
Notes: Est. 2002. Produces plays by and
about Italian authors and Italian themes.
Submit by email.
Preferred Genre: Plays (No Musicals)
Preferred Length: Any length
Submission Materials: 10-pg sample,
synopsis
Submission Fee: No
Agent Only: No

Kansas City Repertory Theatre
Eryn M. Bates, Manager of Artistic &
Literary Resources
4949 Cherry St.
Kansas City, MO 64110
Phone: (816) 235-2727
Fax: (816) 235-5367
batesem@kcrep.org
www.kcrep.org
Notes: Est. 1964. Formerly Missouri
Repertory Theatre. Submissions accepted
year-round.
Preferred Genre: All genres
Preferred Length: Full-length
Submission Fee: No
Agent Only: No

Kids' Entertainment
500 St. Clair Ave
Ste 808
Toronto, ON M6C1A8
Phone: (416) 971-4836
Fax: (416) 971-4841
info@kidsentertainment.net
www.kidsentertainment.net

Notes: Kids' Entertainment: Bringing Imagination to Life
Special Interest: Theatre for Young Audiences
Submission Fee: No
Agent Only: No

Kidworks Touring Theatre Co.
Andrea Salloum, Artistic Director
5681 N. Ridge Ave. #2E
Chicago, IL 60660
Phone: (773) 972-7112
Fax: (773) 883-9932
kidworkstheatre@aol.com
www.kidworkstheatre.org
Notes: Est. 1987. Submissions accepted year-round.
Special Interest: Theatre for Young Audiences
Submission Fee: No
Agent Only: No

Killing Kompany
21 Turn Ln.
Levittown, NY 11756
Phone: (212) 772-2590
Fax: (212) 202-6495
killingkompany@killingkompany.com
www.killingkompany.com
Notes: Interactive shows for dinner theater.
Preferred Genre: Interactive
Preferred Length: Full-length
Submission Fee: No
Agent Only: No

L.A. Theatre Works (LATW)
681 Venice Blvd.
Venice, CA 90291
Phone: (310) 827-0808
Fax: (310) 827-4949
bfox@latw.org
www.latw.org
Notes: Est. 1974. Live performances and studio recordings for broadcast over public radio. Response: 6 months.
Preferred Genre: Radio plays
Preferred Length: Any length
Submission Materials: agent-only
Submission Fee: No
Agent Only: Yes

La Centale Galerie Powerhouse
4296 St-Laurent Boulevard
Montreal, QC H2W 1Z3
Phone: (514) 871-0268

galerie@lacentrale.org
www.lacentrale.org
Notes: Growing out of the feminist art movement and founded in 1973, La Centrale Galerie Powerhouse is one of the oldest artist-run centers in Quebec. The center's mandate expands on a history of feminist art practices and engages a broader spectrum of underrepresented artists and their initiatives within established art institutions. The gallery aims to provide a platform for contemporary art informed by feminist and gender theory, as well as intercultural and transdisciplinary practices.
Special Interest: Women's Interest
Submission Materials: see website
Submission Fee: No
Agent Only: No

La Jolla Playhouse
Gabriel Greene, Director of New Play Development
Box 12039
La Jolla, CA 92039
Phone: (858) 550-1070
Fax: (858) 550-1075
information@ljp.org
www.lajollaplayhouse.org
Notes: Est. 1947. Commissions playwrights and provides developmental support thru Page to Stage readings (est. 2001). Response: 2 months query, 1 year script. Submissions accepted year-round.
Preferred Genre: Plays or Musicals
Preferred Length: Full-length
Submission Materials: see website
Submission Fee: No
Agent Only: No

La MaMa Experimental Theater Club
74-A E. 4th St.
New York, NY 10003
Phone: (212) 254-6468
Fax: (212) 254-7597
web@lamama.org
www.lamama.org
Notes: Est. 1961. Response: 6 months.
Preferred Genre: Plays (No Musicals)
Preferred Length: Any length
Submission Materials: professional referral only
Submission Fee: No
Agent Only: No

LAByrinth Theater Company
Philip S. Hoffman, Co-Artistic Dir.
155 Bank street
New York, NY 10014
Phone: (212) 513-1080
Fax: (212) 513-1123
lab@labtheater.org
www.labtheater.org
Notes: Est. 1992. Labyrinth Theater
Company was founded by a small group of
actors who wanted to push their artistic limits
and tell new, more inclusive stories that
expanded the boundaries of mainstream
theater. In doing so, they created a tightly
knit, uninhibited and impassioned ensemble
that created incendiary and vital new works
for the stage that redefined the landscape of
New York City theater. Today Labyrinth is
one of the nation's leading ensemble theater
companies. Driven by a diverse group of
over 120 actors, directors, playwrights and
designers, Labyrinth produces new works for
the stage, giving voice to new perspectives
that are powerful, groundbreaking and that
have changed the face of America's theatrical
landscape.
Preferred Genre: All genres
Preferred Length: Any length
Submission Fee: No
Agent Only: No

LaMicro Theater
Berioska Ipinza, Executive Director
Box 20019, London Terrace
New York, NY 10011
Phone: (212) 929-0332
info@lamicrotheater.org
www.lamicrotheater.org
Notes: Est. 2003. Bilingual productions of
contemporary and emerging playwrights;
explore new ideas and generate dialogue
concerning the realities faced by our diverse
communities.
Special Interest: Latino
Submission Materials: see website
Submission Fee: No
Agent Only: No

Lark Theatre Company, The
939 8th Ave.
#301
New York, NY 10019
Phone: (212) 246-2676
Fax: (212) 246-2609
submissions@larktheatre.org

www.larktheatre.org
Notes: Est. 1994. The Lark Play
Development Center is a laboratory for new
voices and new ideas. We provide
playwrights and their collaborators with
resources to develop their work in a
supportive yet rigorous environment and
encouraging artists to define their own goals
and creative processes in pursuit of a unique
vision. We embrace new and diverse
perspectives here at home and in all corners
of the world, supporting innovative strategies
to help new work reach audiences through a
network of evolving partnerships. We strive
to reinvigorate the theater's ancient and
enduring role as a public forum for
discussion, debate and community
engagement, and to strengthen society's
capacity to imagine its future through
storytelling.
Preferred Genre: All genres
Preferred Length: Full-length
Submission Materials: see website
Submission Fee: No
Agent Only: No

Leaping Thespians
Karen White, Director
leapingthespians@hotmail.com
www.leapingthespians.ca
Notes: Leaping Thespians is a woman's
theatre company bringing stories of lesbians'
lives to Vancouver audiences. We want to
present original work and nurture emerging
talents on stage and behind the scenes. We
accept new members for every production.
We are always interested in reading scripts of
at least one hour's length, where all parts can
be played by women. If you would like us to
consider producing your work, please send a
production/workshop/dramaturge history of
your script as well as a synopsis.
Special Interest: Women's Interest
Submission Materials: synopsis
Submission Fee: No
Agent Only: No

**Lewis Family Playhouse at the Victoria
Gardens Center**
Susan Sluka-Kelly, Cultural Arts Supervisor
12505 Culture Center Drive
Rancho Cucamonga, CA 91739
Phone: (909) 477-2775
Fax: (909) 477-2774
susan.sluka-kelly@cityofrc.us

www.lewisfamilyplayhouse.com
Notes: Recognizing that the arts create stronger communities and provide life-long benefits, the Lewis Family Playhouse is a dynamic Performing Arts Center where we educate, entertain and ignite high quality theatrical experiences for children and families, and audiences of all ages throughout Southern California.
Submission Fee: No
Agent Only: No

Lexington Children's Theatre
418 West Short Street
Lexington, KY 40507
Phone: (859) 254-4546
Fax: (859) 254-9512
info@lctonstage.org
www.lctonstage.org
Notes: Est. 1938. Lexington Children's Theatre is a fully professional, non-profit organization dedicated to the intellectual and cultural enrichment of young people. LCT creates imaginative compelling theatre experiences for young people and families. We share a collective aspiration to impart, explore, foster and develop artistry at all levels and ages in every theatrical discipline and educational opportunity. We are one of the oldest continuously operating theatres for young people in the country and are proud to be the State Children's Theatre of Kentucky.
Special Interest: Theatre for Young Audiences
Submission Fee: No
Agent Only: No

Lincoln Center Theater
150 W. 65th St.
New York, NY 10023
Phone: (212) 362-7600
info@lct.org
www.lct.org
Notes: Est. 1966. Response: 2 months.
Preferred Genre: All genres
Preferred Length: Full-length
Submission Materials: agent-only
Submission Fee: No
Agent Only: Yes

Literally Alive
The Players Theatre
115 MacDougal St.
New York, NY 10012
Phone: (212) 866-5170

brenda@literallyalive.com
www.literallyalive.com
Notes: The mission of Literally Alive is to ignite children's imagination while instilling a love of reading by bringing literature to life. Our approach combines art forms including theatre, dance, music, art, and puppetry to explore a work of literature. Literally Alive encourages children to become expressive, open-minded, creative and to see the arts as a central part of life.
Preferred Genre: Plays or Musicals
Special Interest: Theatre for Young Audiences
Preferred Length: Any length
Submission Fee: No
Agent Only: No

Little Fish Theatre (LFT)
777 Centre St.
San Pedro, CA 90731
Phone: (310) 512-6030
Fax: (310) 507-0269
holly@littlefishtheatre.org
www.littlefishtheatre.org
Notes: Est. 2002. No longer accepting full length plays, see website for annual Pick of the Vine short play festival.
Preferred Genre: Plays (No Musicals)
Preferred Length: 10-min./10pgs.
Submission Materials: see website
Submission Fee: No
Agent Only: No

Looking Glass Theatre [NY]
Erica Nilson, Literary Manager
New York, NY
lgtlit@yahoo.com
www.lookingglasstheatrenyc.com
Notes: Est. 1993. Plays for ages 3 and up. Casts of five or fewer preferred.
Preferred Genre: Plays (No Musicals)
Special Interest: Theatre for Young Audiences
Preferred Length: 50-60 min.
Submission Materials: full script
Submission Fee: No
Agent Only: No

Lookingglass Theatre [IL]
2936 N. Southport Ave., Fl. 3
Chicago, IL 60657
Phone: (773) 477-9257
info@lookingglasstheatre.org
www.lookingglasstheatre.org

Notes: Ensemble-based theater producing primarily company-developed projects. Shows are highly physical with strong narrative. No kitchen sink or talking heads. Lookingglass Theatre Company does not accept unsolicited scripts for consideration. You may submit a 2 - 10 page synopsis (preferred) or your complete play, if it reflects the above criteria, through a literary agent or accompanied by a letter of recommendation by a theater professional (i.e., an artistic director or literary manager of a professional theater). Please include an explanation of how and why your script would fit well into the Lookingglass aesthetic.
Preferred Genre: Plays (No Musicals)
Preferred Length: Any length
Submission Materials: query letter, S.A.S.E., synopsis
Submission Fee: No
Agent Only: No

Los Angeles Women's Theatre Project
Dee Jea Cox, Co-Founder/Artistic Director
10061 Riverside Dr
Toluca Lake, CA 91602
Phone: (818) 471-9100
info@womenstheatreproject.com
www.LAWomenstheatreproject.com
Notes: A nonprofit 501(c)3 organization dedicated to supporting, empowering and creating opportunities for women in the performing arts.
Special Interest: Women's Interest
Submission Materials: see website
Submission Fee: No
Agent Only: No

Lost Nation Theater
City Hall
39 Main St.
Montpelier, VT 05602
Phone: (802) 229-0492
Fax: (802) 223-9608
info@lostnationtheater.org
www.lostnationtheater.org
Notes: Est. 1977. Production: cast limit 8, unit set, no fly. Response: 2 months query, 4 months script.
Submission Materials: 10-pg sample, query letter, resume, synopsis
Submission Fee: No
Agent Only: No
Deadline(s): November 1, 2014

Luna Stage
Cheryl Katz, Artistic Director
555 Valley Road
West Orange, NJ 07052
Phone: (973) 395-5551
submissions@lunastage.org
www.lunastage.org
Notes: Luna Stage accepts scripts from September 15 - April 15.
Preferred Genre: All genres
Preferred Length: Full-length
Submission Materials: see website
Submission Fee: No
Agent Only: No
Deadline(s): April 15, 2014

Ma-Yi Theatre Company
520 8th Ave, #309
New York, NY 10018
Phone: (603) 924-3886
Fax: (603) 924-9142
admissions@macdowellcolony.org
www.ma-yitheatre.org
Notes: Est. 1989. Submissions not returned.
Preferred Genre: Plays (No Musicals)
Special Interest: Asian-American
Preferred Length: Full-length
Submission Materials: query letter, synopsis
Submission Fee: No
Agent Only: No

Magic Theatre
Dori Jacob, Literary Manager
Ft. Mason Center., Bldg. D
San Francisco, CA 94123
Phone: (713) 524-3622
Fax: (713) 524-3977
rudden@mainstreettheater.com
www.magictheatre.org
Notes: Magic produces world premieres and 2nd and 3rd productions of new work. Production: cast limit 8. Response: 3-9 months script. All local, San Francisco Bay Area playwrights are welcome to submit their work unsolicited and without representation. All other writers must submit via literary/talent agencies. Submissions accepted year-round.
Preferred Genre: Plays (No Musicals)
Preferred Length: Full-length
Submission Materials: see website
Submission Fee: No
Agent Only: No

Main Street Theater
Rebecca Greene Udden, Artistic Director
2540 Times Blvd.
Houston, TX 77005
Phone: (212) 989-0948
Fax: (212) 823-0084
saulzachary@yahoo.com
www.mainstreettheater.com/
Notes: Est. 1975. Production: cast limit 9.
Prefer plays by women. Submissions
accepted year-round.
Submission Materials: see website
Submission Fee: No
Agent Only: No

Marin Theater Company (MTC)
Margot Melcon, Literary Manager
397 Miller Ave.
Mill Valley, CA 94941
Phone: (202) 416-8864
Fax: (202) 416-4892
ghenry@kennedy-center.org
www.marintheatre.org
Notes: Est. 1966. Marin Theatre Company
accepts full scripts for season consideration
when submitted by an agent; playwrights
may submit a letter of inquiry. Response time
approximately 6 - 9 months. Marin Theatre
Company has an open script submission
policy for our two annual new play prizes.
See website for submission guidelines.
Preferred Genre: Plays (No Musicals)
Preferred Length: Full-length
Submission Materials: see website
Submission Fee: No
Agent Only: No
Deadline(s): August 31, 2014

MCC Theater
311 W. 43rd St., #206
New York, NY 10036
Phone: (212) 727-7722
Fax: (212) 727-7780
literary@mcctheater.org
www.mcctheater.org
Notes: Est. 1986. Production: cast limit 10.
Response: 2 months.
Preferred Genre: All genres
Preferred Length: Full-length
Submission Materials: see website
Submission Fee: No
Agent Only: No

McCarter Theater Center
Carrie Hughes, Literary Director
91 University Pl.
Princeton, NJ 08540
Phone: (609) 258-6500
Fax: (609) 497-0369
chughes@mccarter.org
www.mccarter.org
Notes: McCarter Theatre employs a search
rather than submission method when scouting
new work. We do not accept submissions.
This includes submissions from agents,
writers, and other theater artists. We believe a
more focused and directed approach benefits
both McCarter and the artists we serve.
McCarter Theatre is committed to nurturing
new plays and artists through commissions,
readings, workshops, retreats and
productions. We identify new artists by
carefully following the work around us
through contact with other theaters, festivals,
graduate programs and playwright
development organizations, and through
conversations with our colleagues around the
country. Agents and artists with a relationship
with McCarter who have a project they
believe will be of particular interest to
McCarter are invited to contact the artistic
staff. If the project fits our needs and we
believe it may be a possible fit for
development or production in the next few
seasons, we will respond with a request to
read the script.
Preferred Genre: Plays or Musicals
Preferred Length: Full-length
Submission Materials: agent-only
Submission Fee: No
Agent Only: Yes

Merrimack Repertory Theatre
Peter Crewe, Company Manager
132 Warren St.
Lowell, MA 01852
Phone: (978) 654-7550
Fax: (978) 654-7575
peter.crewe@mrt.org
www.merrimackrep.org
Notes: Est. 1979. Production: cast limit 8.
Prefer digital scripts. Response: 12 months.
Preferred Genre: Plays (No Musicals)
Preferred Length: Full-length
Submission Materials: agent-only
Submission Fee: No
Agent Only: Yes

Metro Theater Company
Carol North, Artistic Director
8308 Olive Blvd.
St. Louis, MO 63132
Phone: (314) 997-6777
Fax: (314) 997-1811
carol@metrotheatercompany.org
www.metrotheatercompany.org
Notes: Est. 1973. Mainstage shows, tours and commissions of theater for children and family audiences. We do not accept unsolicited scripts. Commissioned playwrights are individuals who have established a relationship with us over time. Visit our website for submission information. Production: cast limit 10. Response: 3 months.
Preferred Genre: Plays or Musicals
Special Interest: Theatre for Young Audiences
Preferred Length: 50-60 min.
Submission Materials: 10-pg sample, S.A.S.E., synopsis
Submission Fee: No
Agent Only: Yes

MetroStage
Carolyn Griffin, Producing Artistic Director
1201 N. Royal St.
Alexandria, VA 22314
Phone: (703) 548-9044
Fax: (703) 548-9089
info@metrostage.org
www.metrostage.org
Notes: Est. 1984. Production: cast limit 6 - 8, orchestra limit 5, unit set. Musicals must already be workshopped and have a demo cd. Small musicals and small intimate contemporary plays with an emotional core preferred. Agent submissions preferred. Submissions accepted year-round.
Preferred Genre: Musical theatre
Preferred Length: Full-length
Submission Materials: 10-pg sample, S.A.S.E., synopsis
Submission Fee: No
Agent Only: Yes

Miami Theater Center, Inc.
Elaiza Irizarry, Executive Director
9806 NE 2nd Ave
Miami Shores, FL 33138
Phone: (305) 751-9550
Fax: (305) 751-9556
elaiza@mtcmiami.org
www.mtcmiami.org
Submission Fee: No
Agent Only: No

Milk Can Theatre Company
Julie Fei Fan Balzer, Artistic Dir.
19-19 23rd Drive
Astoria, NY 01105
Phone: (212) 561-0618
info@milkcantheatre.org
www.milkcantheatre.org
Notes: Est. 2003. The Milk Can Theatre Company is a collective of directors and playwrights. The name of the company reflects our belief that there is power and elegance in simplicity. We provide a collaborative home for artists. Each season allows every company member to take risks: the chance to explore, the opportunity to fail, it's all a process. The selected playwrights will have the opportunity to present their work for an audience and receive valuable feedback and commentary.
Submission Materials: see website
Submission Fee: No
Agent Only: No

Milwaukee Chamber Theatre
Marcella Kearns, Literary Manager
158 N. Broadway
Milwaukee, WI 53202
Phone: (414) 276-8842
Fax: (414) 277-4477
marcella@milwaukeechambertheatre.com
www.chamber-theatre.com
Notes: Est. 1975. Production: small cast, unit set. Response: 6 months. Only interested in Wisconsin writers or those writing about Wisconsin locations and themes. Submissions accepted year-round.
Preferred Genre: All genres
Preferred Length: Full-length
Submission Materials: 10-pg sample, query letter, S.A.S.E., synopsis
Submission Fee: No
Agent Only: No

Milwaukee Repertory Theater
Leda Hoffmann, Literary Coordinator
108 E. Wells St.
Milwaukee, WI 53202
Phone: (414) 224-1761
Fax: (414) 224-9097
lhoffmann@milwaukeerep.com
www.milwaukeerep.com

Notes: Est. 1954. The Rep produces over 600 performances annually of new and contemporary work, classics, and musical theater pieces plus a new short-play festival showcasing its intern company which is one of the oldest internship programs in regional theater. Accompanying The Rep's productions is an array of audience enrichment programs from nightly pre-show talks to Play Guides, Talkbacks, extensive lobby displays and a full array of patron access services. For general submission information, please see website.
Preferred Genre: Plays or Musicals
Preferred Length: Any length
Submission Materials: see website
Submission Fee: No
Agent Only: Yes

Miracle Theatre Group
Olga Sanchez, Artistic Director
425 SE 6th Ave.
Portland, OR 97214
Phone: (503) 236-7253
Fax: (503) 236-4174
olga@milagro.org
www.milagro.org
Notes: Est. 1985. Author must be Hispanic. Production: cast limit 10, no fly. Response: 1 year. Seeking plays but will consider musicals. Submissions accepted year-round.
Preferred Genre: Plays (No Musicals)
Special Interest: Latino
Preferred Length: Full-length
Submission Materials: full script
Submission Fee: No
Agent Only: No

Missouri Repertory Theatre
4949 Cherry St.
Kansas City, MO 64110
Phone: (816) 235-2727
Fax: (816) 235-6562
theatre@umkc.edu
www.missourireptheatre.org
Notes: Est. 1964.
Preferred Genre: Plays (No Musicals)
Preferred Length: Full-length
Submission Materials: agent-only
Submission Fee: No
Agent Only: Yes

Mixed Blood Theatre Company
1501 S. 4th St.
Minneapolis, MN 55454

Phone: (612) 338-0937
Fax: (612) 338-1851
literary@mixedblood.com
www.mixedblood.com
Notes: Est. 1976. Mixed Blood welcomes submissions of contemporary plays that pursue and realize the company's mission and aesthetic. Mixed Blood uses theatre to address pluralism, usually manifest in race, culture, language, disability, gender, nationality, affectional orientation, and political worldview. Predictably unpredictable, the theatre particularly invites polyglot plays, scripts from the global stage, and work that advances the art form. We prefer e-submissions. If you think your play might be a good fit for us, please send a query letter, your bio or resume, a brief synopsis, and a 10-page sample of your play. Response: 4 months.
Preferred Genre: All genres
Preferred Length: Full-length
Submission Materials: see website
Submission Fee: No
Agent Only: No

Moving Arts
Box 481145
Los Angeles, CA 90048
Phone: (323) 666-3259
Fax: (323) 666-2841
info@movingarts.org
www.movingarts.org
Notes: Est. 1992. Currently not accepting submissions. To stay informed of changes to these guidelines and other company news, sign up for our e-mail list.
Preferred Genre: Plays (No Musicals)
Preferred Length: Full-length
Submission Fee: No
Agent Only: No

National Theatre of the Deaf
Betty Beekman, Executive Director
325 Pequot Ave
New London, CT 06320
Phone: (860) 574-9063
Fax: (860) 574-9107
bbeekman@ntd.org
www.ntd.org
Notes: Est. 1967. Looking for work unproduced professionally. Production: cast limit 10, touring set. Response: 1 month query, 6 months script. We are a company

comprised of Deaf and Hearing actors.
Submissions accepted year-round.
Preferred Genre: All genres
Special Interest: Deaf
Preferred Length: Full-length
Submission Materials: 10-pg sample, query
letter, S.A.S.E., synopsis
Submission Fee: No
Agent Only: No

National Yiddish Theater -- Folksbiene
135 W. 29th St.
Room 504
New York, NY 10001
Phone: (212) 213-2120
Fax: (212) 213-2186
info@folksbiene.org
www.folksbiene.org
Notes: Seeking material in Yiddish or based
on Yiddish source material.
Preferred Genre: Plays or Musicals
Preferred Length: Any length
Submission Materials: see website
Submission Fee: No
Agent Only: No

Near West Theatre (NWT)
Carole L. Hedderson, Business Director
6514 Detroit Avenue
Cleveland, OH 44102
Phone: (216) 961-9750
Fax: (216) 961-6381
LDoerr@nearwesttheatre.org
www.nearwesttheatre.org
Notes: Near West Theatre builds loving
relationships and engages diverse people in
strengthening their sense of identity, passion,
and purpose, individually and in community,
through transformational theatre arts
experiences.
Submission Fee: No
Agent Only: No

New Conservatory Theatre Center
Ed Decker, Artistic Director
25 Van Ness Ave., Lower Lobby
San Francisco, CA 94102
Phone: (415) 861-4914
Fax: (415) 861-6988
ed@nctcsf.org
www.nctcsf.org
Notes: Est. 1981. Material must be
unoptioned. Response: 2-4 months. Agent
submissions preferred. Submissions accepted
year-round.

Preferred Genre: No translation or
adaptation
Special Interest: LGBT
Preferred Length: Any length
Submission Materials: see website
Submission Fee: No
Agent Only: No

New Federal Theatre
292 Henry St.
New York, NY 10002
Phone: (212) 353-1176
Fax: (212) 353-1088
newfederal@aol.com
www.newfederaltheatre.com
Notes: Est. 1970. Production: cast limit 5,
unit set. Response: 6 months.
Preferred Genre: Plays (No Musicals)
Preferred Length: Full-length
Submission Materials: full script, S.A.S.E.
Submission Fee: No
Agent Only: No

New Georges
Kara-Lynn Vaeni, Literary Manager
109 W. 27th St., #9-A
New York, NY 10001
Phone: (646) 336-8077
Fax: (646) 336-8077
info@newgeorges.org
www.newgeorges.org
Notes: New Georges does not read
submissions for production, but to discover
compelling writers to bring into relationship
with the company, with an eye for future
collaboration.
Preferred Genre: Plays (No Musicals)
Special Interest: Women's Interest
Preferred Length: Full-length
Submission Materials: full script
Submission Fee: No
Agent Only: No

New Ground Theatre
Chris Jansen, Artistic Director
2113 E. 11th St.
Davenport, IA 52803
Phone: (563) 326-7529
Fax: (563) 359-7576
cjansen@hotmail.com
www.newgroundtheatre.org
Notes: Est. 2001. Author must be resident of
Iowa, Illinois or quad city area. Production:
cast limit 6, unit set, no fly. Response: 6
months.

Preferred Genre: All genres
Preferred Length: Full-length
Submission Materials: full script
Submission Fee: No
Agent Only: No

New Group, The
410 W. 42nd St.
New York, NY 10036
Phone: (212) 244-3380
Fax: (212) 244-3438
info@thenewgroup.org
www.thenewgroup.org
Notes: Est. 1991. Workshops and readings.
US mail submissions only. Response: 2
months for samples, 9 months for full scripts.
Preferred Genre: Plays (No Musicals)
Preferred Length: Full-length
Submission Materials: see website
Submission Fee: No
Agent Only: No

New Jersey Repertory Company
179 Broadway
Long Branch, NJ 07740
Phone: (732) 229-3166
Fax: (732) 229-3167
njrep@njrep.org
www.njrep.org
Notes: Est. 1997. Seeking
unproduced/unpublished via email only. US
mail submits not returned. Production: cast
limit 4 for plays and musicals. 6-7 Full
length plays produced each year. 15-20
readings produced each year. See website for
specific guidelines. Submissions accepted
year-round.
Preferred Genre: Plays or Musicals
Preferred Length: Full-length
Submission Materials: audio CD, character
breakdown, full script, synopsis
Submission Fee: No
Agent Only: No

New Repertory Theatre
Bridget Kathleen O'Leary, Associate Artistic
Director
200 Dexter Ave.
Watertown, MA 02472
Phone: (617) 923-7060
Fax: (617) 923-7625
bridgetoleary@newrep.org
www.newrep.org
Notes: Est. 1984. New Repertory Theatre is
only accepting submissions to participate in

our Next Voices Fellowship program. We
have an open submission policy for New
England area playwrights looking to
participate in the program. Participants must
be able to meet regularly at the New Rep
offices in Watertown, Massachusetts.
Interested writers may send a cover letter and
a synopsis of their proposed play along with
a 10-page sample.
Preferred Genre: Plays (No Musicals)
Preferred Length: Full-length
Submission Materials: 10-pg sample, query
letter, synopsis
Submission Fee: No
Agent Only: No

New Theatre
Steven Chambers, Literary Manager
Roxy Performing Arts Center
1645 SW 107th Avenue
Miami, FL 33165
Phone: (305) 443-5373
Fax: (305) 443-1642
schambers@new-theatre.org
www.new-theatre.org
Notes: Est. 1986. New works and new
adaptations of Shakespeare sought.
Production: cast limit 6, minimal set.
Response: 6-9 months. Submissions accepted
year-round. Best times to submit are July-
August to be considered for the following
season.
Preferred Genre: All genres
Preferred Length: Full-length
Submission Materials: character breakdown,
query letter, synopsis
Submission Fee: No
Agent Only: No

New Works/Vantage Theatres
Dori Salois, Artistic Manager
1251 W. Muirlands Dr.
La Jolla, CA 92037
Phone: (858) 456-9664
vantagetheatre@gmail.com
www.vantagetheatre.com
Notes: Seeking work with big
political/spiritual ideas.
Preferred Genre: Plays (No Musicals)
Preferred Length: Any length
Submission Materials: full script, S.A.S.E.,
synopsis
Submission Fee: No
Agent Only: No

New World Theater (NWT)
100 Hicks Way, #16 Curry Hicks
Amherst, MA 01003
Phone: (413) 545-1972
Fax: (413) 545-4414
nwt@admin.umass.edu
Notes: Hosts "New Works for a New World" every summer & invite up to 4 artists for a development residency.
Preferred Genre: All genres
Preferred Length: Any length
Submission Materials: query letter
Submission Fee: No
Agent Only: No

New York Stage and Film (NYSAF)
214 West 29th Street, Suite 1001
New York, NY 10001
Phone: (212) 736-4240
Fax: (212) 736-4241
info@newyorkstageandfilm.org
www.newyorkstageandfilm.org
Notes: Est. 1985. Summer season (Jun-Aug) in residence as part of Powerhouse program at Vassar College. Response: 6 months.
Preferred Genre: Plays (No Musicals)
Preferred Length: Full-length
Submission Materials: full script, S.A.S.E.
Submission Fee: No
Agent Only: No

New York Theatre Workshop (NYTW)
83 E. 4th St.
New York, NY 10003
Phone: (212) 780-9037
Fax: (212) 460-8996
litern@nytw.org
www.nytw.org
Notes: Est. 1979. Works of innovative form & language about socially relevant issues. Response: 3 months query, 8 months script.
Preferred Genre: Plays (No Musicals)
Preferred Length: Full-length
Submission Materials: 10-pg sample, query letter, resume, S.A.S.E., synopsis
Submission Fee: No
Agent Only: No

Next Theater Company
Jenny Avery, Artistic Director
927 Noyes St.
Suite 108
Evanston, IL 60201
Phone: (847) 475-1875
Fax: (847) 475-6767

info@nexttheatre.org
www.nexttheatre.org
Notes: Est. 1981. Commissions 1 world premiere per season. Production: cast limit 10. Next does not accept unsolicited scripts for consideration. Any writer with representation should submit his or her play through a literary agent. Submissions will also be accepted if accompanied by a letter of recommendation by a theater professional. See website for submission guidelines.
Preferred Genre: Plays (No Musicals)
Preferred Length: Full-length
Submission Materials: 10-pg sample, query letter, S.A.S.E., synopsis
Submission Fee: No
Agent Only: No

Nightwood Theatre
55 Mill Street
Suite 301
Case Goods Warehouse, Bldg. No. 71
Toronto, ON M5A 3C4
Phone: (416) 944-1740
Fax: (416) 944-1739
info@nightwoodtheatre.net
www.nightwoodtheatre.net
Notes: The oldest professional women's theatre company in Canada. Founded in1979 by Cynthia Grant, Kim Renders, Mary Vingoe and Maureen White, Nightwood has produced, developed and toured landmark, award-winning plays by and about Canadian women.
Special Interest: Women's Interest
Submission Materials: see website
Submission Fee: No
Agent Only: No

Nora Theatre Company, The
450 Massachusetts Ave
Cambridge, MA 02139
Phone: (617) 576-9278
info@thenora.org
www.thenora.org
Notes: The Nora Theatre Company produces illuminating contemporary and modern classic theater and champions the voice of women.
Special Interest: Women's Interest
Submission Materials: see website
Submission Fee: No
Agent Only: No

North Carolina Theatre for Young People
Jody Kaizen, UNCG Theatre Manager
406 Tate Street
PO Box 26170
Greensboro, NC 27402-6170
Phone: (336) 334-4601
Fax: (336) 334-5100
jtcauthe@uncg.edu
http://performingarts.uncg.edu/theatre
Special Interest: Theatre for Young
Audiences
Submission Fee: No
Agent Only: No

Northern Stage
Carol Dunne, Artistic Director
Box 4287
White River Junction, VT 05001
Phone: (802) 291-9009
Fax: (802) 291-9156
info@northernstage.org
www.northernstage.org
Notes: Est. 1997. Submissions accepted year-round.
Preferred Genre: All genres
Preferred Length: Full-length
Submission Materials: query letter, S.A.S.E.
Submission Fee: No
Agent Only: No

Northlight Theatre
Kristin Leahey, Resident Dramaturg
9501 N. Skokie Blvd.
Skokie, IL 60077
Phone: (847) 679-9501
Fax: (847) 679-1879
kleahey@northlight.org
www.northlight.org
Notes: Est. 1975. Preference given to writers
from Illinois.
Preferred Genre: All genres
Preferred Length: 10-min./10pgs.
Submission Materials: see website
Submission Fee: No
Agent Only: No

Obsidian Theatre Company
1089 Dundas Street East
Toronto, ON M4M-1R9 Canada
Phone: (416) 463-8444
obsidiantheatre@bellnet.ca
www.obsidiantheatre.com
Notes: Check website for submission details.
Submissions accepted year-round.
Preferred Genre: Plays (No Musicals)

Preferred Length: Full-length
Submission Materials: E-mail only
Submission Fee: No
Agent Only: No

Omaha Theater Company at The Rose
Michael Miller, Literary Manager
2001 Farnam St.
Omaha, NE 68102
Phone: (402) 502-4624
Fax: (402) 344-7255
michaelm@rosetheater.org
www.rosetheater.org
Notes: Est. 1949. Production: cast limit 10,
unit set. Response: 6 months. Please submit a
cover letter with contact information and a
script sample.
Preferred Genre: Plays (No Musicals)
Special Interest: Theatre for Young
Audiences
Preferred Length: One-Act
Submission Materials: see website
Submission Fee: No
Agent Only: No

Open Eye Theater
Amie Brockway, Producing Artistic Director
PO Box 959
Margaretville, NY 12455
Phone: (845) 586-1660
Fax: (845) 586-1660
openeye@catskill.net
www.theopeneye.org
Notes: Est. 1972. Readings and productions
for a multigenerational audience. Production:
small cast, modest set. Response: 6 months.
Preferred Genre: All genres
Special Interest: Theatre for Young
Audiences
Preferred Length: Any length
Submission Materials: query letter, synopsis
Submission Fee: No
Agent Only: No

Opera Cleveland
1422 Euclid Ave, #1052
Cleveland, OH 44115
Phone: (216) 575-0903
Fax: (216) 575-1918
williamson@operacleveland.org
www.operacleveland.org
Notes: Est. 2006 (merger of Lyric Opera
Cleveland, Cleveland Opera). Spring-fall
season and summer festival of 3 full-length
operas. Response: 1 month.

Preferred Genre: Opera
Preferred Length: Full-length
Submission Materials: audio CD, full script, query letter, S.A.S.E., synopsis
Submission Fee: No
Agent Only: No

Oregon Shakespeare Festival
Box 158
Ashland, OR 97520
Phone: (541) 482-2111
Fax: (541) 482-0446
literary@osfashland.org
www.osfashland.org
Notes: Est. 1935. Response: 6 months.
Preferred Genre: Plays (No Musicals)
Preferred Length: Full-length
Submission Materials: query letter
Submission Fee: No
Agent Only: No

Orlando Repertory Theatre
Brian Diaz, Company Manager
1001 East Princeton St
Orlando, FL 32803
Phone: (407) 896-7365
Fax: (407) 897-3284
briand@orlandorep.com
www.orlandorep.com
Notes: The Rep is a professional theatre for young audiences with a mission to enlighten, entertain and enrich children and adults by producing theatre of exceptional quality. The award winning Rep Youth Academy provides classes, camps and workshops for children along with professional development opportunities to local classroom teachers. Housed in a three-theatre complex in Loch Haven Park. The Rep is also home to the University of Central Florida's MFA in Theatre for Young Audiences graduate programs.
Special Interest: Theatre for Young Audiences
Submission Fee: No
Agent Only: No

Passage Theatre
P.O. Box 967
Trenton, NJ 08605
Phone: (609) 392-0766
Fax: (609) 392-0318
info@passagetheatre.org
www.passagetheatre.org

Notes: Est. 1985. Seeks boundary-pushing & stylistically adventurous new works. Production: Modest cast size 4-6 actors, no fly. Response: 5 months. Passage Theatre is no longer accepting unsolicited submissions.
Preferred Genre: Plays or Musicals
Preferred Length: Any length
Submission Materials: agent-only
Submission Fee: No
Agent Only: No

Patrick's Cabaret
3010 Minnesota Ave.
Minneapolis, MN 55406
Phone: (612) 724-6273
amy@patrickscabaret.org
www.patrickscabaret.org
Notes: Est. 1986. Primarily a rental house for shared evenings of short works (up to 15 minutes). Production: all ages, cast 2-20, minimal sets. Response: 1 month
Preferred Genre: All genres
Preferred Length: 15 min.
Submission Materials: query letter
Submission Fee: Yes
Agent Only: No

PCPA Theatrefest
800 S. College Dr.
Santa Maria, CA 93454
Phone: (805) 928-7731
Fax: (805) 928-7506
literary@pcpa.org
www.pcpa.org
Notes: Est. 1964. Response: 3 months query, 6 months script.
Preferred Genre: Plays (No Musicals)
Preferred Length: Full-length
Submission Materials: query letter, synopsis
Submission Fee: No
Agent Only: No

Pearl Theatre Company, Inc.
307 West 38th St.
Suite 1805
New York, NY 10018
Phone: (212) 505-3401
Fax: (212) 505-3404
kfarrington@pearltheatre.org
www.pearltheatre.org
Notes: Est. 1982. Focusing on classical adaptations/translations or based on classical themes/characters only. Production: age 18-75, cast size 6-13, 1 set. Response: 4-6 months.

Preferred Genre: Adaptation
Preferred Length: Any length
Submission Materials: character breakdown, synopsis
Submission Fee: No
Agent Only: No

Pegasus Theater Company
Box 942
Monte Rio, CA 95462
Phone: (707) 522-9043
director@pegasustheater.com
www.pegasustheater.com
Notes: Est. 1998. Our purpose is to produce thought provoking theater that reflects, enriches and educates the diverse community that it serves, and to enhance tourism, so essential to our local economy.
Submission Materials: see website
Submission Fee: No
Agent Only: No

Penguin Rep Theatre
Angelo Parra, Literary Manager
Box 91
Stony Point, NY 10980
Phone: (845) 786-2873
Fax: (845) 786-3638
playrite@optonline.net
www.penguinrep.org
Notes: Est. 1977. Agent Submission ONLY. Full length plays, single set, four actors or fewer. No calls please. Response: Up To One Year. Response: 6-12 months.
Preferred Genre: Plays (No Musicals)
Preferred Length: Full-length
Submission Materials: full script
Submission Fee: No
Agent Only: Yes

Pennsylvania Youth Theatre
25 W 3rd St
Bethlehem, PA 18015
Phone: (610) 332-1400
Fax: (610) 332-1405
office@123pyt.org
www.123pyt.org
Notes: Pennsylvania Youth Theatre (PYT) is a nonprofit performing arts organization with the mission of educating, entertaining, and enriching the lives of young people and their families through the art of theatre. PYT was founded with the commitment to provide opportunities for all children to participate and learn through the art of theatre.

Special Interest: Theatre for Young Audiences
Submission Fee: No
Agent Only: No

Penumbra Theatre Company
270 N. Kent St.
St. Paul, MN 55102
Phone: (651) 288-6795
Fax: (651) 224-3180
sarah.bellamy@penumbratheatre.org
www.penumbratheatre.org
Notes: Est. 1976. Response: 9 months.
Preferred Genre: Plays (No Musicals)
Preferred Length: Any length
Submission Materials: see website
Submission Fee: No
Agent Only: No

People's Light and Theatre Company
39 Conestoga Rd.
Malvern, PA 19355
Phone: (610) 647-1900
www.peopleslight.org
Notes: Est. 1974. We are currently not accepting unsolicited scripts.
Preferred Genre: Plays (No Musicals)
Preferred Length: Full-length
Submission Materials: 10-pg sample, full script, query letter, synopsis
Submission Fee: No
Agent Only: No

Performance Network Theatre
120 E. Huron St.
Ann Arbor, MI 48104
Phone: (734) 663-0696
Fax: (734) 663-7396
david@performancenetwork.org
www.performancenetwork.org
Notes: Est. 1981. Production: cast limit 10, no fly. Response: 6 months. E-mail submissions Only.
Preferred Genre: Plays (No Musicals)
Preferred Length: Full-length
Submission Materials: see website
Submission Fee: No
Agent Only: No

Philadelphia Theatre Company (PTC)
Carrie Chapter, Literary Manager
230 S. Broad St.
Ste. 1105
Philadelphia, PA 19102
Phone: (215) 985-1400

Fax: (215) 985-5800
literary@philadelphiatheatrecompany.org
www.philadelphiatheatrecompany.org
Notes: Est. 1974. Agent submissions or local
writers only. 4 contemporary US plays/season
(September-July). Production: cast limit 8.
Response: an e-letter of acknowledgement
only; 6 months to 1 year. No phone calls,
please.
Preferred Genre: Plays (No Musicals)
Preferred Length: Full-length
Submission Materials: see website
Submission Fee: No
Agent Only: No

Phoenix Arts Association Theatre [CA]
Linda Ayres-Frederick, Executive Artistic
Director
414 Mason St. #601
San Francisco, CA 94102
Phone: (415) 336-1020
Fax: (415) 664-5001
Lbaf23@aol.com
www.phoenixtheatresf.org
Notes: Est. 1985. NOTE: Due to economics,
we have taken a hiatus from receiving new
scripts. Production: cast limit 7, unit set.
Response: 6 weeks query, 6 months script.
Preferred Genre: Plays (No Musicals)
Submission Materials: see website
Submission Fee: No
Agent Only: No

Phoenix Theatre [IN]
Bryan Fonseca, Literary Manager
749 N. Park Ave.
Indianapolis, IN 46202
Phone: (317) 635-7529
bfonseca@phoenixtheatre.org
www.phoenixtheatre.org
Notes: Est. 1983. Production: cast limit 6.
Response: 6 months. Submissions accepted
year-round.
Preferred Length: Any length
Submission Materials: agent-only
Submission Fee: No
Agent Only: Yes

Pier One Theatre
Lance Petersen, Artistic Director
Box 894
Homer, AK 99603
Phone: (907) 235-7333
Fax: (907) 235-7333
info@pieronetheatre.net

www.pieronetheatre.org
Notes: Est. 1973. Non-Equity community
theater. Response: 6 months.
Preferred Genre: Plays or Musicals
Preferred Length: Full-length
Submission Materials: full script, S.A.S.E.
Submission Fee: No
Agent Only: No

Pillsbury House Theatre
3501 Chicago Ave. S.
Minneapolis, MN 55407
Phone: (612) 825-0459
Fax: (612) 827-5818
raymondn@pillsburyhousetheatre.org
www.pillsburyhousetheatre.org
Notes: Est. 1992. Submit by invitation only.
Production: cast limit 10. Response: 5
months query, 6 months script.
Preferred Genre: Plays (No Musicals)
Preferred Length: Full-length
Submission Materials: agent-only
Submission Fee: No
Agent Only: Yes

Pioneer Theatre Company
Karen Azenberg, Artistic Director
300 South 1400 East, #325
Salt Lake City, UT 84112
Phone: (801) 581-7188
Fax: (801) 581-5472
karen.azenberg@PTC.utah.edu
www.pioneertheatre.org
Notes: Est. 1962. Response: 6 months. We
accept submissions either by agent or with a
letter of recommendation. Submissions
accepted year-round.
Preferred Genre: All genres
Preferred Length: Full-length
Submission Materials: agent-only
Submission Fee: No
Agent Only: No

Pittsburgh Public Theater
621 Penn Ave.
Pittsburgh, PA 15222
Phone: (412) 316-8200
Fax: (412) 316-8216
www.ppt.org
Notes: Est. 1975. Not accepting submissions
at this time.
Submission Fee: No
Agent Only: No

Plan-B Theatre Company
Jerry Rapier, Producing Director
138 W. 300 S.
Salt Lake City, UT 84101
Phone: (801) 297-4200
jerry@planbtheatre.org
www.planbtheatre.org
Notes: Est. 1995. Submit script via email in PDF format. Focused on work by Utah-based playwrights (playwrights with legitimate, actual ties to Utah will also be considered - coming here to ski or attend Sundance does not qualify.). Production: cast limit 5, minimal set. Response: 3 months.
Preferred Genre: Plays (No Musicals)
Special Interest: LGBT
Preferred Length: 90 min./no intermission
Submission Materials: E-mail only
Submission Fee: No
Agent Only: No
Deadline(s): January 31, 2014

Play With Your Food
PO Box 2161
Westport, CT 06880
Phone: (203) 247-4083
carole@jibproductions.org
www.jibproductions.org
Notes: Looking for first rate one-act plays for Connecticut's popular lunchtime play-reading series, Play With Your Food.
Preferred Genre: Plays (No Musicals)
Preferred Length: One-Act
Submission Materials: full script
Submission Fee: No
Agent Only: No

Playhouse on the Square
Jordan Nichols, Director of New Works
51 S. Cooper St.
Memphis, TN 38104
Phone: (901) 725-0776
jordan@playhouseonthesquare.org
www.playhouseonthesquare.org
Notes: Est. 1968. Playhouse on the Square, now in its 43rd Season, is accepting scripts for the 1st Annual "New Works @ The Works" Competition. A panel of local directors, actors, and designers will review all submitted scripts and select six to receive staged readings during the 2013-14 season. After the six readings have been presented, Playhouse on the Square will select two that will receive full productions during the 2014-15 season. These two new works will receive world premieres at Playhouse's third performance space, TheatreWorks. The two winning works will each be awarded a prize of $500. The playwright of each play will also be flown to Memphis to take part in the rehearsals and development of the new work. $10 entry fee must be paid along with submitted script for consideration (check or money order). Cast size up to 10. Submissions that have been previously produced or published will not be accepted. Scripts will be accepted between January 1-May 30.
Submission Materials: see website
Submission Fee: No
Agent Only: No
Deadline(s): May 30, 2014

Playmakers of Baton Rouge
Karli Henderson
Reilly Theatre Tower Drive, LSU
Baton Rouge, LA 70803
Phone: (225) 578-6996
karli@playmakers.net
http://playmakersbr.org/
Notes: Est. 1982. Playmakers of Baton Rouge, Inc.'s mission is to provide entertaining educational experiences for young audiences through quality professional theatre. We are Louisiana's only professional theatre dedicated to bringing quality live theatrical productions to young audiences across the state. Playmakers is proud to continue providing excellent educational and entertaining opportunities to thousands of children and adults, through the annual Summer Neighborhood Tour, Spring Elementary School Tour, Drama Classes and Camps, Season Productions including Youth Company productions, and the Wally Wise Guy Educational Safety Mini-Tour.
Submission Fee: No
Agent Only: No

Plays for Young Audiences
c/o The Children's Theatre Co,
2400 3rd Ave S
Minneapolis, MN 55404
Phone: (612) 872-5108
Fax: (612) 874-8119
mwright@playsforyoungaudiences.org
www.playsforyoungaudiences.org
Special Interest: Theatre for Young Audiences

Submission Fee: No
Agent Only: No

Playwrights Horizons
Adam Greenfield, Director, New Play
Development
416 W. 42nd St.
New York, NY 10036
Phone: (212) 410-9234
emilyandren@earthlink.net
www.playwrightshorizons.org
Notes: Est. 1971. Offering 6
productions/season and numerous readings to
new American voices. See website for
material preferences. Production: cast limit
10. Response: 6 months for plays; 9 months
for musicals. Hard copy, full manuscripts
only. No synopses, samples, or electronic
submissions.
Preferred Genre: Plays or Musicals
Preferred Length: Full-length
Submission Materials: audio CD, bio, full
script, S.A.S.E.
Submission Fee: No
Agent Only: No

Playwrights Theatre of New Jersey
John Pietrowski, Artistic Director
Box 1295
Madison, NJ 07940
Phone: (301) 816-0569
pforum7@yahoo.com
www.ptnj.org
Notes: Est. 1986. Submissions are limited.
Please check website for specific guidelines.
Works accepted through New Play
Development Program. Production: ages 10
and above; casts up to 6. Response: 1 year.
Preferred Genre: Plays (No Musicals)
Preferred Length: Full-length
Submission Materials: 10-pg sample,
S.A.S.E., synopsis
Submission Fee: No
Agent Only: No

**Playwrights/Actors Contemporary Theatre
(PACT)**
Juel Wiese, Managing Director
105 W. 13th St., #5-G
New York, NY 10011
Phone: (212) 242-5888
Fax: (212) 242-5888
juelwiese@msn.com
Notes: We are not accepting submissions at
this time.

Preferred Genre: Drama
Special Interest: American
Preferred Length: Full-length & 10-min.
Submission Fee: No
Agent Only: No

Polarity Ensemble Theatre
Richard Engling, Artistic Director
135 Asbury Ave.
Evanston, IL 60202
Phone: (847) 475-1139
richard@petheatre.com
www.petheatre.com
Notes: Visit our website and register on our
auditions list to be notified when we
accept/read scripts. We work exclusively with
Chicago-Area playwrights.
Preferred Genre: Plays or Musicals
Preferred Length: Full-length
Submission Materials: full script
Submission Fee: No
Agent Only: No

Poplar Pike Playhouse (PPP)
Frank Bluestein, Director
7653 Old Poplar Pike
Germantown, TN 38138
Phone: (901) 755-7775
Fax: (901) 755-6951
PopPikePlayhouse@aol.com
www.ppp.org
Notes: Est. 1976. Occasionally produce
original work. Production: ages 14-19, full
orchestra. Response: 3 months.
Preferred Genre: Plays or Musicals
Special Interest: Theatre for Young
Audiences
Preferred Length: Any length
Submission Materials: full script, S.A.S.E.
Submission Fee: No
Agent Only: No

Porchlight Music Theatre
4200 W. Diversey Ave.
Chicago, IL 60639
Phone: (773) 777-9884
Fax: (773) 777-9886
info@porchlightmusictheatre.org
www.porchlightmusictheatre.org
Notes: Est. 1994. Response: 6 months. See
website for submission guidelines.
Preferred Genre: Musical theatre
Preferred Length: Full-length
Submission Materials: audio CD, bio,
S.A.S.E., synopsis

Submission Fee: No
Agent Only: No

Portland Center Stage [OR]
Brandon Woolley, Producing Associate
128 NW 11th Ave.
Portland, OR 97209
Phone: (503) 445-3839
Fax: (503) 445-3721
brandonw@pcs.org
www.pcs.org
Notes: Est. 1988. At this time, not accepting
unsolicited script submission for general
season consideration. If you are interested in
submitting a script for JAW: A Playwrights
Festival, visit the JAW Script Submission
page: http://www.pcs.org/jaw/#scripts. Scripts
will be accepted between November 1, 2013-
February 1, 2014.
Preferred Genre: All genres
Preferred Length: Full-length
Submission Materials: see website
Submission Fee: No
Agent Only: No
Deadline(s): February 1, 2014

Portland Stage Company [ME]
PO Box 1458
Portland, ME 04104
Phone: (207) 774-1043
Fax: (207) 774-0576
dburson@portlandstage.org
www.portlandstage.org
Notes: Est. 1974. Response: 6 months script.
Submissions accepted year-round.
Preferred Genre: Plays (No Musicals)
Preferred Length: Full-length
Submission Materials: full script, synopsis
Submission Fee: No
Agent Only: Yes

Prairie Fire Children's Theatre
PO Box 82
Barrett, MN 56311
Phone: (320) 528-2596
prairiefirechildrenstheatre@gmail.com
www.prairiefirechildrenstheatre.com
Notes: Est. 1987. Prairie Fire Children's
Theatre (or PFCT) is a professional touring
theatre company based in Barrett, Minnesota
bringing a theatrical experience to
communities across the upper Midwest.
Prairie Fire tours a variety of original musical
adaptations of classic tales. Throughout the
entire year, Prairie Fire Children's Theatre

sends two professional Actors/Directors to a
community for a one week residency. Local
children fill the roles, and PFCT provides
everything needed to do the show. After a
week of rehearsing, the cast will perform the
play twice on the weekend.
Special Interest: Theatre for Young
Audiences
Submission Fee: No
Agent Only: No

Pregones Theater
Rosalba Rolon, Artistic Director
571-575 Walton Ave.
Bronx, NY 10451
Phone: (718) 585-1202
Fax: (718) 585-1608
rrolon@pregones.org
www.pregones.org
Notes: Create and perform original musical
theatre and plays rooted in Puerto
Rican/Latino cultures.
Special Interest: Latino
Submission Materials: 10-pg sample
Submission Fee: No
Agent Only: No

Premiere Stages at Kean University
Clare Drobot, Producing Associate
Hutchinson Hall, 1000 Morris Ave.,
Union, NJ 07083
Phone: (908) 737-4092
Fax: (908) 737-4636
premiere@kean.edu
www.kean.edu/premierestages
Submission Materials: see website
Submission Fee: No
Agent Only: No

Present Company
520 Eighth Ave., #311
New York, NY 10018
Phone: (212) 279-4488
Fax: (212) 279-4466
info@presentcompany.org
www.fringenyc.org
Notes: Creators and producers of the New
York International Fringe Festival featuring
200+ shows every August in New York City.
Applications are accepted December -
February.
Preferred Genre: All genres
Preferred Length: Any length
Submission Materials: see website

Submission Fee: Yes
Agent Only: No
Deadline(s): February 1, 2014

Primary Stages
307 W. 38th St, #1510
New York, NY 10018
Phone: (212) 840-9705
Fax: (212) 840-9725
info@primarystages.org
www.primarystages.org
Notes: Est. 1984. Founded to produce new
plays and develop playwrights. Response: 1
year. Primary Stages would like to offer DG
members 10% off Online Playwriting classes
summer at Primary Stages. This unique
resource allows our curriculum and award-
winning faculty to reach all corners of the
artistic world. This summer we are bringing
back the popular "Online First Draft", as well
as introducing "Online Adaptation". These
classes begin the weeks of June 4th & 11th,
respectively. Guild members use the code
"DGA" to receive the discount.
Preferred Genre: All genres
Preferred Length: Full-length
Submission Materials: agent-only
Submission Fee: No
Agent Only: Yes

Prime Stage Theatre
Wayne Brinda, Producing Artistic Director
Box 99446
Pittsburgh, PA 15233
Phone: (724) 773-0700
wbrinda@primestage.com
www.primestage.com
Notes: Literature based youth and adult
theatre. Production: age 12 - senior citizen.
Submissions accepted year-round.
Preferred Genre: Adaptation
Special Interest: Theatre for Young
Audiences
Preferred Length: Full-length
Submission Materials: 30-pg sample, query
letter, S.A.S.E., synopsis
Submission Fee: No
Agent Only: No

Public Theater [NY]
Liz Frankel, Literary Manager
425 Lafayette St.
New York, NY 10003
Phone: (212) 539-8530
submissions@publictheatre.org

www.publictheater.org
Notes: Est. 1954. Response: 6 months.
Submissions accepted year-round.
Preferred Genre: Plays or Musicals
Preferred Length: Full-length
Submission Materials: 10-pg sample, query
letter, synopsis
Submission Fee: No
Agent Only: No

Puerto Rican Traveling Theatre
304 W. 47th St.
New York, NY 10036
Phone: (212) 354-1293
Fax: (212) 307-6769
allen@prtt.org
www.prtt.org
Notes: est. 1977.
Readings/workshops/productions for
beginning and professional playwrights.
Prefer author to be Latino/minority.
Preferred Genre: All genres
Special Interest: Latino
Preferred Length: Full-length
Submission Materials: full script, S.A.S.E.
Submission Fee: No
Agent Only: No

Puerto Rican Traveling Theatre (PRTT)
Miriam Colon Valle, Artistic Director
304 W. 47th St.
New York, NY 10036
Phone: (212) 354-1293
Fax: (212) 307-6769
miriam@prtt.org
www.prtt.org
Notes: Est. 1977. Present and produce truly
bilingual professional theater. Offer artistic
development to emerging and established
artists.
Special Interest: Latino
Submission Fee: No
Agent Only: No

Pulse Ensemble Theatre
Alexa Kelly, Artistic Director
248 W 35th Street, 15th Fl.
New York, NY 10018
Phone: (212) 695-1596
Fax: (212) 594-4208
theatre@pulseensembletheatre.org
www.pulseensembletheatre.org
Notes: Est. 1989. Only developing new
works in Playwrights' Lab. Response: up to 1
year.

Preferred Genre: Plays (No Musicals)
Preferred Length: Full-length
Submission Materials: 10-pg sample,
S.A.S.E., synopsis
Submission Fee: No
Agent Only: No

Purple Rose Theatre Company
Michelle Mountain, Literary Manager
137 Park St.
Chelsea, MI 48118
Phone: (734) 433-7782
Fax: (734) 475-0802
mountain@purplerosetheatre.org
www.purplerosetheatre.org
Notes: Est. 1991. Prefer comedy. Must be
unoptioned/unpublished/unproduced.
Production: ages 18-80, cast of 2-10.
Response: 8 months. See website for full
submission guidelines. Submissions accepted
year-round.
Preferred Genre: Plays (No Musicals)
Preferred Length: Full-length
Submission Materials: 15-pg sample,
character breakdown, S.A.S.E., synopsis
Submission Fee: No
Agent Only: No

Queens Theatre
Rob Urbinati, Director, New Play
Development
Box 520069
Flushing, NY 11352
Phone: (718) 760-0064
Fax: (718) 760-1972
roburbinati@gmail.com
www.queenstheatre.org
Notes: Est. 2001. New play development
series for immigrant and minority writers.
Production: cast limit 10. Response: 6
months. Submissions accepted year-round.
Preferred Genre: All genres
Preferred Length: Full-length
Submission Materials: see website
Submission Fee: No
Agent Only: No

Rainbow Dinner Theatre
David DiSavino, Executive Producer
3065 Lincoln Hwy East
Box 56
Paradise, PA 17562
Phone: (717) 687-4300
Fax: (717) 687-8280
david@rainbowdinnertheatre.com

www.rainbowdinnertheatre.com
Notes: Est. 1984. Professional non-Equity
dinner theater. Production: ages 18 and older,
cast of 2-12, set limit 2. Response: 6 months.
Preferred Genre: Plays (No Musicals)
Preferred Length: Full-length
Submission Materials: 10-pg sample,
S.A.S.E., synopsis
Submission Fee: No
Agent Only: No

Rattlestick Playwrights Theatre
244 Waverly Pl.
New York, NY 10014
Phone: (212) 627-2556
Fax: (630) 839-8352
info@rattlestick.org
www.rattlestick.org
Notes: Yearlong development program,
culminating in annual spring Exposure
Festival. Production: cast of up to 8.
Preferred Genre: All genres
Preferred Length: Full-length
Submission Materials: see website
Submission Fee: No
Agent Only: No

Raven Theatre New Play Workshop
Susan Lieberman, Literary Manager
6157 North Clark Street
Chicago, IL 60660
Phone: (773) 338-2177
Fax: (773) 338-6547
susan@RavenTheatre.com
www.RavenTheatre.com
Notes: Est. 1992. Scripts accepted ONLY for
New Play Workshops. See website for
specific details.
Preferred Genre: No musicals or
adaptations
Preferred Length: Full-length
Submission Materials: see website
Submission Fee: No
Agent Only: No

Red Bull Theater
Literary Submission
P.O. Box 250863
New York, NY 10025
Phone: (212) 414-5168
info@redbulltheater.com
www.redbulltheater.com
Notes: Est. 2003. Interested in new full-
length plays and adaptations that relate to our
mission of exploring Jacobean

themes/heightened language. US mail only.
Response: six months.
Preferred Genre: Plays or Musicals
Preferred Length: Any length
Submission Materials: see website
Submission Fee: No
Agent Only: Yes

Repertorio Espanol
Robert Federico, Executive Director
138 E. 27th St.
New York, NY 10016
Phone: (212) 225-9999
Fax: (212) 225-9085
r.federico@repertorio.org
www.repertorio.org
Notes: Est. 1968. Introduce the best of Latin
American, Spanish, and Hispanic-American
theatre in distinctive, quality productions, and
bring theatre to a broad audience.
Special Interest: Latino
Preferred Length: Full-length
Submission Materials: see website
Submission Fee: No
Agent Only: No

Rivendell Theatre Ensemble
Rachel Walshe, Literary Manager
5775 N Ridge Ave
#1
Chicago, IL 60660
Phone: (773) 334-7728
rachel@rivendelltheatre.net
www.rivendelltheatre.org/
Notes: Committed to cultivating the talents
of women theatre artists and to seeking out
innovative plays that explore the unique
female experience in an intimate, salon
environment. You may submit your play
through a literary agent or accompanied by a
letter of recommendation by a theater
professional (i.e. an artistic director or
literary manager at a professional theater). If
neither of these apply to you, you may write
a letter of inquiry and submit it, along with a
brief synopsis and your resume.
Special Interest: Women's Interest
Submission Materials: query letter, resume,
synopsis
Submission Fee: No
Agent Only: No

Riverside Theatre [FL]
Allen D. Cornell, Artistic Director
3250 Riverside Park Dr.

Vero Beach, FL 32963
Phone: (772) 231-5860
Fax: (772) 234-5298
info@riversidetheatre.com
www.riversidetheatre.com
Notes: Est. 1985. Production: cast limit 10.
Preferred Genre: Plays or Musicals
Special Interest: Theatre for Young
Audiences
Preferred Length: Full-length
Submission Materials: query letter, synopsis
Submission Fee: No
Agent Only: No

Riverside Theatre [IA]
Jody Hovland, Artistic Director
213 N. Gilbert St.
Iowa City, IA 52245
Phone: (319) 887-1360
Fax: (319) 887-1362
artistic@riversidetheatre.org
www.riversidetheatre.org
Notes: Est. 1981. Open submissions for
Riverside Theatre's annual monologue
festival, Walking The Wire. Due to staff
limitations, we unfortunately cannot accept
unsolicited scripts directly from playwrights.
Scripts may be submitted by agents &
professional representatives as well as all
NNPN member theatres. Some unsolicited
work may be considered based on the
strength of a professional recommendation.
See website for annual deadline and complete
guidelines.
Preferred Length: 10-min./10pgs.
Submission Materials: agent-only
Submission Fee: No
Agent Only: Yes
Deadline(s): September 15, 2014

RoaN Productions
C. Abeydeera, Literary Manager
30-43 41st St.
Ste. 1
Astoria, NY 11103
Phone: (646) 415-8206
corina@roanproductions.com
www.roanproductions.com
Notes: RoaN Productions is dedicated in
producing works with a strong feminine
perspective in a collaborative environment,
with non-traditional casting. Presently
accepting submissions for reading series.
Special Interest: Women's Interest
Preferred Length: Full-length

Submission Materials: see website
Submission Fee: No
Agent Only: No

Rosalind Productions
P.O. Box 480820
Los Angeles, CA 90048
Phone: (310) 422-1636
abigail@rosalindproductions.com
www.rosalindproductions.com
Notes: Rosalind Productions explores stories in which the female characters are as vital, complex and influential as the male characters.
Special Interest: Women's Interest
Submission Materials: see website
Submission Fee: No
Agent Only: No

Round House Theatre
Box 30688
Bethesda, MD 20824
Phone: (240) 644-1099
Fax: (240) 644-1090
productionstaff@roundhousetheatre.org
www.roundhousetheatre.org
Notes: Est. 1978. Literary Works Project in Bethesda, and New Works Series in Silver Spring. Production: cast limit 8, piano only, unit set. Response: 2 months query, 1 year script.
Preferred Genre: All genres
Preferred Length: Any length
Submission Materials: query letter
Submission Fee: No
Agent Only: No

Royal Court Theatre
Sloane Sq.
London SW1W 8AS United Kingdom
infor@royalcourttheater.com
www.royalcourttheatre.com
Notes: Est. 1956. Production/development for both international writers and young writers. See website for details. US mail material only.
Preferred Genre: All genres
Preferred Length: Full-length
Submission Materials: S.A.S.E., synopsis
Submission Fee: No
Agent Only: No

Salt Lake Acting Company
168 West 500 North
Salt Lake City, UT 84103

Phone: (801) 363-7522
Fax: (801) 532-8513
andra@saltlakeactingcompany.org
www.saltlakeactingcompany.org
Notes: Est. 1970. SLAC works with writers to workshop new pieces and produces new works (plays/musicals/adaptations).
Preferred Genre: Plays or Musicals
Preferred Length: Any length
Submission Materials: see website
Submission Fee: No
Agent Only: No

San Diego Repertory Theatre
79 Horton Plz.
San Diego, CA 92101-6144
Phone: (619) 231-3586
Fax: (619) 235-0939
arasbeary@sdrep.org
www.sdrep.org
Notes: Est. 1976. We no longer accept unsolicited scripts from unrepresented writers. However, given our commitment to supporting new work, writers who reside in the Southern California area may submit a query letter that includes a current email contact and brief biography of your writing history, noting awards and production history, a paragraph about why your play is a good match for the San Diego Rep, a one-page synopsis of the play including number of cast, genre, and run-time for musicals, please also include a CD with sample songs from the score.
Preferred Genre: All genres
Preferred Length: Full-length
Submission Materials: full script
Submission Fee: No
Agent Only: Yes

Santa Monica Playhouse
Cydne Moore, Dramaturg
1211 4th St.
Suite #201
Santa Monica, CA 90401
Phone: (310) 394-9779
Fax: (310) 393-5573
theatre@SantaMonicaPlayhouse.com
www.santamonicaplayhouse.com
Notes: Est. 1960. Production: cast limit 10. Response: 9 months query, 12 months script. Submissions accepted year-round.
Preferred Genre: Plays (No Musicals)
Preferred Length: Full-length
Submission Materials: 10-pg sample, query

letter, resume
Submission Fee: No
Agent Only: No

Seacoast Repertory Theatre
125 Bow St.
Portsmouth, NH 03801
Phone: (603) 433-4793
Fax: (603) 431-7818
craig@seacoastrep.org
www.seacoastrep.org
Notes: Est. 1986. Offers 8 mainstage and 6 youth works each year. Submissions must be unoptioned. Response: 6 months.
Preferred Genre: All genres
Special Interest: Theatre for Young Audiences
Preferred Length: Any length
Submission Materials: 10-pg sample, S.A.S.E., synopsis
Submission Fee: No
Agent Only: No

Seattle Children's Theatre
201 Thomas St.
Seattle, WA 98109
Phone: (206) 443-0807
Fax: (206) 443-0442
info@sct.org
www.sct.org
Notes: Est. 1975. No unsolicited works, professional recommendation only.
Special Interest: Theatre for Young Audiences
Submission Fee: No
Agent Only: Yes

Seattle Jewish Theater Company
Art Feinglass, Artistic Director
5225 50th Avenue NE, #203
Seattle, WA 98105
Phone: (212) 581-8655
seattlejewishtheatercompany@gmail.com
www.seattlejewishtheater.com
Notes: SJTC presents classic and contemporary Jewish theatre throughout the Seattle area. Submissions accepted year-round.
Preferred Genre: Plays (No Musicals)
Special Interest: Jewish
Preferred Length: Any length
Submission Materials: query letter, synopsis
Submission Fee: No
Agent Only: No

Seattle Repertory Theatre
155 Mercer St.
Box 900923
Seattle, WA 98109
Phone: (206) 443-2210
Fax: (206) 443-2379
bradena@seattlerep.org
www.seattlerep.org
Notes: Est. 1963. 8-9 plays/year on 2 proscenium stages: 850-seat Bagley Wright; 300-seat Leo K. Staff: Response: 6 months. We welcome submissions from playwrights, literary agents and theatre colleagues with whom we have an existing professional relationship. Unfortunately, due to the staffing needs, we do not accept unsolicited script submissions or queries.
Preferred Genre: Plays (No Musicals)
Preferred Length: Any length
Submission Materials: full script, S.A.S.E.
Submission Fee: No
Agent Only: Yes

Second Stage Theatre
Kyle Frisina, Director of Play Development
305 W. 43rd St.
New York, NY 10036
Phone: (212) 787-8302
Fax: (212) 397-7066
kfrisina@2st.com
www.2st.com
Notes: Est. 1979. 2 Off-Broadway theaters, 6 shows per season; work featuring heightened realism and sociopolitical issues.
Preferred Genre: Plays or Musicals
Preferred Length: Full-length
Submission Materials: agent-only
Submission Fee: No
Agent Only: Yes

Seventh Street Playhouse, LLC
Anthony Gallo, Artistic Director
PO Box 15414
Washington, DC 20003
Phone: (202) 544-6973
aegallo2368@verizon.net
http://seven.aegallo.com
Notes: Agent only or prior professional recommendation. Unpublished submissions accepted by email only to agallo2368@verizon.net
Preferred Genre: Plays or Musicals
Preferred Length: Full-length
Submission Materials: synopsis

Submission Fee: No
Agent Only: Yes

Shadowlight Productions
22 Chattanooga St.
San Francisco, CA 94114
Phone: (415) 648-4461
Fax: (415) 641-9734
info@shadowlight.org
www.shadowlight.org
Notes: Est. 1972. Production: cast limit 15.
Response: 1 month.
Preferred Genre: Plays (No Musicals)
Preferred Length: Full-length
Submission Materials: see website
Submission Fee: No
Agent Only: No

Shakespeare & Company
70 Kemble St.
Lenox, MA 01240
Phone: (413) 637-1199 Ext 111
Fax: (413) 637-4274
tsimotes@shakespeare.org
www.shakespeare.org
Notes: Est. 1978. Not accepting submissions
at this time. Production: cast of 2-8.
Response: 3 months.
Preferred Genre: Plays (No Musicals)
Preferred Length: Full-length
Submission Materials: 10-pg sample, query
letter, S.A.S.E., synopsis
Submission Fee: No
Agent Only: No

Shakespeare Theatre Company
Drew Lichtenberg, Literary Associate
516 8th St. SE
Washington, DC 20003-2834
Phone: (202) 547-3230 Ext 2225
dlictenberg@shakespearetheatre.org
www.shakespearetheatre.org
Notes: Est. 1986. The Shakespeare Theatre
Company is currently accepting submissions
of original and new shows for all ages geared
toward intelligent children and their families
to be commissions for the 2015-2016 season.
The shows can have music incorporated, but
it is not required. It is also not required to be
classical in form. It will be performed during
the holiday season but need not be a holiday
show. Please e-mail all submissions.
Preferred Genre: All genres
Special Interest: Theatre for Young
Audiences

Preferred Length: Any length
Submission Materials: 15-20 pg sample
Submission Fee: No
Agent Only: No

She Said Yes! Theatre
64 Quidi Vidi Rd
St. John, NL A1A 1C1 Canada
Phone: (709) 739-0702
sara@shesaidyestheatre.ca
www.shesaidyestheatre.ca
Notes: She Said Yes! is an unincorporated,
non-profit, artist-driven feminist theatre
company based in St. John's, Newfoundland.
She Said Yes! endeavors to push the artistic
boundaries of its artists by introducing
challenging, well-developed scripts, new
methods of creation and new acting
techniques to the creative community of St.
John's. Through developmental programming
such as the Mail-Order Dramaturgy program
and the Women's Work Festival, we also aim
to provide a secure and open environment for
female playwrights to hone and perfect their
works in progress.
Special Interest: Women's Interest
Submission Materials: see website
Submission Fee: No
Agent Only: No
Deadline(s): October 15, 2014

Shotgun Productions Inc.
Patricia Klausner, Managing Director
165 E. 35 St., #7-J
New York, NY 10016
Phone: (212) 689-2322
Fax: (212) 689-2322
literary@shotgun-productions.org
www.shotgunproductions.org
Notes: Est. 1989. 3-step development,
includes staged readings, workshops and full
productions for unoptioned/unproduced work.
Response: 1 year. NOT accepting unsolicited
submissions at this time.
Preferred Genre: Plays (No Musicals)
Preferred Length: Full-length
Submission Materials: query letter, synopsis
Submission Fee: No
Agent Only: No

Signature Theatre Company [NY]
630 9th Ave., #1106
New York, NY 10036
Phone: (212) 967-1913
Fax: (212) 967-2957

kbowen@signaturetheatre.org
www.signaturetheatre.org
Notes: Est. 1990. Premieres and revivals
produced in a season of work by current and
past playwrights in residence.
Submission Materials: agent-only
Submission Fee: No
Agent Only: Yes

SignStage
William Morgan, Artistic Manager/Producer
11635 Euclid Ave.
Cleveland, OH 44106
Phone: (216) 325-7559
Fax: (216) 325-7659
wmorgan@chsc.org
www.chsc.org
Notes: Est. 1975. In-school residencies,
educational performances about deaf
awareness. Response only if interested.
Submissions accepted year-round.
Special Interest: Deaf
Submission Materials: S.A.S.E., synopsis
Submission Fee: No
Agent Only: No

Silk Road Theatre Project
680 S. Federal
Ste 301
Chicago, IL 60605
Phone: (312) 857-1234 Ext 202
Fax: (312) 577-0849
jamil@srtp.org
www.srtp.org
Notes: We are currently not accepting
unsolicited scripts. We accept full-length
scripts only by US mail. Work must be from
playwrights and about protagonists of Asian,
Middle Eastern, and Mediterranean descent.
Preferred Genre: Plays (No Musicals)
Special Interest: Multi-Ethnic
Preferred Length: One-Act
Submission Materials: 15-pg sample, query
letter, synopsis
Submission Fee: No
Agent Only: No

Six Figures Theatre Company
Box 88, Planetarium Sta.
New York, NY 10024
Phone: (212) 946-1737
info@sixfigures.com
www.sixfigures.com
Notes: Not accepting submissions at this
time.

Preferred Genre: Musical theatre
Preferred Length: Full-length
Submission Materials: see website
Submission Fee: No
Agent Only: No

Society Hill Playhouse
Deen Kogan
507 S. 8th St.
Philadelphia, PA 19147
Phone: (215) 923-0210
Fax: (215) 923-1789
shp@erols.com
www.societyhillplayhouse.org
Notes: Submit by US mail only. Production:
cast of up to 8. Response: 3 months.
Preferred Genre: Plays or Musicals
Preferred Length: Full-length
Submission Materials: query letter, S.A.S.E.
Submission Fee: No
Agent Only: No

SoHo Repertory Theatre Inc.
401 Broadway, Suite 300
New York, NY 10013
Phone: (212) 941-8632
Fax: (212) 941-7148
sohorep@sohorep.org
www.sohorep.org
Notes: Est. 1975. Soho Rep. is a leading hub
for innovative contemporary theater in New
York City. We are dedicated to artistic
excellence by supporting distinctive, diverse
and pioneering theater. We empower artists to
make their boldest work and invite audiences
to share in that intimate and transformative
live experience. Soho Rep. creates a dynamic
context for both artists and audiences that
promotes and sustains conversation in the
field and the cultural fabric of the city.
Preferred Genre: All genres
Preferred Length: Any length
Submission Materials: see website
Submission Fee: No
Agent Only: No

South Camden Theatre Company
Joseph M. Paprzycki, Artistic Director
Waterfront South Theatre
400 Jasper Street
Camden, NJ 08104
Phone: (856) 409-0365
info@southcamdentheatre.org
www.southcamdentheatre.org

Notes: South Camden Theatre Company, now producing its 8th season of thought provoking theatre at our new Waterfront South Theatre in Camden, NJ announces its open call for its "Staged Reading Series". We seek 3 full-length plays for directed, script in hand readings to be held over the summer. We seek plays that adhere to the company's mission, have no more than 5 characters, and have single or simple set requirements. The playwright must be in attendance at the reading to hear his/her work and be onstage for audience feedback. Email a synopsis, character breakdown, and how the play meets SCTC's mission to the attention of Susan Schwartz Paschkes. Do not send full plays. ONLY Dramatists Guild members will be considered. Submissions accepted year-round.
Submission Materials: character breakdown, synopsis
Submission Fee: No
Agent Only: No

South Coast Repertory Theatre
Kimberly Colburn, Assistant Literary Manager
PO Box 2197
Costa Mesa, CA 92628
Phone: (714) 708-5500
Fax: (714) 545-0391
kimberly@scr.org
www.scr.org
Notes: Est. 1964. Mainstage programming, family programming, reading series, playwrights new work fest. Response: 2 months query; 6 months script.
Preferred Genre: Plays or Musicals
Special Interest: Theatre for Young Audiences
Preferred Length: Full-length
Submission Materials: 10-pg sample, query letter, S.A.S.E., synopsis
Submission Fee: No
Agent Only: No

Stage 773
1225 W. Belmont Ave.
Chicago, IL 60657
Phone: (773) 929-7367
Fax: (773) 327-1404
info@stage773.com
www.stage773.com
Notes: Stage 773 acts to embody the vibrant spirit of Chicago off-loop theater: We celebrate the creative process, supporting the work of actors, directors, writers, composers, and designers. We nurture the artist, offering material, technical, organizational and emotional support. We honor our audience, presenting accessible, affordable and exceptional entertainment.
Submission Materials: see website
Submission Fee: No
Agent Only: No

Stage One Family Theatre
Peter Holloway, Producing Artistic Director
323 W. Broadway
Suite #600
Louisville, KY 40202
Phone: (502) 498-2436
Fax: (502) 589-4344
stageone@stageone.org
www.stageone.org
Notes: Est. 1946. Classic and contemporary tales of childhood with strong social and emotional content. Production: cast limit 12, touring set. Response: 3 months. Submissions accepted year-round.
Preferred Genre: Plays or Musicals
Special Interest: Theatre for Young Audiences
Preferred Length: Any length
Submission Materials: 10-pg sample, query letter
Submission Fee: No
Agent Only: No

Stages Repertory Theatre [TX]
3201 Allen Pkwy., #101
Houston, TX 77019
Phone: (713) 527-0220
Fax: (713) 527-8669
www.stagestheatre.com
Notes: Est. 1978. Production cast limit: 6. Response: 9 months.
Preferred Genre: Plays (No Musicals)
Preferred Length: Full-length
Submission Materials: full script
Submission Fee: No
Agent Only: No

Stages Theatre Company [MN]
1111 Main St.
Hopkins, MN 55343
Phone: (952) 979-1120
Fax: (952) 979-1124
brow@stagestheatre.org
www.stagestheatre.org

Notes: Est. 1984. Material must be 60 - 70 min. Production: ages 10-21 in primary roles. Response: 3 months.
Preferred Genre: Plays (No Musicals)
Special Interest: Theatre for Young Audiences
Preferred Length: One-Act
Submission Materials: full script, query letter, S.A.S.E., synopsis
Submission Fee: No
Agent Only: No

Stageworks/Hudson [NY]
Laura Margolis, Executive Artistic Director
41-A Cross St.
Hudson, NY 12534
Phone: (518) 828-7843
Fax: (518) 828-4026
literary@stageworkshudson.org
www.stageworkshudson.org/index.html
Notes: Est. 1996. Also known as Stageworks/Hudson, Stageworks is dedicated to bringing adventurous theater productions and programs of high artistic quality to the City of Hudson, Columbia County and the greater Hudson Valley. Central to our mission is Futures, an integrative program designed to move Stageworks to the forefront of new play development. Stageworks is both the experiment and the resource to infuse the whole life of the theater with a creative process that produces new ways of expressing, interpreting and sharing the human experience. Stageworks maintains a series of Principal Programs to encourage and engage traditional theatergoers and new audiences. See website for specific submission guidelines.
Submission Materials: see website
Submission Fee: No
Agent Only: No

Statement Productions
Box 496
Kittredge, CO 80457
Phone: (303) 670-8397
Fax: (303) 670-1897
freerobbie@aol.com
Notes: Not accepting work at this time. Usually, productions mostly of 2-women plays. Production: age 30-50, cast of up to 10. Response: 90 days.
Preferred Genre: Musical theatre
Preferred Length: Any length
Submission Materials: full script, S.A.S.E.

Submission Fee: No
Agent Only: No

Steppenwolf Theatre Company
758 W. North Ave., 4th Fl.
Chicago, IL 60610
Phone: (312) 335-1888
Fax: (312) 335-0808
acarter@steppenwolf.org
www.steppenwolf.org
Notes: Est. 1976. Actor's collective performing in three spaces. Production: cast limit 10. Response: 6-8 months. See website for specific guidelines.
Preferred Genre: Plays (No Musicals)
Preferred Length: Full-length
Submission Materials: 10-pg sample, query letter, resume, synopsis
Submission Fee: No
Agent Only: No

Steppingstone Theatre
55 Victoria Street N
Saint Paul, MN 55104
Phone: (651) 225-9265
Fax: (651) 225-1225
info@steppingstonetheatre.org
www.steppingstonetheatre.org
Notes: Est. 1987. SteppingStone Theatre's mission is to develop the whole child by using educational theatre programs, and fully staged productions to build self-esteem, confidence, and a sense of community while celebrating diversity in a supportive, non-competitive atmosphere. Our programs foster creativity, self-expression and self-confidence; teach children and youth about history, diverse cultures, literature and the arts while making learning engaging and entertaining; and help to create in youth a lifelong appreciation for the arts. We serve youth from diverse ethnic, social and economic backgrounds by teaching life skills through theatre.
Submission Fee: No
Agent Only: No

Strand Theater Company
1823 North Charles
Baltimore, MD 21201
Phone: (443) 874-4917
info@strand-theatre.org
www.strand-theater.org
Notes: The Strand accepts new play submissions year round! We need new and

interesting works to wow Baltimore. We like plays that use magical realism, tell stories about real people, and focus on relevant issues. We love plays by women and want to tell their stories.
Special Interest: Women's Interest
Submission Fee: No
Agent Only: No

Sundance Institute Theatre
Christopher Hibma, Associate Director
180 Varick St, Suite 1330
New York, NY 10014
Phone: (646) 822-9563
Fax: (310) 360-1975
theatre@sundance.org
www.sundance.org/programs/theatre
Notes: Est. 2003. Equity Special Agreement. 2-week developmental workshop focusing on musical theater and ensemble-created work. Assistance: stipend,room/board,travel. Frequency: annual. By invitation only.
Submission Fee: No
Agent Only: No

Sundog Theatre
Susan Fenley, Artistic Director
Box 10183
Staten Island, NY 10301
Phone: (718) 816-5453
info@sundogtheatre.org
www.SundogTheatre.org
Notes: Ferry Plays: looking for six 10-25 minute unproduced/unoptioned plays with Staten Island Ferry as setting. Full length work: cast of 2-10, orchestra limit 4, minimal set.
Preferred Genre: Plays or Musicals
Preferred Length: Any length
Submission Materials: see website
Submission Fee: No
Agent Only: No
Deadline(s): December 1, 2014

Sweetwood Productions
Pat Hazell, Chief Creative Officer
3406 Riva Ridge Rd.
Austin, TX 78746
Phone: (512) 383-9498
Fax: (512) 383-1680
pat@sweetwoodproductions.com
www.sweetwoodproductions.com
Notes: Not accepting submissions at this time.
Preferred Genre: Comedy

Preferred Length: Full-length
Submission Fee: No
Agent Only: No

Synchronicity Performance Group
Box 6012
Atlanta, GA 31107
Phone: (404) 523-1009
Fax: (404) 325-5168
info@synchrotheatre.com
www.synchrotheatre.com
Notes: Est. 1997. Dedicated to strong women characters, scripts with depth, meaning and social content and powerful stories. Production: cast limit 12, no fly. Response only if interested.
Preferred Genre: Plays (No Musicals)
Preferred Length: Full-length
Submission Materials: 10-pg sample, query letter, S.A.S.E., synopsis
Submission Fee: No
Agent Only: No

Syracuse Stage
820 E. Genesee St.
Syracuse, NY 13210
Phone: (315) 443-4008
Fax: (315) 443-9846
kebass@syr.edu
www.syracusestage.org
Notes: Est. 1974. Production: small cast. Syracuse Stage is not accepting unsolicited scripts at this time.
Preferred Genre: Plays (No Musicals)
Preferred Length: Full-length
Submission Materials: agent-only
Submission Fee: No
Agent Only: Yes

TADA! Youth Theater
Joanna Greer, Artistic Director
15 W 28th St, Fl. 3
New York, NY 10001
Phone: (212) 252-1619
Fax: (212) 252-8763
jgreer@tadatheater.com
www.tadatheater.com
Notes: Est. 1984. Production: age 8-18. Response: 6 months. Submissions accepted year-round.
Preferred Genre: Musical theatre
Special Interest: Theatre for Young Audiences
Preferred Length: Full-length
Submission Materials: see website

Submission Fee: No
Agent Only: No

Teatro Circulo
Jose Oliveras, Artistic Director
65 East 4th Street
New York, NY 10003
Phone: (212) 505-1808
Fax: (212) 505-1806
joliveras@teatrocirculo.org
http://teatrocirculowordpress.wordpress.com/
Notes: Illustrate works of Spanish and Latin American playwrights.
Special Interest: Latino
Submission Fee: No
Agent Only: No

Teatro Dallas
Cora Cordona, Artistic Director
1331 Record Crossing Rd.
Dallas, TX 75235
Phone: (214) 689-6492
Fax: (214) 670-3243
teatro@airmail.net
www.teatrodallas.org
Notes: Est. 1985. Work (in English or Spanish) about Latino issues; priority given to Latino or Iberian playwrights. US mail. Production: cast limit 6, unit set. Response if interested.
Preferred Genre: Plays (No Musicals)
Special Interest: Latino
Preferred Length: Any length
Submission Materials: query letter, S.A.S.E., synopsis
Submission Fee: Yes
Agent Only: No

Teatro Latea Latin American Theater Experiment & Associates
Nelson Landrieu, Executive Director
Clemente Soto Velez Cultural & Education Center
107 Suffolk St.
New York, NY 10002
Phone: (212) 529-1948
Fax: (212) 529-7362
nelson@teatrolatea.com
www.teatrolatea.com
Notes: Est. 1982. Provide opportunities to New York's emerging and professional artists.
Special Interest: Latino
Submission Fee: No
Agent Only: No

Teatro SEA
Manuel Moran, Founder, CEO & Artistic Director
Clemente Soto Velez Cultural & Education Center
107 Suffolk Street, 2nd floor
New York, NY 10002
Phone: (212) 529-1545
Fax: (212) 529-1567
mmoran@sea-ny.org
www.teatrosea.org
Notes: Gives a voice to young people through theater and the arts, facilitates learning, provides training and motivates and challenges young people to stay in school. Also specializes in puppeteering and works for children.
Submission Fee: No
Agent Only: No

Teatro Vista
Laurie Dahl, Lit. Mgr.
3712 N Broadway
#275
Chicago, IL 60613
Phone: (312) 666-4659
Fax: (312) 666-4659
info@teatrovista.org
www.teatrovista.org
Notes: We focus on works by, about or for Latinos.
Preferred Genre: Plays or Musicals
Special Interest: Latino
Preferred Length: Full-length
Submission Materials: character breakdown, synopsis
Submission Fee: No
Agent Only: No

Tectonic Theater Project
204 W 84th St
New York, NY 10024
Phone: (212) 579-6111
Fax: (212) 579-6112
literary@tectonictheaterproject.org
www.tectonictheaterproject.org
Notes: Est. 1992. Lab led by Moises Kaufman. Response: 1 month.
Preferred Genre: All genres
Preferred Length: Full-length
Submission Materials: full script, S.A.S.E., synopsis
Submission Fee: No
Agent Only: No

Ten Grand Productions
Jason Hewitt, Managing Director
123 E 24th Street
New York, NY 10010
Phone: (212) 253-2058
Fax: (917) 591-9398
elana@elanagartner.com
Notes: Est. 2003.
Preferred Genre: Drama
Preferred Length: Full-length
Submission Materials: 20-pg sample,
S.A.S.E.
Submission Fee: No
Agent Only: No

Tennessee Repertory Theatre
161 Rains Ave.
Nashville, TN 37203
Phone: (615) 244-4878
Fax: (615) 782-4001
represervations@gmail.com
www.tennesseerep.org
Notes: Est. 1985. Production: small cast,
small orchestra. Response: 1 year.
Preferred Genre: Plays or Musicals
Preferred Length: Full-length
Submission Materials: see website
Submission Fee: No
Agent Only: No

Tennessee Women's Theatre Project
P.O. Box 158525
(Performing at:
Z. Alexander Looby Theatre
2301 Rosa L. Parks Blvd)
Nashville, TN 37215
Phone: (615) 681-7220
maryanna@twtp.org
www.twtp.org
Notes: Giving voice to women through
theater arts. See website for submission
guidelines.
Special Interest: Women's Interest
Submission Materials: see website
Submission Fee: Yes
Agent Only: No

Thalia Spanish Theatre
Angel Gil Orrios, Artistic/Executive Director
41-17 Greenpoint Ave.
Sunnyside, NY 11104
Phone: (718) 729-3880
agil@thaliatheatre.org
www.thaliatheatre.org

Notes: Est. 1977. First and only bilingual
Hispanic theatre in Queens. Unique
productions of plays, musicals and dance of
Spanish and Latin American culture.
Submissions accepted year-round.
Special Interest: Latino
Submission Fee: No
Agent Only: No

The Eugene O'Neill Theater Center
Anne G. Morgan, Literary Manager
The O'Neil
305 Great Neck Rd.
Waterford, CT 06385
Phone: (860) 443-5378
Fax: (860) 440-3161
litoffice@theoneill.org
www.theoneill.org
Notes: Home of the National Playwrights
Conference, National Music Theater
Conference, National Puppetry Conference,
Cabaret and Performance Conference,
National Theater Institute, and National
Critics Institute. See website for details.
Preferred Genre: All genres
Preferred Length: Full-length
Submission Materials: see website
Submission Fee: Yes
Agent Only: No

The Little Theatre of Alexandria
Rich Amada, Instructor
600 Wolfe St.
Alexandria, VA 22314
Phone: (703) 683-5778
richardamada@gmail.com
www.thelittletheatre.com
Notes: Beginning Playwriting classes and
Advanced Playwriting workshops offered
every spring and fall semester. Public reading
opportunities available for selected works of
advanced playwrights.
Submission Materials: see website
Submission Fee: Yes
Agent Only: No

Theater 2020, Inc.
Judith Jarosz, Producing Artistic Director
Theater 2020, Inc.
57 Montague Street, Suite 7-I
New York, NY 11201
theater2020@gmail.com
www.theater2020.com
Notes: Only e-mail submissions will be
accepted. We will get back to you only if we

need more information. We prefer shows with casts with 10 or fewer roles (doubling parts is fine) and that require one unit set, or sets that can be suggested with limited set pieces and props. As part of our mission to create more opportunities for women in the arts, the cast must contain equal number of parts for men and women or more for women! Submissions accepted year-round.
Preferred Genre: All genres
Special Interest: Women's Interest
Preferred Length: Any length
Submission Materials: character breakdown, synopsis
Submission Fee: No
Agent Only: No

Theater at Monmouth
Box 385
Monmouth, ME 04259
Phone: (207) 933-2952
Fax: (207) 933-2952
TAMOffice@TheaterAtMonmouth.org
www.theateratmonmouth.org
Notes: Est. 1970. Only adaptations of popular classics for adults and children. Response: 2 months.
Preferred Genre: Plays (No Musicals)
Special Interest: Theatre for Young Audiences
Preferred Length: Any length
Submission Materials: query letter, synopsis
Submission Fee: No
Agent Only: No

Theater Breaking Through Barriers
Ike Schambelan, Artistic Director
306 W. 18th St. #3A
New York, NY 10011
Phone: (212) 243-4337
Fax: (212) 243-4337
ischambelan@nyc.rr.com
www.tbtb.org
Notes: Est. 1979. Work must be about disability or by a disabled writer. Production: cast of 1-6. Either US Mail or Electronic submissions are accepted. Response: 2 months.
Preferred Genre: All genres
Special Interest: Disabled
Preferred Length: Any length
Submission Materials: full script, S.A.S.E.
Submission Fee: No
Agent Only: No

Theater for the New City (TFNC)
Crystal Field, Executive Artistic Director
155 1st Ave.
New York, NY 10003
Phone: (212) 254-1109
Fax: (212) 979-6570
crystalfield@theaterforthenewcity.net
www.theaterforthenewcity.net
Notes: Est. 1970. Experimental new works. Submissions accepted year-round.
Preferred Genre: Experimental
Preferred Length: Any length
Submission Materials: 10-pg sample, query letter, S.A.S.E., synopsis
Submission Fee: No
Agent Only: No

Theater J
Shirley Serotsky, Director of Literary and Public Programs
1529 16th St. NW
Washington, DC 20036
Phone: (202) 777-3228
Fax: (202) 518-9421
shirleys@washingtondcjcc.org
www.theaterj.org
Notes: Est. 1991. Offers readings, workshops, and productions of work that celebrates the distinctive urban voice and social vision of the Jewish culture. Response: 6 months. Inquiries and submissions accepted by email ONLY. Submissions accepted year-round.
Preferred Genre: Plays or Musicals
Preferred Length: Full-length
Submission Materials: 10-pg sample, synopsis
Submission Fee: No
Agent Only: No

Theatre at the Center / Lawrence Arts Center
940 New Hampshire St.
Lawrence, KS 66044
Phone: (785) 843-2787
Fax: (785) 843-6629
ricaverill@lawrenceartscenter.org
www.lawrenceartscenter.com
Notes: Est. 1973. Submit by email. Production: cast limit 6 adults or 30 youth. Response: 6 weeks query, 3 months script.
Preferred Genre: Plays or Musicals
Special Interest: Theatre for Young Audiences
Preferred Length: Full-length

Submission Materials: 10-pg sample, synopsis
Submission Fee: No
Agent Only: No

Theatre for a New Audience
154 Christopher St. #3-D
New York, NY 10014
Phone: (212) 229-2819
Fax: (212) 229-2911
info@tfana.org
www.tfana.org
Notes: We do not accept unsolicited scripts.
Submission Materials: agent-only
Submission Fee: No
Agent Only: Yes

Theatre of Yugen
Jubilith Moore, Artistic Director
2840 Mariposa St.
San Francisco, CA 94110
Phone: (415) 621-0507
Fax: (415) 621-0223
info@theatreofyugen.org
www.theatreofyugen.org
Notes: Est. 1978. Traditional and new works of East-West fusion primarily based on Noh and Kyogen. Our plays tend to incorporate music and dance and as such we prefer short poetic scripts with minimal dialogue. Submissions accepted year-round.
Preferred Genre: Experimental
Preferred Length: One-Act
Submission Materials: query letter, S.A.S.E.
Submission Fee: No
Agent Only: No

Theatre Rhinoceros
1360 Mission St. Ste #200
San Francisco, CA 94103
Phone: (415) 552-4100
Fax: (415) 552-2615
info@therhino.org
www.therhino.org
Notes: Est. 1977. Response: 6 months
Preferred Genre: Plays or Musicals
Special Interest: LGBT
Preferred Length: Full-length
Submission Materials: agent-only
Submission Fee: No
Agent Only: Yes

Theatre Three [NY]
Jeffrey Sanzel, Executive Director
Box 512/412 Main St.

Port Jefferson, NY 11777
Phone: (631) 928-9202
Fax: (631) 928-9120
scrooooge@aol.com
www.theatrethree.com
Notes: Est. 1969. Theatre Three Production Inc. is seeking unproduced plays for its Seventeenth Annual One-Act Play Festival to be held January-February 2014. Winners receive full production and a small stipend. To date, the festival has produced over 75 original works. For submission guidelines send SASE to Jeffrey Sanzel or visit our website.
Preferred Genre: All genres
Preferred Length: One-Act
Submission Materials: see website
Submission Fee: No
Agent Only: No
Deadline(s): September 30, 2014

Theatreworks/USA [NY]
151 W. 26th St., Fl. 7
New York, NY 10001
Phone: (212) 647-1100
Fax: (212) 924-5377
info@theatreworksusa.org
www.theatreworksusa.org
Notes: Est. 1961. Production: age 20-50, cast of up to 6, piano only, touring set.
Preferred Genre: All genres
Special Interest: Theatre for Young Audiences
Preferred Length: Full-length
Submission Materials: agent-only
Submission Fee: No
Agent Only: Yes

Thunderclap Productions
Aaron Alon, President, Board of Directors
5248 Arboles Drive
Houston, TX 77035
Phone: (281) 954-4399
info@thunderclapproductions.com
www.thunderclapproductions.com
Notes: Est. 2011. Dedicated to developing and performing new and underrepresented works of theatre. No children's or liturgical plays. Please see website for further details. In addition to our rolling call, we often post specific calls for submissions on our site. Join our writers and/or composers mailing lists to stay informed. Submissions accepted year-round.
Preferred Genre: Plays or Musicals

Preferred Length: Any length
Submission Materials: see website
Submission Fee: No
Agent Only: No

Touchstone Theatre
James P. Jordan, Producing Director
321 E. 4th St.
Bethlehem, PA 18015
Phone: (610) 867-1689
jp@touchstone.org
www.touchstone.org
Notes: Est. 1981. We only accept proposals
for collaborative work with movement-based
company ensemble. Response: 8 months.
Submission Materials: query letter
Submission Fee: No
Agent Only: No

Transport Group
Jack Cummings, Artistic Director
520 Eighth Ave.
Ste. 305
New York, NY 10018
Phone: (212) 564-0333
Fax: (212) 564-0331
info@transportgroup.org
www.transportgroup.org
Notes: Est. 2001. Transport Group is a not-
for-profit, off-Broadway theatre company in
New York City that stages new works and
re-imagines revivals by American writers.
Our visually progressive productions of
emotionally classic stories explore the
challenges of relationships and identity in
modern America.
Preferred Genre: All genres
Special Interest: American
Preferred Length: Full-length
Submission Materials: see website
Submission Fee: No
Agent Only: No

TriArts at the Sharon Playhouse
Box 1187
Sharon, CT 06069
Phone: (860) 364-7469
Fax: (860) 364-8043
info@triarts.net
www.triarts.net
Notes: Est. 1989. We are not accepting
submissions at this time.
Preferred Genre: Plays or Musicals
Preferred Length: Any length
Submission Materials: audio CD, query

letter, synopsis
Submission Fee: No
Agent Only: No

Trinity Repertory Company
Tyler Dobrowsky, Associate Artistic Director
201 Washington St.
Providence, RI 02903
Phone: (401) 351-4242
tdobrowsky@trinityrep.com
www.trinityrep.com
Notes: Trinity Rep is committed to the
development and production of new theater
works. Each season, we seek to produce at
least one premiere production, as well as
readings and workshops of plays in
development. Our Mabel T. Woolley Literary
Department reads and reviews hundreds of
scripts, looking for new plays which support
our aesthetic vision and our resident acting
company. We are no longer accepting
unsolicited scripts from playwrights without
representation. Please see our website for
further guidelines.
Preferred Genre: Plays (No Musicals)
Preferred Length: Full-length
Submission Materials: 10-pg sample, query
letter, synopsis
Submission Fee: No
Agent Only: Yes

Trustus Theatre
Sarah Hammond, Literary Manager
Box 11721
Columbia, SC 29211
Phone: (803) 254-9732
Fax: (803) 771-9153
shammond@trustus.org
www.trustus.org
Notes: Est. 1985. Trustus Theatre Announces
its Annual Playwrights' Festival, a National
Contest Culminating in the Professional
World Premier of an Original Play. Now in
our 24th year, we're one of America's
longest-running play festivals. Since 1988,
many of our winners have been published
and produced off-Broadway, in Hollywood or
at the Actors Theatre of Louisville. THE
WINNING PLAY will receive a staged-
reading at our Festival and $250. During the
following year, the playwright will develop
the script for production as he/she wishes and
in consultation with members of the Trustus
staff and company. In August, the play will
receive a full production--and the playwright

an additional $500, plus travel/lodging for the Festival opening.
Preferred Genre: Plays (No Musicals)
Submission Materials: see website
Submission Fee: Yes
Agent Only: No

Turtle Shell Productions
300 W. 43rd St.
#403
New York, NY 10036
Phone: (646) 765-7670
jcooper@TurtleShellProductions.com
Preferred Genre: All genres
Preferred Length: Any length
Submission Materials: full script
Submission Fee: No
Agent Only: No

Two River Theatre Company (TRTC)
21 Bridge Ave.
Red Bank, NJ 07701
Phone: (732) 345-1400
Fax: (732) 345-1414
info@trtc.org
www.trtc.org
Notes: Est. 1994. Does not accept unsolicited material.
Preferred Genre: Adaptation
Submission Materials: agent-only
Agent Only: Yes

Urban Stages
555 8th Ave. Room 1800
New York, NY 10018
Phone: (212) 421-1380
Fax: (212) 421-1387
urbanstage@aol.com
www.urbanstages.org
Notes: Production: cast size 5 or less, minimal sets. Response: 8 months. Submission: e-mailed submissions will not be accepted. ALL plays should be mailed.
Preferred Genre: Plays (No Musicals)
Preferred Length: Full-length
Submission Materials: full script
Submission Fee: No
Agent Only: No

Valley Youth Theatre (VYT)
807 N. 3rd St.
Phoenix, AZ 85004
Phone: (602) 253-8188 Ext 305
Fax: (602) 253-8282
bobb@vyt.com

www.vyt.com
Notes: Est. 1989. Response: 2 weeks query, 2 months script.
Preferred Genre: Plays or Musicals
Special Interest: Theatre for Young Audiences
Preferred Length: Full-length
Submission Materials: audio CD, query letter, synopsis
Submission Fee: No
Agent Only: No

Venture Theatre (MT)
PO Box 112
Billings, MT 59103
venture@venturetheatre.org
www.venturetheatre.org/
Notes: See website for submission guidelines.
Preferred Genre: All genres
Preferred Length: One-Act
Submission Materials: full script, resume, synopsis
Submission Fee: Yes
Agent Only: No

Venus Theatre
The Venus Theatre Play Shack
21 C St
Laurel, MD 20707
Phone: (202) 236-4078
www.venustheatre.org
Notes: A women's theatre company that perform plays by talented women playwrights and employs talented female actors, directors, designers and others.
Special Interest: Women's Interest
Submission Materials: see website
Submission Fee: No
Agent Only: No

Victory Gardens Theater
Aaron Carter, Literary Manager
2433 N. Lincoln Ave.
Chicago, IL 60614
Phone: (773) 549-5788
Fax: (773) 549-2779
acarter@victorygardens.org
www.victorygardens.org
Notes: Est. 1974. 5 productions/season. Agent submissions accepted year-round.
Preferred Genre: All genres
Preferred Length: Full-length
Submission Materials: see website

Submission Fee: No
Agent Only: Yes

Victory Theatre Center
Maria Gobetti, Artistic Director
3326 W. Victory Blvd.
Burbank, CA 91505
Phone: (818) 841-4404
Fax: (818) 841-6328
thevictory@mindspring.com
www.thevictorytheatrecenter.org
Notes: Est. 1979. Includes 99-seat Big
Victory and 50-seat Little Victory theaters.
Production: unit set. Response: 1 year.
Submissions accepted year-round.
Preferred Genre: Plays or Musicals
Preferred Length: Full-length
Submission Materials: full script, S.A.S.E.
Submission Fee: No
Agent Only: No

Village Theatre
Robb Hunt, Executive Producer
303 Front St. N.
Issaquah, WA 98027
Phone: (425) 392-1942 Ext 113
Fax: (425) 391-3242
rhunt@villagetheatre.org
www.villagetheatre.org
Notes: Est. 1979. Readings, workshops and
productions of new musicals. Production:
cast limit 20. Response: 6 months.
Submissions accepted year-round.
Preferred Genre: Musical theatre
Preferred Length: Full-length
Submission Materials: audio CD, full script,
S.A.S.E.
Submission Fee: No
Agent Only: No

Vineyard Theatre
108 E. 15th St..
New York, NY 10003
Phone: (212) 353-3366
Fax: (212) 353-3803
literary@vineyardtheatre.org
www.vineyardtheatre.org
Notes: Est. 1981. Response: 1 year query.
Submissions not returned.
Preferred Genre: All genres
Preferred Length: Full-length
Submission Materials: 10-pg sample, audio
CD, query letter, resume, synopsis
Submission Fee: No
Agent Only: No

Virginia Repertory Theatre
Jessical Daugherty, Internet Services
Manager
114 W. Broad Street
Richmond, VA 23220
Phone: (804) 783-1688
vareptheatre@gmail.com
va-rep.org
Notes: Response time: 6 months query, 1
year script. Children's genres include fairy
tales, folk tales, fables, history, African
American history, safety, outreach, science.
Production: cast of 3-5, touring set,
performances in schools. Virginia Repertory
Theatre was formerly two organizations:
Barksdale Theatre and Theatre IV. After
sharing one staff for over a decade, we
merged to become Virginia Rep in 2012.
(Barksdale Est. 1953, Theatre IV Est. 1975).
Theatre for Young Audiences (Theatre IV on
Tour division). Small cast, no fly or wing
space. We also offer adult main stage season
that range from classics to world premieres.
E-Mail submissions preferred. Submissions
accepted year-round.
Preferred Genre: Plays or Musicals
Special Interest: Theatre for Young
Audiences
Preferred Length: Any length
Submission Materials: full script, query
letter, synopsis
Submission Fee: No
Agent Only: No

Virginia Stage Company (VSC)
Patrick Mullins, Associate Artistic Director
Box 3770
Norfolk, VA 23514
Phone: (757) 627-6988
Fax: (757) 628-5958
pmullins@vastage.com
www.vastage.com
Notes: Est. 1979. Production: cast limit 8.
Response: 1 month query, 6 months script.
Preferred Genre: All genres
Submission Materials: query letter, synopsis
Submission Fee: No
Agent Only: No

Vital Theatre Company
Stephanie Usis, Company Manager
2162 Broadway, Fl. 4
New York, NY 10024
Phone: (212) 579-0528
Fax: (212) 579-0646

susis@vitaltheatre.org
www.vitaltheatre.org
Notes: Not accepting unsolicited scripts at this time.
Preferred Genre: Theatre for Young Audiences
Preferred Length: 50-60 min.
Submission Materials: agent-only
Submission Fee: No
Agent Only: Yes

VS. Theatre Company
Box 2293
Los Angeles, CA 91610
Phone: (323) 816-2471
Fax: (323) 850-6045
info@vstheatre.org
www.vstheatre.org
Notes: Est. 2003. Production: cast limit 6. Response: 6 months.
Preferred Genre: Plays (No Musicals)
Preferred Length: Full-length
Submission Materials: agent-only
Submission Fee: No
Agent Only: Yes

Walnut Street Theatre
Beverly Elliott, Literary Manager
825 Walnut St.
Philadelphia, PA 19103
Phone: (215) 574-3550
Fax: (215) 574-3598
literary@walnutstreettheatre.org
www.walnutstreettheatre.org
Notes: As America's oldest theatre, the Walnut has been in existence as a theatre since 1809. We are actively looking for new scripts for possible production in our 2 theatre venues: Our Studio space has a cast limit of 4-5, and our mainstage has a cast limit of 14 (plays) and 20 (musicals). As one of the few theatres in the country to accept unsolicited material, please allow greater response time: 3 months query, 6 months script. Submissions accepted year-round.
Preferred Genre: Plays or Musicals
Preferred Length: Full-length
Submission Materials: see website
Submission Fee: No
Agent Only: No

Weird Sisters Women's Theatre Collective
ally@weirdsisterscollective.com
www.weirdsisterscollective.com

Notes: A group of women in Austin, Texas dedicated to promoting women in the arts. The Collective embraces the feminist ideology of collaboration; each participant is encouraged to use her voice. The collaborative approach, in an all-female and so more risk-free setting, empowers women. The Weirds explore feminism and theater through theater productions, readings, lectures, salons, and parties throughout the year. Our process has been one of continual exploration.
Special Interest: Women's Interest
Submission Materials: see website
Submission Fee: No
Agent Only: No

Wellfleet Harbor Actors Theater
Daniel Lombardo, Artistic Director
Box 797
Wellfleet, MA 02667
Phone: (508) 349-3011 Ext 107
Fax: (508) 349-9082
lombardo.what@gmail.com
www.what.org
Notes: Est. 1985. Cast size: 6 maximum. Response: 3 months query, 6 months script.
Preferred Genre: All genres
Preferred Length: Full-length
Submission Materials: 10-pg sample, bio, synopsis
Submission Fee: No
Agent Only: No

West End Studio Theatre
402 Ingalls St, Ste 3
Santa Cruz, CA 95060
Phone: (831) 425-9378
Fax: (831) 425-3333
admin@westperformingarts.com
www.westperformingarts.com
Notes: The mission of WEST Performing Arts is to provide youth and families a creative outlet and training ground that cultivates and treasures the imaginative process. We provide educational experiences in literature, performing, expressive and creative arts through classes and productions. We give young artists and audiences the invaluable knowledge that their imaginations have had a positive and profound impact on their world.
Submission Fee: No
Agent Only: No

Western Stage
Jon Selover, Artistic Director
411 Central Ave.
Salinas, CA 93901
Phone: (831) 755-6987
Fax: (831) 755-6954
jselover@hartnell.edu
www.westernstage.com
Notes: Est. 1974. The Western Stage (TWS) has evolved over the last four decades into one of the most respected regional theatres on California's Central Coast. Supported in part by a grant from The National Endowment for the Arts, TWS is committed to enriching the culture of its community by bringing together professional artists, theatre students, and community members to produce a dynamic season of plays that enhances the lives of both the artist and audience; developing new works that speak to the history and culture of the Salinas Valley; and providing educational opportunities to allow students of all skill levels to explore and develop their unique talents.
Preferred Genre: All genres
Special Interest: Theatre for Young Audiences
Preferred Length: Full-length
Submission Materials: audio CD, query letter, synopsis
Submission Fee: No
Agent Only: No

Westport Arts Center
51 Riverside Ave.
Westport, CT 06880
Phone: (203) 222-7070
Fax: (203) 222-7999
cara@westportartscenter.org
www.westportartscenter.org
Notes: Programs in visual and performing arts.
Preferred Genre: All genres
Preferred Length: Any length
Submission Materials: see website
Submission Fee: No
Agent Only: No

What Girls Know
info@whatgirlsknow.com
www.whatgirlsknow.com
Notes: Theater program for adolescent girls in NYC from different ethnic and economic backgrounds.

Special Interest: Women's Interest
Submission Materials: see website
Submission Fee: No
Agent Only: No

White Horse Theater Company
Cyndy A. Marion, Producing Artistic Director
205 3rd Ave., #6-N
New York, NY 10003
Phone: (212) 592-3706
cymarion@whitehorsetheater.com
www.whitehorsetheater.com
Notes: Est. 2002. Work must be unproduced in NYC. Response: 4-6 months. Special Interests: Female Playwrights; plays about the American experience. Submissions accepted year-round.
Preferred Genre: Plays (No Musicals)
Preferred Length: Full-length
Submission Materials: see website
Submission Fee: No
Agent Only: No

WildClaw Theatre
Scott T. Barsotti, Literary Manager
Chicago, IL 60613
deathscribe2014@gmail.com
www.wildclawtheatre.com
Notes: We exclusively produce original plays and adaptations that are of the horror genre. Please read our mission statement and literary policy before submitting.
Preferred Genre: Radio plays
Preferred Length: Full-length & 10-min.
Submission Materials: see website
Submission Fee: No
Agent Only: No

Wilma Theater
Walter Bilderback, Dramaturg/Literary Manager
265 S. Broad St.
Philadelphia, PA 19107
Phone: (215) 893-9456
Fax: (215) 893-0895
WBilderback@wilmatheater.org
www.wilmatheater.org
Notes: Est. 1979. Produces 4 plays/year, 6-week runs. LORT-D 300-seat theater. Highly theatrical, poetic, imaginative, politically evocative (not provocative), arousing, artful, bold, inventive. Production: cast limit 8. Response: 1 year.
Preferred Genre: All genres
Preferred Length: Full-length

Submission Materials: see website
Submission Fee: No
Agent Only: Yes

Woman Made Gallery
685 North Milwaukee Ave
Chicago, IL 60642
Phone: (312) 738-0400
Fax: (312) 738-0404
gallery@womanmade.org
www.womanmade.org
Notes: The goal of Woman Made Gallery is
to support all women in the arts by providing
opportunities, awareness, and advocacy while
building an alternative community where
artistic values and criteria are determined by
women, for women.
Special Interest: Women's Interest
Submission Materials: see website
Submission Fee: No
Agent Only: No

Women's Project and Production, Inc.
Megan Carter, Associate Artistic Director
55 West End Ave.
New York, NY 10023
Phone: (510) 868-5096
Fax: (650) 244-9136
info@womenarts.org
www.womensproject.org
Notes: As the nation's oldest and largest
company dedicated to producing and
promoting theater created by women,
Women's Project is the magnetic force field
for innovative artists and adventurous theater-
goers from around the world. Scripts are
accepted May-December. See website for full
submission guidelines.
Special Interest: Women's Interest
Submission Materials: see website
Submission Fee: No
Agent Only: No

Women's Theatre Company
P.O. Box 5924
Parsippany, NJ 07054
Phone: (312) 408-9910
wtachicago@gmail.com
www.womenstheater.org
Notes: A professional theatre company
dedicated to the development, promotion and
inclusion of women in all aspects of theatre
production.
Special Interest: Women's Interest
Submission Materials: see website

Submission Fee: No
Agent Only: No

Women's Theatre Project
1314 E. Las Olas Blvd
#31
Lauderdale, FL 33301
Phone: (973) 316-3033
info@womenstheater.org
www.womenstheatreproject.com
Notes: A company of professional female
theatre artists dedicated to producing
theatrical works exploring the female voice,
TWTP was founded from a need for
women's voices to be heard and a desire to
break down the stereotypes of women
propelled by the media and to create more
professional theatrical opportunities for
women of all shapes, sizes, races, and ages.
Produces 4 productions each calendar year.
Royalties paid to playwrights/publishing
companies. TWTP seeks full-length plays
with all-female casts by female playwrights
for their intimate black box theatre.
Special Interest: Women's Interest
Preferred Length: Full-length
Submission Materials: see website
Submission Fee: No
Agent Only: No

WomenArts
Martha Richards, Executive Director
1442A Walnut Street #67
Berkeley, CA 94709
Phone: (954) 462-2334
twtp@bellsouth.net
www.womenarts.org
Notes: A worldwide community of artists
and allies that work for empowerment,
opportunity, and visibility for women artists.
We provide a variety of free online
networking, fundraising and advocacy
services, and we organize Support Women
Artists Now Day (SWAN Day), an annual
international holiday celebrating women's
creativity in all its forms. We believe in the
power of women artists to create, connect,
and change the world.
Special Interest: Women's Interest
Submission Materials: see website
Submission Fee: No
Agent Only: No

Woolly Mammoth Theatre Company
641 D St. NW
Washington, DC 20004
Phone: (202) 289-2443
submissions@woollymammoth.net
www.woollymammoth.net
Notes: Est. 1980. Production: cast limit 6.
Response: 1 year., electronic submissions
only, only accepts unsolicited submissions
from dramatists in the Washington D.C. area.
Preferred Genre: Plays (No Musicals)
Preferred Length: Full-length
Submission Materials: 10-pg sample, query
letter, synopsis
Submission Fee: No
Agent Only: No

WOW Cafe
59-61 E 4th St
New York, NY 10003
Phone: (212) 777-4280
wowcafetheatre@gmail.com
www.wowcafe.org
Notes: WOW Café Theater is a women's
theater collective in NYC's East Village,
which promotes the empowerment of women
through the performing arts. Historically,
WOW has been a majority lesbian woman's
space. WOW welcomes the full participation
of all women and transpeople in solidarity
with women. WOW especially welcomes
women and transpeople of color, and women
and transpeople who identify as lesbians,
bisexual and queer. We provide a working
theater space to our members & the technical
support to create and produce works,
regardless of economic status. Attend a
Tuesday night meeting, 6:30 at our space.
Special Interest: Women's Interest
Submission Materials: see website
Submission Fee: No
Agent Only: No

Writers' Theatre
Stuart Carden, Associate Artistic Director
376 Park Ave.
Glencoe, IL 60022
Phone: (416) 504-8222
Fax: (416) 504-9090
www.writerstheatre.org
Notes: Est. 1992. Response: 6 months.
Preferred Genre: Plays or Musicals
Preferred Length: Full-length
Submission Materials: 10-pg sample,
S.A.S.E., synopsis

Submission Fee: No
Agent Only: No

Yale Repertory Theatre
Amy Boratko, Literary Manager
Box 208244
New Haven, CT 06520
Phone: (203) 436-9098
literary.office@yale.edu
www.yalerep.org
Notes: Est. 1965. Response: 2 months query,
4 months script.
Preferred Genre: Plays or Musicals
Preferred Length: Full-length
Submission Materials: agent-only
Submission Fee: No
Agent Only: Yes

Yangtze Repertory Theatre of America
Dr. Joanna Chan, Artistic Director
22 Howard St., #2-B
New York, NY 10013
Phone: (212) 732-2799
joannawychan@juno.com
www.yangtze-rep-theatre.org
Notes: Founded in 1992; welcomes
submission of multi-lingual (English and
Chinese) dramatic works with an Asian
theme for a large (18-20) multi-ethnic cast;
and usually responds in less than a month.
Submissions accepted year-round.
Special Interest: Asian-American
Preferred Length: Full-length
Submission Materials: see website
Submission Fee: No
Agent Only: No

York Shakespeare Company
Seth Duerr, Artistic Director
1852 West 4th Street, #2R
Brooklyn, NY 11223
Phone: (646) 623-7117
Fax: (646) 964-6575
info@yorkshakespeare.org
www.yorkshakespeare.org
Notes: Est. 2001. Seeking Classical-oriented,
unoptioned work. Need professional
recommendation. Submissions accepted year-
round.
Preferred Genre: Plays or Musicals
Preferred Length: Full-length
Submission Materials: full script
Submission Fee: No
Agent Only: No

York Theatre Company
619 Lexington Ave.
New York, NY 10022
Phone: (212) 935-5820
Fax: (212) 832-0037
mail@yorktheatre.org
www.yorktheatre.org
Notes: Est. 1985. Opportunities include
developmental reading series. Production:
cast of 3-6, piano only. Submit via US mail.
Response: 6 months.
Preferred Genre: Musical theatre
Preferred Length: Full-length
Submission Materials: audio CD, full script,
S.A.S.E.
Submission Fee: No
Agent Only: No

Youth Performance Co
Sherilyn Howes, Associate Director
3338 University Ave SE
Minneapolis, MN 55414
Phone: (612) 623-9180
Fax: (612) 623-1020
showes@youthperformanceco.org
www.youthperformanceco.com
Notes: Youth Performance Company fuels
the creative spirit of youth by developing,
empowering and advancing young artists.
Through direct programming that includes
productions, classes, in-school residencies,
community appearances, and a leadership
development component, YPC provides
affordable and meaningful arts experiences
for Twin Cities families, children, and teens.
Special Interest: Theatre for Young
Audiences
Submission Fee: No
Agent Only: No

Youth Stages
Jean P. Rosolino, Founder
287 Walnut Lane
Princeton, NJ 08540-3459
Phone: (609) 430-9000
manager@youthstages.com
www.youthstages.com
Notes: Youth Stages will accept submissions
of audience participation plays for 1-2 adult
actors for audience ages 3-9 years old.
Integrated audience participation is a must.
Preferred length: 30 minutes - 1 hour.
Submissions accepted year-round.
Preferred Genre: Theatre for Young
Audiences
Special Interest: Theatre for Young
Audiences
Submission Fee: No
Agent Only: No

Educational Opportunities

Colleges and Universities

Academy of Art University
79 New Montgomery Street
San Francisco, CA 94105
Phone: (800) 544-2787
Fax: (415) 618-6287
info@academyart.edu
www.academyart.edu
Notes: Est. 1929. Rolling admissions.
Undergraduate and Graduate degree
programs. Certificates, Continuing Art
Education, and Pre-college programs
available online and on campus. Fees:
$785/unit (undergrad), $885/unit (grad).
Agent Only: No

Adelphi University
P.O. Box 701
Garden City, NY 11530
Phone: (516) 877-4044
mfa@adelphi.edu
http://academics.adelphi.edu/artsci/
creativewriting
Notes: The English Department offers the
Master of Fine Arts (M.F.A.) program in
Creative Writing, with advanced workshops
in fiction, poetry, creative non-fiction, and
dramatic writing, and courses in literature,
language, and theory. The M.F.A. in Creative
Writing offers students the opportunity to
specialize in three major genres: fiction,
poetry, and dramatic writing.
Submission Materials: see website
Submission Fee: Yes
Agent Only: No

**American Lyric Theatre - Development
Program**
Phone: (646) 216-8298
Fax: (212) 541-4944
www.altnyc.org/composer-librettist-
development-program
Notes: Est. 2007. Until ALT started the
Composer Librettist Development Program
(CLDP), there was not a single full-time
training program for opera composers and
librettists at any opera company in the United
States. Almost every opera company in the
country has a Young Artist Program to
mentor emerging singers, and over the past
25 years, these programs have proved
immensely successful at improving both the
artistic level and the career success of

American singers around the globe. Imagine
what could happen if the same sort of
opportunities were available for operatic
writers. ALT is doing more than imagining
this - we are making it happen. The CLDP
has been designed to address the absence of
appropriate mentorship for our writers.
Submission Materials: see website
Submission Fee: No
Agent Only: No
Deadline(s): April 1, 2014

Angelo State University (ASU)
Bill Doll, Director of University Theater
Box 10895, ASU Station
San Angelo, TX 76909
Phone: (325) 942-2146 Ext 6191
Fax: (325) 942-2033
bill.doll@angelo.edu
www.angelo.edu
Notes: BA in Theatre Arts.
Preferred Genre: Plays or Musicals
Preferred Length: Full-length
Submission Materials: full script
Submission Fee: No
Agent Only: No

Arizona State University (ASU)
Guillermo Reyes, Professor
School of Theatre and Film
Box 872002
Tempe, AZ 85287
Phone: (480) 965-0519
Fax: (480) 965-5351
Guillermo.Reyes@asu.edu
www.theatrefilm.asu.edu/degrees/grad/
mfa_theatre/dramatic_writing.php
Notes: BA, MFA, PHD in Theatre. Available
concentrations: directing, dramatic writing,
interdisciplinary digital media and
performance, interdisciplinary concentration
with the School of Arts, Media and
Engineering), performance, performance
design and theatre for youth.
Submission Fee: Yes
Agent Only: No
Deadline(s): February 1, 2014

Artistic New Directions
Janice Goldberg, Artistic Co-Director
250 W. 90th St. #15-G
New York, NY 10024

Phone: (212) 875-1857
Fax: (212) 875-1857
artnewdir@aol.com
www.artisticnewdirections.org
Notes: Ongoing Wednesday night
development lab, Anything Goes, open to all
from which we cull material. We produce
works-in-progress, workshops, and Equity
Showcases. No unsolicited material. We
sponsor Playwrights Retreat and Masters
Improv Retreat every summer. Also, annual
Eclectic Evening of Shorts.
Workshops/Classes in solo work and improv
to develop character and script, among
others. Also, Jeffery Sweet's From Improv To
Script.
Preferred Genre: All genres
Submission Materials: see website
Submission Fee: No
Agent Only: No

Bard College
JoAnne Akalaitis, Chair, Theater Department
Box 5000
Annandale-on-Hudson, NY 12504
Phone: (845) 758-7957
rbangiola@bard.edu
www.bard.edu
Notes: BA in Theatre. MFA in music.
Submission Fee: No
Agent Only: No

Bates College
Schaeffer Theater, #302
Lewiston, ME 04238
Phone: (207) 786-8294
mreidy@bates.edu
www.bates.edu
Submission Fee: No
Agent Only: No

**Boston Playwrights' Theatre at Boston
University**
K. Alexa Mavromatis, Program Coordinator
949 Commonwealth Ave.
Boston, MA 02215
Phone: (617) 353-5443
Fax: (617) 353-6196
newplays@bu.edu
www.bu.edu/bpt/playwriting-program.html
Notes: After more than 30 years of building
our nationally recognized Playwriting
program (Founded by Nobel Laureate Derek
Walcott in 1981), we now offer a three-year
MFA in Playwriting-a collaboration between

Boston University's College of Arts &
Sciences and award-winning School of
Theatre. Our students' voices are encouraged,
nurtured, and challenged, and we have a
profound and positive impact on their artistry
by incorporating them into a vibrant
community of artists. We accept only four or
five graduate students every two years-2014,
2016, and so on.
Preferred Genre: All genres
Preferred Length: Any length
Submission Materials: see website
Submission Fee: No
Agent Only: No
Deadline(s): March 1, 2014

Bowling Green State University (BGSU)
338 South Hall
Bowling Green, OH 43403
Phone: (419) 372-2222
Fax: (419) 372-7186
theatrefilm@bgsu.edu
www.bgsu.edu/theatrefilm
Notes: BA, MA, PHD in Theatre.
Submission Fee: Yes
Agent Only: No

Brigham Young University
Elizabeth Funk, Administrative Assistant
Dept. of Theatre and Media Arts
D-581 HFAC
Provo, UT 84602
Phone: (801) 422-6645
Fax: (801) 422-0654
tmaweb@byu.edu
www.byu.edu
Submission Fee: Yes
Agent Only: No

Brooklyn College-CUNY
Eliza Hornig, MFA Administrator
English Dept.
2900 Bedford Ave.
Brooklyn, NY 11210
Phone: (718) 951-5197
EHornig@brooklyn.cuny.edu
http://depthome.brooklyn.cuny.edu/english/
graduate/mfa/pwriting.htm
Notes: MFA in Playwriting. The playwriting
program is dedicated to the proposition that
writing for the theater is not a business of
finished thought and dead rules. Rather, we
endeavor to pursue kinds of writing that
involve an ongoing conversation with theater
of the past and (hopefully) the future.

Submission Materials: see website
Submission Fee: Yes
Agent Only: No
Deadline(s): January 15, 2014

Brown University
Erik Ehn, Department Chair
Box 1852, Waterman St.
Providence, RI 02912
Phone: (401) 863-3283
erik_ehn@brown.edu
www.brown.edu/Departments/
    Theatre_Speech_Dance/grad/
    playwritingmfa.html
Notes: MFA in Playwriting. Brown is a chief
and storied site for the formation of
playwrights, established to grant broad
inventive license while offering close
mentorship and profound resources (in the
department, the university, and the greater
community, locally to internationally).
Alumni distinguish themselves by their
professional credits, and by their collegial
élan.
Submission Materials: see website
Submission Fee: Yes
Agent Only: No

California College of the Arts
Joseph Lease, Department Chair
1111 8th Street
San Francisco, CA 94107
Phone: (415) 703-9523
eblack2@cca.edu
www.cca.edu/academics/graduate/writing
Notes: MFA in Writing: The MFA Program
in Writing at California College of the Arts is
a two-year course of study. Our program
offers workshops in fiction, poetry, creative
nonfiction, cross-genre writing, playwriting,
and screenwriting. Rather than require you to
declare a specific genre, we instead leave
open the option to take workshops in various
genres.
Submission Fee: No
Agent Only: No

California Institute of the Arts
24700 McBean Pkwy.
Valencia, CA 91355
Phone: (661) 253-7716
jrutzmoser@calarts.edu
http://theater.calarts.edu/programs/writing
Notes: MFA in Writing. A Writing Program
located in an Art School offers different

opportunities than those found in the more
traditional habitat of an English department.
Not only do writers benefit from taking
courses and collaborating with others in
different métiers, the pedagogical ethos of art
schools is different. The program is non-
tracking, and all faculty have multi-
disciplinary practices, with experience in
publishing, editing, reviewing, criticism,
scholarship, collaboration and translation.
Submission Materials: see website
Submission Fee: Yes
Agent Only: No

Campbell University
Box 128
Buries Creek, NC 27506
Phone: (910) 893-1507
buildyourfuture@campbell.edu
www.campbell.edu/artsandsciences/theater/
Notes: Degree offered: B.A.
Submission Materials: see website
Submission Fee: Yes
Agent Only: No

Carnegie Mellon University
Rob Handel, Coordinator, Graduate
Admissions
Purnell Center A32
Pittsburgh, PA 15213
Phone: (412) 268-2398
rhandel@andrew.cmu.edu
www.drama.cmu.edu/
Notes: Carnegie Mellon is uniquely
positioned to offer an intense experience that
combines training in playwriting,
screenwriting, television writing, and
theatrical entrepreneurship. As an integral
part of the Carnegie Mellon School of
Drama, the oldest degree-granting theatre
program in the United States, the Dramatic
Writing program provides ongoing
collaboration with the next generation of
important actors, directors, and designers.
Dramatic Writing MFA candidates have the
opportunity to see their thesis play fully
produced in the New Works Series and have
two teleplays fully produced in studio
conditions. Interested students have the
opportunity to teach undergraduate
playwriting and screenwriting classes.
Submission Materials: see website
Submission Fee: Yes
Agent Only: No
Deadline(s): January 1, 2014

Catholic University of America
Jon Klein, Head of MFA Writing Program
Catholic University, Dept. of Drama
620 Michigan Ave. NE
Washington, DC 20064
Phone: (202) 319-5351
kleinj@cua.edu
http://drama.cua.edu/graduate/mfa-playwriting.cfm
Notes: MFA in Playwriting. Full tuition fellowships available to selected candidates. In this three year program, playwrights collaborate with actors and directors to shape and reshape their works in classrooms, readings and workshops. They will come in contact with a variety of dramaturgical techniques for the development of dramatic action, character, language and structure. The focus is on a professional and practical approach to scriptwriting, culminating in the writing of five or more stage plays, a screenplay and a television script.
Submission Materials: see website
Submission Fee: Yes
Agent Only: No
Deadline(s): January 31, 2014

Central Washington University (CWU)
Scott Robinson, Department Chair
CWU Theater Dept.
400 E. University Way
MS: 7460
Ellensburg, WA 98926
Phone: (509) 963-2020
scott.robinson@cwu.edu
www.cwu.edu/theatre
Notes: BA and MA in Theatre.
Special Interest: Multi-Ethnic
Preferred Length: Any length
Submission Materials: see website
Submission Fee: No
Agent Only: No

Chapman University
1 University Dr.
Orange, CA 92866
Phone: (714) 997-6711
pjquinn@chapman.edu
www.chapman.edu/wilkinson/graduate-studies/ma-mfa-english.aspx
Notes: MFA in Creative Writing. The M.F.A. program at Chapman fosters the growth of fiction writers and poets through workshops, technique courses, literature courses, the John Fowles Literary Forum Core, and the literary journal Elephant Tree. The culmination of each M.F.A. student's work is a book-length thesis project in fiction or poetry. (Students may complete a thesis in creative nonfiction, stage drama, or screenplay, with the approval of the graduate program director.)
Submission Fee: No
Agent Only: No

College of the Holy Cross
1 College St.
Worcester, MA 01610
Phone: (508) 793-3490
eisser@holycross.edu
www.holycross.edu
Submission Materials: see website
Submission Fee: Yes
Agent Only: No

Columbia College [IL]
John Green, Allen and Lynn Turner Theatre Chair
72 E. 11th St.
Chicago, IL 60605
Phone: (312) 344-6100
theatre@colum.edu
www.colum.edu/theatre
Notes: The Columbia College Theatre Department is the largest undergraduate department of its kind in the nation, offering a comprehensive education in the theory and practice of contemporary Western theatre and performance. Located in the heart of Chicago, with over 200 producing theaters, the department provides the ideal environment for you to develop your artistic talents and apply them in production. We currently offer three different degree programs designed to suit your level of interest in theatre and performance including a collaborative Playwriting program.
Submission Materials: see website
Submission Fee: Yes
Agent Only: No

Columbia University School of the Arts Theatre Program
Julie Rossi, Director of Academic Administration
2960 Broadway MC 1807, 601 Dodge Hall
New York, NY 10027-7021
Phone: (212) 854-3408
Fax: (212) 854-3344
theatre@columbia.edu
www.arts.columbia.edu/mfa-playwriting-

concentration
Notes: MFA in Playwriting. The playwriting program takes a pragmatic approach, stressing the process and development of a writer's skills, with the understanding that there is not one way to write a wonderful play but many ways, as Aeschylus and Shakespeare and Chekhov have proven. The philosophy of the program is based on the idea that the work must come from within the playwright.
Submission Materials: see website
Submission Fee: Yes
Agent Only: No

DePaul University
2350 North Racine Ave
Chicago, IL 60614
Phone: (773) 325-7932
dcorrin@depaul.edu
http://theatreschool.depaul.edu
Notes: The Theatre School at DePaul University, educates, trains and inspires students of theatre in a conservatory setting that is rigorous, disciplined, culturally diverse and that strives for the highest level of professional skill and artistry.
Submission Fee: Yes
Agent Only: No

Drexel University, Westphal College
3141 Chestnut St.
Philadelphia, PA 19104
Phone: (215) 895-1920
Fax: (215) 895-2452
nick.anselmo@drexel.edu
www.drexel.edu/westphal
Submission Materials: see website
Submission Fee: Yes
Agent Only: No

Duke University
Jody McAuliffe, Chair, Theater Studies
Box 90680
Durham, NC 27708
Phone: (919) 660-3343
Fax: (919) 684-8906
theater@duke.edu
www.theaterstudies.duke.edu/
Notes: We do not accept unsolicited scripts of any kind.
Submission Fee: Yes
Agent Only: No

Eastern Michigan Univ. Applied Drama & Theatre for Young
Patricia Zimmer, Professor
103 Quirk Street
Ypsilanti, MI 48197
Phone: (734) 487-0033
Fax: (734) 487-3443
pzimmer@emich.edu
http://catalog.emich.edu/
  preview_program.php?catoid=17&poid=7952
Submission Materials: see website
Submission Fee: No
Agent Only: No

Emerson College
10 Boylston Pl., 5th Floor
Department of Performing Arts
Boston, MA 02116
Phone: (617) 824-8780
stagedoor@emerson.edu
www.emerson.edu/academics/departments/performing
Notes: Degree offered: BA
Submission Materials: see website
Submission Fee: Yes
Agent Only: No

Florida State University
Barbara Thomas, Program Assistant
239 Fine Arts Bldg.
Tallahassee, FL 32306
Phone: (850) 644-7257
Fax: (850) 644-7246
bgthomas@admin.fsu.edu
www.theatre.fsu.edu/Graduate/MFA/Stage-
  and-Screen-Writing
Notes: MFA in Stage and Screen Writing. The course of study in Writing for the Stage & Screen is offered jointly by the College of Motion Picture, Television and Recording Arts, and The School of Theatre. Only six writing students are admitted each fall. The program is comprised of six consecutive semesters (61 hours of completed coursework) that lead to a Master of Fine Arts Degree.
Submission Materials: application
Submission Fee: Yes
Agent Only: No

Goddard College (Plainfield, VT & Pt. Townsend, WA)
David DeLucca, Admissions Counselor, MFA in Creative Writing
123 Pitkin Road
Plainfield, VT 05667

Phone: (802) 322-1619
david.delucca@goddard.edu
www.goddard.edu/mfa-creative-writing
Notes: Our low-residency Master of Fine
Arts in Creative Writing Program includes a
nationally recognized playwriting and
screenwriting program in Vermont &
Washington State, led by an award-winning
faculty who are actively involved in the
professional theatre. A 48-credit, rigorous,
student-centered program for writers,
Goddard's MFA in Creative Writing Program
is ideal for people with commitments to
family, work,or other personal obligations,
who choose to live their lives and hone their
writing skills at the same time. The
playwriting/screenwriting program regularly
hosts luminaries from the theatre and film
industries.
Submission Fee: No
Agent Only: No

Hollins University Playwright's Lab
Todd Ristau, Program Director
PO Box 9603
Roanoke, VA 24020
Phone: (540) 556-5396
Fax: (540) 362-6465
tristau@hollins.edu
www.hollins.edu/grad/playwriting/index.html
Notes: Summer Intensive in MFA program in
Playwriting: Hollins' M.F.A. program in
playwriting is designed for those interested in
playwriting as well as those who want an
academic study of theatre with the playscript
as the central foundation. In addition to
ongoing academic programming, the
Playwright's Lab produces two reading series
at local theatres with an open submission
policy. Please contact for specific information
about submission guidelines. NO
SUBMISSION FEE FOR GUILD
MEMBERS.
Submission Materials: see website
Submission Fee: No
Agent Only: No
Deadline(s): February 15, 2014

Hunter College - CUNY
Mark Bly, Director MFA Playwriting
Program
695 Park Ave
New York, NY 10065
Phone: (713) 448-0079
mbly@hunter.cuny.edu

Notes: The Rita and Burton Goldberg MFA
in Playwriting is a selective two year
program with a strong emphasis on
production. Under the guidance of award
wining playwright Tina Howe, Playwright in
Residence, and internationally known new
play dramaturg and playwriting professor
Mark Bly, you will study the craft of
playwriting, theater history, dramatic
literature, and play analysis in Hunter's
Department of Theatre as well as be
encouraged to take electives. The second year
students also participate in the unique Hunter
Playwrights Festival where they receive a
fully staged workshop production featuring
professional directors, designers and student
actors in support of their work presented
before an invited industry audience of theatre
professionals.
Submission Fee: No
Agent Only: No

Indiana University
Ken Weitzman, Head of Playwriting
257 N. Jordan Ave., Rm. A300U
Bloomington, IN 47405
Phone: (812) 855-4535
Fax: (812) 856-0698
kweitzma@indiana.edu
www.indiana.edu/~thtr/academics/
  MFA_playwriting.shtml
Notes: The M.F.A. in playwriting is a three-
year program designed for writers with
original voices who are committed to making
an impact on the profession. The training is
comprised of coursework, productions, and
professional engagement. Classes are
designed to give the writer a broad education
in dramatic writing, in order to explore and
develop multiple ways to tell a story as well
as multiple ways to make a living.
Submission Materials: see website
Submission Fee: Yes
Agent Only: No
Deadline(s): February 1, 2014

Johnson County Community College
12345 College Blvd.
Overland Park, KS 66210
Phone: (913) 469-8500
Fax: (913) 469-2585
bpettigr@jccc.net
www.jccc.net
Notes: No original play submissions
accepted.

Submission Fee: Yes
Agent Only: No

Kansas State University (KSU)
John Uthoff, Program Director - Theatre
School of Music, Theatre & Dance
109 McCain Auditorium
Manhattan, KS 66506
Phone: (785) 532-6864
Fax: (785) 532-6899
jsutd@ksu.edu
www.k-state.edu/theatre
Notes: BA/BS in Theatre, MA in Theatre,
MA in Theatre with a Concentration in
Drama Therapy, NAST Accredited
Submission Materials: see website
Submission Fee: Yes
Agent Only: No

Lesley University
Jana M. Van der Veer
29 Everett Street
Cambridge, MA 02138
jvanderv@lesley.edu
www.lesley.edu/master-of-fine-arts/
  creative-writing/low-residency/
Notes: The MFA Program in Creative
Writing at Lesley University takes your
writing as seriously as you do, working with
you to turn your promise into settled
accomplishment. Students may choose one of
five program concentrations: fiction,
nonfiction, poetry, writing for stage and
screen, writing for young people. The
residency includes workshops, seminars,
lectures, and readings, providing a forum for
collaboration and for constructive critique of
students' work.
Submission Fee: No
Agent Only: No

Louisiana Tech University
PO Box 8608
Ruston, LA 71272
Phone: (318) 257-2711
Fax: (318) 257-4571
lulu@latech.edu
http://performingarts.latech.edu
Notes: Degree offered: BA, MA
Submission Materials: see website
Submission Fee: Yes
Agent Only: No

Loyola Marymount University
Stephen Shepherd, Program Director
1 LMU Dr.
MS 8210
Los Angeles, CA 90045
Phone: (310) 568-6225
sshephe1@lmu.edu
www.lmu.edu
Notes: MFA in Creative Writing - The
Creative Writing Emphasis offers a range of
coursework in several genres and modes of
writing. In addition to strong fiction and
poetry workshops, the Emphasis offers
innovative classes including The Novella,
Prose Poetry, The Memoir, Constraint Based
Writing, Playwriting, and more. Students may
also work with faculty in other departments,
including film and theatre.
Preferred Genre: All genres
Preferred Length: Any length
Submission Materials: see website
Submission Fee: No
Agent Only: No

Loyola University New Orleans
Cherie Roberts, Office Manager
6363 St. Charles Ave., Box 155
New Orleans, LA 70118
Phone: (504) 865-3840
Fax: (504) 865-2284
theatre@loyno.edu
www.loyno.edu/theatrearts
Notes: Degree offered: BA.
Submission Materials: see website
Submission Fee: Yes
Agent Only: No

Minnesota State University Moorhead
1104 7th Avenue
Moorhead, MN 56563
Phone: (218) 477-2134
graduate@mnstate.edu
Notes: The Master of Fine Arts (MFA) in
Creative Writing is a degree for students who
wish to improve their creative writing
abilities on the graduate level. The program
is designed to be completed on either a full-
time or a part-time basis. Students usually
complete the program in two and a half to
five years. The MFA is a terminal degree.
Most of the student's work will be in actual
writing courses, in tutorials, and in thesis
preparation.
Submission Fee: No
Agent Only: No

Montclair State University
Randy Mugleston, Department Chair
1 Normal Ave., MSU LI-126G
Montclair, NJ 07043
Phone: (973) 655-4817
muglestonr@mail.montclair.edu
www.montclair.edu/arts/theatre-and-dance/
Notes: Degrees offered: BA, BFA, MA.
Submission Materials: see website
Submission Fee: Yes
Agent Only: No

Mount Holyoke College
50 College St.
South Hadley, MA 01075
Phone: (413) 538-2118
Fax: (413) 538-2838
theatre@mtholyoke.edu
www.mtholyoke.edu/acad/theatre
Notes: Degree offered: BA.
Submission Materials: see website
Submission Fee: Yes
Agent Only: No

Murray State Univ. (MSU)
David Balthrop, Chair, Theater/Dance Dept.
MSU, FA 106
Murray, KY 42071
Phone: (270) 762-4421
Fax: (270) 809-4422
dbalthrop@murraystate.edu
www.murraystate.edu/theatre
Notes: BA/BS. The department is very
hands-on with work required on productions
by all theatre majors and minors. The
student-faculty radio is currently 12:1. We
produce shows from all genres and from all
major time frames in three different theatre
spaces. An interview/audition or portfolio
review is required if scholarship money is
requested. Dramatic and comedic monologue
of 60-90 seconds, or portfolio (CD, DVD,
any format).
Agent Only: No
Deadline(s): January 1, 2014

Nebraska Wesleyan University
500 St. Paul Ave.
Lincoln, NE 68504
Phone: (402) 465-2386
jsc@nebrwesleyan.edu
www.nebrwesleyan.edu
Notes: Degrees offered: BA in Theatre
Education; BFA in Acting, Directing, Musical

Theatre, Theatre Design and Technology,
Theatre Studies.
Submission Materials: see website
Submission Fee: Yes
Agent Only: No

New School For Drama
151 Bank Street
New York, NY 10014
Phone: (212) 229-5859
Fax: (212) 242-5018
hoytr@newschool.edu
www.newschool.edu/drama/
Notes: MFA in Playwriting. The New School
for Drama's playwriting program prepares a
select group of students for professional
careers as skilled dramatic writers in theater,
film and television. We believe that a
complete playwriting education requires
rigorous attention to craft and artistic
exploration as well as consistent
opportunities to apply one's developing skills
through presentations and productions.
Submission Fee: No
Agent Only: No

**New York University, Goldberg
Department of Dramatic Writing**
721 Broadway, Fl. 7
New York, NY 10003
Phone: (212) 998-1940
Fax: (212) 998-4069
tisch.ddw@nyu.edu
www.ddw.tisch.nyu.edu/page/graduate.html
Notes: MFA in Dramatic Writing. Acceptance
into the Department enrolls all students in the
Division of Playwriting and the Division of
Film and TV Writing. Students study in both
divisions, concentrating in at least one
medium as their studies advance. During the
first year, the graduate seminars in theatre
will require an original ten-minute play, a
one-act play, and a full-length play. Students
also start study in either film or television,
completing either a full-length screenplay or
a half hour television script. In the spring,
individual workshops give students the
opportunity to continue their exploration and
assess their suitability for one or more of the
mediums.
Submission Materials: see website
Submission Fee: No
Agent Only: No

Northern Kentucky University
Ken Jones, Chair, Theater Dept.
NKU, FA 205-A
Highland Heights, KY 41099
Phone: (859) 572-6362
Fax: (859) 572-6057
davissa@nku.edu
www.nku.edu/~theatre
Notes: Degrees offered: BA, BFA.
Submission Materials: application
Submission Fee: Yes
Agent Only: No

Northwest Children's Theater & School
1819 NW Everett St., Suite 216
Portland, OR 97209
Phone: (503) 222-2190
Fax: (503) 222-4130
www.nwcts.org
Notes: Est. 1993. NWCT produces four
Mainstage shows per year and administers
one of the largest theater schools on the west
coast. Our Mission is to educate, entertain
and enrich the lives of young audiences.
Submission Materials: see website
Submission Fee: No
Agent Only: No

Northwestern University
Theatre Interpertation Building
1949 Campus Drive
Evanston, IL 60208
Phone: (847) 467-1157
Fax: (847) 467-2019
write@northwestern.edu
www.communication.northwestern.edu/
　programs/mfa_writing_screen_stage/intro
Notes: MFA in Writing for the Screen and
Stage. We've designed our MFA Program
around six core courses, which introduce you
to a set of 'transportable' media writing
concepts, as well as specific idioms/genres.
You'll build a significant portfolio -- at least
a short screenplay, play, TV episode, and
full-length thesis project of your choosing.
You'll understand not just the art and craft of
media writing, but also the business of media
writing as we'll practice pitching, taking
meetings, writing query letters, and
understanding contracts.
Submission Materials: application
Submission Fee: Yes
Agent Only: No

NYU Tisch School of the Arts - Grad.
Musical Theatre Writing
Marie Costanza, Administrative Director
113-A 2nd Ave., Fl. 1
New York, NY 10003
Phone: (212) 998-1830
Fax: (212) 995-4873
mcc1@nyu.edu
www.gmtw.tisch.nyu.edu/
Notes: Est. 1981. MFA for composers,
lyricists and bookwriters from Institution of
Performing Arts at Tisch School of the Arts.
Response: Decisions are made in April for
class starting in September.
Preferred Genre: Musical theatre
Submission Materials: see website
Submission Fee: Yes
Agent Only: No
Deadline(s): February 1, 2014

Oakland University
Music, Theater, Dance
Rochester, MI 48309
Phone: (248) 370-2030
Fax: (248) 370-2041
knox@oakland.edu
www.oakland.edu/mtd
Notes: BA, BFA. Meadow Brook Theater is
on campus.
Submission Materials: application
Submission Fee: No
Agent Only: No

Ohio University
Charles Smith, Head, Playwriting Program
Kantner Hall 307
Athens, OH 45701
Phone: (740) 593-4818
Fax: (740) 593-4817
ohioplaywriting@gmail.com
www.ohioplaywriting.org
Notes: MFA in Playwriting. The Professional
Playwriting Program seeks to train
playwrights to become craftspeople and
artists who contribute to the culture. The
basic and advanced principles of the craft can
be learned through earnest study of our
dramatic literary heritage and intensive
practical application of the craft.
Submission Fee: No
Agent Only: No

Ohio Wesleyan University (OWU)
Elane Denny-Todd
Chappelear Drama Ctr.

Delaware, OH 43015
Phone: (740) 368-3851
eedennyt@owu.edu
http://theatre.owu.edu
Notes: BA in Theatre.
Agent Only: No

Pace University
551 5th Ave
New York, NY 10176
Phone: (212) 346-1531
actorsstudiomfa@pace.edu
www.pace.edu/dyson/academic-departments-
    and-programs/asds
Notes: MFA in Playwriting. Founded in 1947
by Elia Kazan, Robert Lewis, and Cheryl
Crawford, the Actors Studio is a private
space where actors, directors, and
playwrights can practice their craft free from
the pressures of the public world. Over the
years it has provided a unique opportunity for
artists to grow by offering a safe, closed,
protected environment where they can
experiment and stretch their creativity beyond
all boundaries. All students - actors, directors,
playwrights - train side-by-side as actors.
Submission Fee: No
Agent Only: No

Palm Beach Atlantic University
Box 24708
West Palm Beach, FL 33416
Phone: (561) 803-2000
Jofeue_leon@pba.edu
www.pba.edu
Submission Materials: see website
Submission Fee: Yes
Agent Only: No

Purdue University
552 W. Wood Street
West Lafayette, IN 47907
Phone: (765) 494-3074
Fax: (765) 496-1766
theatre@purdue.edu
www.purdue.edu/theatre
Notes: Degree offered: BA, MA, MFA.
Submission Materials: see website
Submission Fee: Yes
Agent Only: No

Queens College - CUNY
Nicole Cooley, Director
6530 Kissena Boulevard
Flushing, NY 11367

Phone: (718) 997-4671
nicole.cooley@qc.cuny.edu
www.qc.cuny.edu/creative_writing
Notes: MFA in Creative Writing and Literary
Translation. Our program is new - We are
now entering its fourth year-and has
galvanized the energies of students and
faculty alike. We are proud to be the latest
MFA program in the City University of New
York system and the only one in the borough
of Queens. We offer degrees in poetry, prose,
playwriting and literary translation.
Submission Fee: No
Agent Only: No

Radford University
Dance and Theatre
RU Station
Radford, VA 24142
Phone: (540) 831-5207
Fax: (540) 831-6313
clefko@radford.edu
http://theatre.asp.radford.edu
Notes: Degree offered: BA.
Submission Materials: see website
Submission Fee: Yes
Agent Only: No

Rutgers University (Camden)
Lisa Zeidner, interim MFA Director
406 Penn Street
Camden, NJ 08102
Phone: (856) 225-6121
mfa@comden.rutger.edu
http://mfa.camden.rutgers.edu/
Notes: MFA in Creative Writing. The
Rutgers-Camden Master of Fine Arts in
creative writing is a 42-credit terminal degree
in the theory and practice of writing - the
first of its kind in the Philadelphia/South
Jersey area. Rutgers-Camden think writers in
one genre can learn from writers in another--
poets from fiction writers, fiction writers
from memoirists, and memoirists from poets.
Our unique multi-genre approach prepares
our students not only to write poetry and
prose but to teach at the college level.
Submission Fee: No
Agent Only: No

Rutgers University (Newark)
Jayne A. Phillips, Director
249 University Avenue
New Brunswick, NJ 07102
Phone: (973) 353-1107

rnmfa@newark.rutgers.edu
www.ncas.rutgers.edu/mfa
Notes: MFA in Creative Writing MFA
Program is a Nationally ranked, 48 credit
hour, studio/research program, which means
that our writers study literature as they
endeavor to write it. The Program focuses
strongly on 20 credit hours of Writing
Workshop in a declared genre (one
workshop, with permission of the department,
may be cross-genre), and requires 7 thesis
hours in which students work one-on-one
with their mentor professors.
Submission Fee: No
Agent Only: No

**Rutgers University (State University of
New Jersey)**
Rutgers University/Mason Gross School of
the Arts,
Theatre Arts Department
2 Chapel Drive
New Brunswick, NJ 08901
Phone: (732) 932-9891
Fax: (732) 932-1409
theatre@masongross.rutgers.edu
www.masongross.rutgers.edu/
Notes: MFA program in playwriting.
Applications accepted Fall through March.
See website for application, fees, submission
requirements.
Submission Materials: see website
Submission Fee: Yes
Agent Only: No

San Francisco State University
Creative Writing Dept.
1600 Holloway Ave.
San Francisco, CA 94132
Phone: (415) 338-1891
cwriting@sfsu.edu
http://online.sfsu.edu/~rconboy
Notes: MFA in Playwriting - Surviving and
thriving is the hallmark of this program,
which has grown in the last ten years from a
program centered on the classroom to one
that continues to value intense classroom
experiences while building active and spirited
"on its feet" components powered by the
communal efforts of faculty, students and
alumni.
Submission Materials: application
Submission Fee: Yes
Agent Only: No

Sarah Lawrence College
Christine Farrell, Director of Theatre
1 Mead Way
Bronxville, NY 10708
Phone: (914) 395-2371
Fax: (914) 395-2666
cfarrell@sarahlawrence.edu
www.slc.edu/graduate/programs/writing/index.html
Notes: MFA in Writing. One of the largest
programs of its kind in the country, Sarah
Lawrence's nationally recognized Graduate
Writing Program brings students into close
mentoring relationships with active,
successful writers. Students concentrate in
fiction, creative nonfiction, or poetry,
developing a personal voice while honing
their writing and critical abilities. In addition
to workshops, students benefit from one-on-
one biweekly conferences with faculty.
Submission Fee: No
Agent Only: No

Smith College
Len Berkman, Graduate Adviser
Theatre Dept., Mendenhall Ctr.
Northampton, MA 01063
Phone: (413) 585-3206
lberkman@email.smith.edu
www.smith.edu/gradstudy/degrees_playwrite.php
Notes: MFA in Playwriting - This program,
offered by the Department of Theatre,
provides specialized training to candidates
who have given evidence of professional
promise in playwriting. The Department of
Theatre places great emphasis on
collaborative work among designers,
performers, directors and writers, thus
offering a unique opportunity for playwrights
to have their work nurtured and supported by
others who work with it at various levels.
Preferred Genre: Plays (No Musicals)
Preferred Length: Full-length
Submission Materials: see website
Submission Fee: Yes
Agent Only: No

Southern Methodist University (SMU)
Box 750369
Dallas, TX 75275
Phone: (214) 768-2937
gesmith@mail.smu.edu
www.smu.edu
Notes: Degrees offered: BFA, MFA.
Submission Materials: see website

Submission Fee: No
Agent Only: No

Spalding University's Brief-Residency MFA in Writing
Karen J. Mann, Administrative Director
851 S. Fourth Street
Louisville, KY 40203
Phone: (502) 873-4400
Fax: (502) 992-2409
kmann@spalding.edu
www.spalding.edu/mfa
Agent Only: No

SUNY Purchase
Howard Enders, Chair, Dramatic Writing Program
735 Anderson Hill Rd.
Purchase, NY 10577
Phone: (914) 251-6833
howard.enders@purchase.edu
www.purchase.edu
Submission Materials: see website
Submission Fee: Yes
Agent Only: No

Texas A&M University, Commerce (TAMU)
Jim Tyler Anderson, KCACTF Vice Chair, Region VI
Pac 103
P.O. Box 3011
Commerce, TX 75429
Phone: (903) 886-5346
Fax: (903) 468-3250
jim.anderson@tamu-commerce.edu
www.tamuc.edu/default.aspx
Notes: BA, MA.
Agent Only: No

Texas State University, San Marcos
601 University Dr.
San Marcos, TX 78666
Phone: (512) 245-2147
Fax: (512) 245-8440
jf18@txstate.edu
www.theatreanddance.txstate.edu
Notes: Degrees offered: BA, BFA.
Submission Materials: see website
Submission Fee: Yes
Agent Only: No

Texas Tech Univ. (TTU)
Norman Bert, Head of Playwriting
Box 42061
Lubbock, TX 79409
Phone: (806) 742-3601
norman.bert@ttu.edu
www.depts.ttu.edu/theatreanddance/
Notes: BA, BFA, MA, MFA, PhD.
Submission Fee: No
Agent Only: No

The Juilliard School
Tanya Barfield
Playwrights Program
60 Lincoln Center Plaza
New York, NY 10023
Phone: (212) 799-5000 Ext 223
Fax: (212) 875-8437
admissions@juilliard.edu
www.juilliard.edu/degrees-
    programs/drama/playwrights.php
Notes: MFA in Playwriting - The Lila Acheson Wallace American Playwrights Program encourages and aids the development of new and diverse voices in the American theater. Students may take any class in the Drama Division and are encouraged to see productions around the city by receiving free or discounted tickets to many events on- and off-Broadway. The essence of the Playwrights Program lies in the weekly master class with the playwright heads focusing on dramatic structure and the cultivation of each writer's individual voice.
Submission Materials: see website
Submission Fee: Yes
Agent Only: No

The Little Theatre of Alexandria Playwriting Class
The Little Theatre of Alexandria
600 Wolfe Street
Alexandria, VA 22314
Phone: (703) 683-5578
Fax: (703) 683-1378
virginia@thelittletheatre.com
www.thelittletheatre.com/
Notes: See website for specific class information.
Agent Only: No

University of California, Los Angeles (UCLA)
Natasha Levy, Graduate Counselor for Theater
10920 Wilshire Blvd 5th Floor
Los Angeles, CA 90024-6502
theatergrad@tft.ucla.edu
www.tft.ucla.edu/programs/theater-

department/graduate-degrees/playwriting-mfa/
Notes: MFA in Playwriting is a three year program that trains and nurtures dramatists whose purpose is to transform the way we see and understand the world. Playwriting faculty includes successful writers whose work has been professionally produced throughout the country. In the first year, playwrights complete two short plays and a full length play. In the second year, playwrights complete a second full length play, a one person play, and an additional writing project such as an adaptation for the stage or a screenplay. The third year typically includes an internship with a professional theater or film studio, or comparative environment.
Submission Fee: No
Agent Only: No

University of California, Riverside (UCR)
Michelle Harding, Program Manager
The Department of Theatre
900 University Ave., ARTS 121
University of California, Riverside
Riverside, CA 92521
Phone: (951) 827-5568
michelle.harding@ucr.edu
www.theatre.ucr.edu
Notes: MFA in Creative Writing, Writing for the Performing Arts. Our low residency program is unique in that it unites your academic pursuits with a real world emphasis on the next stage of your writing career - production and publication. The program was designed and is taught by writers for writers and is open to all genres of writing, including fiction, nonfiction, screenwriting and poetry, and all forms within those genres including crime and science fiction; memoir, essay and single topic nonfiction; commercial Hollywood films and television.
Preferred Genre: All genres
Preferred Length: Any length
Submission Materials: see website
Submission Fee: Yes
Agent Only: No

University of California, San Diego (UCSD)
Marybeth Ward, Graduate Program Coordinator
9500 Gilman Dr., MC0344
La Jolla, CA 92093

Phone: (858) 534-1046
Fax: (858) 534-1080
meward@ucsd.edu
theatre.ucsd.edu/academics/graduatePrograms/playwriting.html
Notes: MFA in Playwriting. Each year we admit one or two individuals who will be nurtured by the close individual attention and extensive production opportunities that are unique to this program. We believe that the theatre itself is a valuable teacher of playwrights and so playwrights work collaboratively with their colleagues in the MFA acting, directing, design, and stage management programs to create stimulating and meaningful works of art. The year-long development process includes a series of readings and a workshop week culminating in the New Play Festival, produced each April.
Submission Materials: see website
Submission Fee: Yes
Agent Only: No

University of California, Santa Barbara (UCSB)
Carlos Morton, Professor, Playwriting Program
552 University Rd.
Santa Barbara, CA 93106
Phone: (805) 893-3241
Fax: (805) 893-7029
cmorton@theaterdance.ucsb.edu
www.theaterdance.ucsb.edu
Notes: Degrees offered: BA., BFA, MA, PhD.
Submission Materials: see website
Submission Fee: Yes
Agent Only: No

University of Idaho (UI)
Box 442008
Moscow, ID 83844
Phone: (208) 885-6465
rcaisley@uidaho.edu
www.uitheatre.com
Notes: Home of Idaho Repertory Theater. MFA in Dramatic Writing offered.
Submission Materials: see website
Submission Fee: Yes
Agent Only: No

University of Iowa
Art Borreca, Head, Playwrights Workshop
200 N. Riverside Dr., #107 TB

Iowa City, IA 52242
Phone: (319) 353-2401
Fax: (319) 335-3568
art-borreca@uiowa.edu
http://theatre.uiowa.edu/academic-
programs/mfa-programs/playwrights-
workshop
Notes: The Iowa Playwrights Workshop-The
University of Iowa's MFA Program in
Playwriting-is an intensive three-year
program dedicated to educating playwrights
for the professional theatre. The Playwrights
Workshop seeks to create conditions in which
writers can develop their unique voices while
freely experimenting with a variety of
creative processes and theatrical forms.
Submission Materials: see website
Submission Fee: Yes
Agent Only: No

University of Michigan (UM)
1226 Murfin Ave.
2230 Walgreen Drama Center
Ann Arbor, MI 48109
Phone: (734) 764-5350
Fax: (734) 647-2297
theatre.info@umich.edu
www.music.umich.edu/departments/theatre
Notes: Degrees offered: BA and BFA.
Submission Materials: see website
Submission Fee: Yes
Agent Only: No

University of Minnesota Duluth (UMD)
Dept. of Theatre
141 MPAC
1215 Ordean Ct.
Duluth, MN 55812
Phone: (218) 726-8778
pdennis@d.umn.edu
www.d.umn.edu/theatre/
Notes: Degrees offered: BFA, BA.
Submission Materials: see website
Submission Fee: Yes
Agent Only: No

University of Missouri
129 Fine Arts Bldg.
Columbia, MO 65211
Phone: (573) 882-2021
Fax: (573) 884-4034
ruffinc@missouri.edu
www.theatre.missouri.edu
Notes: Degrees offered: BA, MA, PhD.
Submission Materials: see website

Submission Fee: Yes
Agent Only: No

University of Missouri, Kansas City
4949 Cherry St.
Kansas City, MO 64110
Phone: (816) 235-2702
fhwriter@aol.com
http://cas.umkc.edu/theatre/
Submission Materials: see website
Submission Fee: Yes
Agent Only: No

University of Nevada, Las Vegas (UNLV)
Department of Theatre
4505 Maryland Pkwy., Box 455036
Las Vegas, NV 89154
Phone: (702) 895-3666
Fax: (702) 895-0833
theatre@unlv.edu
http://theatre.unlv.edu
Notes: Est. 1967. Home of Nevada
Conservatory Theatre.
Submission Materials: see website
Submission Fee: Yes
Agent Only: No

University of New Mexico (UNM)
1 UNM, MSC04-2570
Department of Theatre & Dance
Albuquerque, NM 87131
Phone: (505) 277-4332
Fax: (505) 277-8921
wliotta@unm.edu
www.unm.edu/
Notes: University established 1892. Theater
Department established 1930. Degree offered:
MFA, dramatic writing.
Submission Materials: see website
Submission Fee: Yes
Agent Only: No

University of New Orleans (UNO)
Film, Theatre and Communication Arts
2000 Lake Shore Drive-PAC 307
New Orleans, LA 70148
Phone: (504) 280-6317
Fax: (504) 280-6318
dhoover@uno.edu
www.uno.edu
Notes: Degrees offered: BA, MFA.
Submission Materials: see website
Submission Fee: Yes
Agent Only: No

University of South Florida (USF)
Marc Powers, Director, School of Theatre
and Dance
4202 E. Fowler Ave., FAD 204
Tampa, FL 33620
Phone: (813) 974-2015
Fax: (813) 974-2026
mpowers@usf.edu
http://theatreanddance.arts.usf.edu/theatre
Notes: Degree offered: BA.
Submission Materials: see website
Submission Fee: Yes
Agent Only: No

University of Southern California
University Park, DRC 107
Los Angeles, CA 90089
Phone: (213) 740-1286
thtrinfo@usc.edu
http://theatre.usc.edu/graduate-
  programs/graduate-degrees/mfa-dramatic-
  writing.aspx
Notes: The MFA in Dramatic Writing is an
intimate, dynamic three-year program that
approaches the craft through its critical roots
in playwriting and extends this exploration
into other genre of dramatic writing. The
program encompasses stage, film and
television studies for today's dramatic writer.
Submission Materials: see website
Submission Fee: Yes
Agent Only: No

University of Texas, Austin
Pamela Christian, Director of Graduate
Studies
Department of Theate and Dance
The Unversity of Texas At Austin
1 University Station, D3900
Austin, TX 78712
Phone: (512) 232-5325
Fax: (512) 471-0824
suzanz@mail.utexas.edu
www.utexas.edu/finearts/tad/
Notes: The MFA in Playwriting Program at
the University of Texas at Austin is a
demanding, three-year course of study
designed for artists committed to professional
dramatic writing and its teaching. The
curriculum emphasizes the generation and
revision of new work, both by the individual
playwright and in progressive collaborations
with other writers and artists within the
department.
Submission Materials: see website

Submission Fee: Yes
Agent Only: No

University of Texas, El Paso (UTEP)
Fox Fine Arts, Rm. 371
500 W. Univ. Ave.
El Paso, TX 79968
Phone: (915) 747-5746
Fax: (915) 747-5438
jmurray@utep.edu
www.theatredance.utep.edu
Notes: Special interested in plays by
Hispanic writers, especially those about
Hispanic and border culture. Please send
resume, character ages and descriptions,
synopsis, and 10-page sample electronically
only to listed email.
Preferred Genre: Plays (No Musicals)
Special Interest: Latino
Preferred Length: Any length
Submission Materials: see website
Submission Fee: No
Agent Only: No

University of Toledo
Edmund Lingan, Chair
2801 W. Bancroft Ave.
Theatre & Film MS611
Toledo, OH 43606
Phone: (419) 530-2202
Fax: (419) 530-8439
edmund.lingan@utoledo.edu
www.utoledo.edu/as/theatrefilm
Notes: Cutting Edge Theatre. Our trademark
is innovative theatre comparable to the latest
in theatre hubs like New York and Los
Angeles: Color blind casting, video and live
feeds with live performances, reinvention of
the classics, devised work, medical
simulations/mock trials teach students other
avenues for theatre professionals. Scholarship
deadline is March 1st.
Agent Only: No

University of Tulsa (TU)
Michael Wright, Director, Creative Writing
Kendall Hall, 600 S. College Ave. Tucker
Drive
Tulsa, OK 74104
Phone: (918) 631-2566
Fax: (918) 631-5155
michael-wright@utulsa.edu
www.cas.utulsa.edu/writing
Notes: Degree offered: BA.
Submission Materials: see website

Submission Fee: Yes
Agent Only: No

University of Wyoming
1000 E. University Ave.
Dept. 3951
Laramie, WY 82071
Phone: (307) 766-2198
jchapman@uwyo.edu
www.uwyo.edu/th&d
Notes: Degrees offered: BA, BFA.
Submission Materials: see website
Submission Fee: Yes
Agent Only: No

Villanova Theatre
800 Lancaster Ave., Vasey 5
Villanova, PA 19085
Phone: (610) 519-4897
Fax: (610) 519-6803
elisa.hibbs@villanova.edu
http://theatre.villanova.edu
Submission Materials: see website
Submission Fee: Yes
Agent Only: No

Virginia Tech (VT)
250 E. Henderson Hall
Blacksburg, VA 24061
Phone: (540) 231-5335
Fax: (540) 231-7321
praun@vt.edu
www.theatrecinema.vt.edu
Notes: Degrees offered: BA, MFA.
Submission Materials: see website
Submission Fee: Yes
Agent Only: No

Wayne State University
4841 Cass Ave.
Detroit, MI 48201
Phone: (313) 577-6508
d_magidson@wayne.edu
www.wayne.edu
Notes: Degrees offered: BA, BFA, MFA,
MFA, PhD.
Submission Materials: see website
Submission Fee: Yes
Agent Only: No

Wellesley College
Nora Hussey, Director, Theater Studies
106 Central St.
Wellesley, MA 02181
Phone: (781) 283-2029
Fax: (781) 283-3654
nhussey@wellesley.edu
http://theatre.wellesley.edu
Notes: BA.
Agent Only: No

Wright State University
Victoria Oleen, Managing Director
Department of Theatre, Dance & Motion
Pictures
3640 Col. Glenn Hwy.
Dayton, OH 45435
Phone: (937) 775-3702
Fax: (973) 775-3787
victoria.oleen@wright.edu
www.wright.edu/tdmp
Notes: Stuart McDowell, Chair. BA, BFA.
Agent Only: No

Yale University School of Drama
Maria Leveton, Admissions Administrator
Box 208325
New Haven, CT 06520
Phone: (203) 432-0254
maria.leveton@yale.edu
http://drama.yale.edu/program/playwriting
Notes: MFA in Playwriting - Yale School of
Drama's Playwriting department is designed
to guide the writer in finding honest and
vivid strategies that articulate the personal
and cultural impulses for writing and making
theatre. Yale School of Drama's playwriting
program believes that every voice is unique:
by intense submersion into a spectrum of
aesthetics, literature and theory, the writer's
singular voice is strengthened.
Submission Materials: see website
Submission Fee: Yes
Agent Only: No

Workshops

Academy for New Musical Theatre (ANMT)
Elise Dewsberry, Artistic Director
5628 Vineland Ave.
North Hollywood, CA 91601
Phone: (818) 506-8500
Fax: (818) 506-8500
academy@anmt.org
www.anmt.org
Notes: Est. 1981.Commercial development (production, but with an emphasis on readings, workshops, contest) of new musicals. Additional programs include online curriculum, mentoring/development/feedback. Submit via website.
Preferred Genre: Musical theatre
Preferred Length: Any length
Submission Materials: query letter
Submission Fee: Yes
Agent Only: No
Deadline(s): July 15, 2014

ASCAP Musical Theatre Workshop [NY]
Michael A. Kerker, Director Musical Theatre
1 Lincoln Plaza, Fl. 7
New York, NY 10023
Phone: (212) 621-6234
Fax: (212) 621-6558
mkerker@ascap.com
www.ascap.com
Notes: Directed by Stephen Schwartz, program of 50-minutes from works-in-progress before a panel of professional directors, musical directors, producers, critics and fellow writers. All sessions begin 7pm, May-June.
Preferred Genre: Musical theatre
Preferred Length: 50-60 min.
Submission Materials: audio CD (4 songs), bio, song descriptions, synopsis
Submission Fee: No
Agent Only: No

ASCAP/Dream Works Musical Theatre Workshop [CA]
Michael Kerker, Director Musical Theatre
7920 W. Sunset Blvd., Fl. 3
Los Angeles, CA 90046
Phone: (323) 883-1000
Fax: (323) 883-1049
mkerker@ascap.com
www.ascap.com

Notes: Directed by Stephen Schwartz, 50-min presentation of works-in-development before a professional panel. All sessions begin 7pm, January-February in Los Angeles. See website for complete submission guidelines.
Preferred Genre: Musical theatre
Preferred Length: 50-60 min.
Submission Materials: audio CD (4 songs), bio, song descriptions, synopsis
Submission Fee: No
Agent Only: No

Asian American Theater Company NewWorks Incubator Project
Duy Nguyen, Artistic Director
1695 18th Street, C101
San Francisco, CA 94577
Phone: (415) 913-7366
Fax: (415) 543-5638
duy@asianamericantheater.org
www.asianamericantheater.org
Notes: Est. 2003. Combines San Francisco's best emerging playwrights and actors to create original new plays. Led by Sean Lim and mentored by Philip Kan Gotanda, the group meets twice monthly to test new material and ideas. After six months, four new plays are presented. Joining the New Works Incubator Program is the best way to introduce your work to AATC. Playwrights can submit materials between October 15 to December 15 of each year. See website for submission guidelines.
Agent Only: No
Deadline(s): December 15, 2014

BMI Lehman Engel Musical Theatre Workshop
BMI
7 World Trade Center
250 Greenwich Street
New York, NY 10007
Phone: (212) 220-3181
Fax: (212) 220-4450
pcook@bmi.com
www.bmi.com/genres/theatre
Notes: Weekly 2-hour sessions (Sept - May) Monday evenings (First Year) or Tuesday evenings (Second Year) in NYC. No housing available.
Preferred Genre: Musical theatre

Preferred Length: Any length
Submission Materials: application, audio CD
Submission Fee: No
Agent Only: No
Deadline(s): August 1, 2014

BMI Lehman Engel Musical Theatre Workshop - Librettists
BMI
7 World Trade Center
250 Greenwich Street
New York, NY 10007
Phone: (212) 830-2508
Fax: (212) 262-2508
jbanks@bmi.com
www.bmi.com
Notes: The workshop's goal is to develop the skills unique to musical theatre bookwriters through round-table presentations and critiques of its members' ongoing musical theatre scriptwriting projects. The workshop is moderated by veteran Broadway and Off-Broadway literary manager Nancy Golladay. The workshop meets Monday evenings in New York City from September through May. No housing available. See website for submission guidelines.
Preferred Genre: Musical theatre
Preferred Length: Any length
Submission Materials: see website
Submission Fee: No
Agent Only: No

Broadway Tomorrow Musical Theatre
Elyse Curtis, Artistic Director
191 Claremont Ave., #53
New York, NY 10027
Phone: (212) 531-2447
Fax: (212) 532-2447
solministry@earthlink.net
Notes: Est. 1983. New musicals with new age, transformative, spiritual themes. Concert readings with writer/composer involvement. Response time: 6 months.
Preferred Genre: Musical theatre
Preferred Length: Any length
Submission Materials: audio CD (3 songs), S.A.S.E., synopsis
Submission Fee: No
Agent Only: No

Centennial Theatre Foundation
1606 East Laguna Drive
Tempe, AZ 85282

Phone: (480) 336-3653
bentyler@centennitltf.com
www.centennialtheatrefoundation.com
Preferred Length: Full-length
Submission Materials: bio, full script, synopsis
Agent Only: No

Cherry Lane Theatre Mentor Project
38 Commerce St.
New York, NY 10014
Phone: (212) 989-2020
Fax: (212) 989-2867
company@cherrylanetheatre.org
www.cherrylanetheatre.org
Notes: Est. 1997. Pairs young writers by professional recommendation with masters to work on scripts for full season, ending with Equity Showcase. Production: medium cast size, no orchestra. Submissions not returned. See website for deadlines and submission guidelines.
Preferred Genre: All genres
Preferred Length: Any length
Submission Materials: see website
Submission Fee: No
Agent Only: No
Deadline(s): June 15, 2014

Chesterfield Writer's Film Project
1158 26th St., Box 544
Santa Monica, CA 90401
Phone: (213) 683-3977
Fax: (310) 260-6116
www.chesterfield-co.com
Notes: Based at Paramount Pictures, Writer's Film Project began with support of Steven Spielberg's Amblin Entertainment. Currently on hiatus, please see our website for the most updated information.
Submission Fee: No
Agent Only: No

Colorado New Play Summit
1101 13th St.
Denver, CO 80204
Phone: (303) 893-4000
Fax: (303) 825-2117
playsubmissions@dcpa.org
www.dcpa.org
Notes: Est. 1979. Yearly play festival seeks unproduced scripts. Agent submissions only, except for the Rocky Mountain states (Arizona, Colorado, Idaho, Montana, New

Mexico, Utah, Wyoming). Response time: 6 months. Submissions accepted year-round.
Preferred Genre: Plays (No Musicals)
Preferred Length: Full-length
Submission Materials: agent-only
Submission Fee: No
Agent Only: Yes

David Henry Hwang Writers Institute
Jeff Liu, Literary Manager
120 N. Judge John Aiso St.
Los Angeles, CA 90012
Phone: (213) 625-7000
Fax: (213) 625-7111
jliu@eastwestplayers.org
www.eastwestplayers.org
Notes: Est. 1991. 2 workshops per year (fall, spring). Submissions are accepted year-round.
Special Interest: Asian-American
Submission Materials: query letter
Submission Fee: Yes
Agent Only: No

Fieldwork
Pele Bauch, Associate Director, Programming
161 6th Ave, Fl. 14
New York, NY 10013
Phone: (212) 691-6969
Fax: (212) 255-2053
pele@thefield.org
www.thefield.org
Notes: Est. 1986. Fieldwork is a unique forum for artists to share developing works and exchange feedback, peer to peer. As a method for giving feedback, Fieldwork reveals how each piece is perceived by others and fosters a detailed information exchange. Incisive and stimulating critiques are guided by an experienced facilitator. Participants meet weekly to share their developing works.
Preferred Genre: All genres
Submission Fee: Yes
Agent Only: No

Florida Playwrights' Process
736 Scotland St.
Dunedin, FL 34698
Phone: (727) 734-0880
Fax: (727) 734-0880
flplaypro@yahoo.com
Notes: Unproduced/unoptioned musical development with technical support. Request application via email. Production: cast up to

6, simple set, simple props & costumes. Response: 3 months.
Preferred Genre: Musical theatre
Preferred Length: Any length
Submission Materials: 30-pg sample, full script, S.A.S.E., synopsis
Submission Fee: No
Agent Only: No

Frank Silvera Writers' Workshop
Garland Lee Thompson, Founding Executive Director
P.O. Box 1791,
Manhattanville Station
New York, NY 10027
Phone: (212) 281-8832
Fax: (212) 281-8839
playrite@earthlink.net
www.fsww.org
Notes: Est. 1973. Playwright development program. Submit via US mail or hand deliver. Work must be unoptioned/unproduced/unpublished.
Preferred Genre: All genres
Submission Materials: full script, S.A.S.E.
Submission Fee: No
Agent Only: No

Hangar Theatre
Nick Saldivar, Literary Manager
Box 205
Ithaca, NY 14851
Phone: (607) 273-8588
literary@hangartheatre.org
www.hangartheatre.org
Notes: The Hangar Theatre is NOT accepting any submissions at this time.
Preferred Genre: All genres
Preferred Length: Any length
Submission Materials: see website
Submission Fee: Yes
Agent Only: No

Harold Prince Musical Theatre Program
311 W. 43rd St., #307
New York, NY 10036
Phone: (212) 246-5877
Fax: (212) 246-5882
directorscompany@gmail.com
www.directorscompany.org
Notes: The mission of THE HAROLD PRINCE MUSICAL THEATRE PROGRAM is to mentor the next generation of musical theatre artists; and simultaneously to ensure the future vitality of American musical

theatre by fostering the creation, development and production of original musical theatre works.
Preferred Genre: Musical theatre
Preferred Length: Full-length
Submission Materials: see website
Submission Fee: Yes
Agent Only: No

Horse Trade Theater Group
Erez Ziv, Managing Director
85 E. 4th St.
New York, NY 10003
Phone: (212) 777-6088
Fax: (212) 777-6120
submissions@horsetrade.info
www.horsetrade.info
Notes: Horse Trade is a self-sustaining theater development group; with a focus on new work featuring a resident artist program. The Horse Trade Playwriting Workshop brings together a playwright cohort that work together to develop and polish completed full length drafts of plays. The workshop sessions are designed to clarify storytelling, develop craft, and provide resources for professional playwright development. Each playwright will have the opportunity to receive feedback from professional dramaturges and directors, submit revisions for critique, and use writing tactics that strategically develop their scripts. The workshop will culminate in the presentation of 10 minutes of each script directed and performed by The Drafts Ensemble. Based on audience feedback and the input of workshop facilitators, one script will be choses for a full length reading in the Red Room. Submissions accepted year-round.
Preferred Genre: All genres
Preferred Length: Any length
Submission Materials: full script
Submission Fee: No
Agent Only: No

Jeffrey Sweet's Improv for Playwrights
Kristine Niven, Artistic Co-Director
250 W. 90th St., #15-G
New York, NY 10024
Phone: (212) 875-1857
artnewdir@aol.com
www.artisticnewdirections.org
Notes: Est. 1986. Jeffrey Sweet teaches technique for setting up scenes to improvise toward first drafts of one-acts, plus revising,

introducing characters, and using improv for full-lengths. Monthly sessions. Fees: vary per length of session
Agent Only: No

Manhattan Playwrights Unit (MPU)
Saul Zachary, Artistic Director
338 W. 19th St., #6-B
New York, NY 10011
Phone: (215) 567-1512
mklain1011@aol.com
Notes: Est. 1979. Ongoing biweekly in-house workshop for professional-level playwrights and screenwriters. Informal and intense. Submissions not returned.
Preferred Genre: All genres
Preferred Length: Any length
Submission Materials: query letter, resume
Submission Fee: No
Agent Only: No

Missouri Playwrights Workshop (MPW)
David Crespy, Artistic Director
129 Fine Arts Bldg.
Columbia, MO 65211
Phone: (573) 882-0535
Fax: (573) 884-4034
crespyd@missouri.edu
www.theatre.missouri.edu/mpw/index.htm
Notes: Est. 1998. Weekly salon for developing work by playwrights residing in Missouri as well as MU theatre alumni, faculty, and staff who can attend workshop. Submissions not returned. Submissions accepted year-round.
Preferred Genre: All genres
Preferred Length: Any length
Submission Materials: query letter, synopsis
Submission Fee: No
Agent Only: No

New Directors/New Works (ND/NW)
Roger Danforth, Artistic Director
Drama League
520 8th Ave., #320
New York, NY 10018
Phone: (212) 244-9494
Fax: (212) 244-9191
directorsproject@dramaleague.org
www.dramaleague.org
Notes: Directors Project program to support new works by directors and collaborating artists.
Preferred Genre: Plays or Musicals
Preferred Length: Any length

Submission Materials: see website
Submission Fee: Yes
Agent Only: No

Pataphysics
The Flea
41 White St.
New York, NY 10013
Phone: (212) 226-0051
Fax: (212) 965-1808
garyw@theflea.org
www.theflea.org
Notes: Pataphysics workshops are scheduled sporadically and occur unexpectedly. To receive notification of upcoming classes, please email.
Submission Materials: see website
Submission Fee: No
Agent Only: No

PlayGround
Jim Kleinmann, Artistic Director
3286 Adeline Street, #8
Berkeley, CA 94703
Phone: (415) 992-6677
Fax: (415) 704-3177
jim@playground-sf.org
www.playground-sf.org
Notes: PlayGround offers playwriting master classes with leading Bay Area playwrights, dramaturgs and producers. These classes are open to the public and take place at the PlayGround Play Space on the first Monday of the month. Advance registration required.
Submission Fee: No
Agent Only: No

Playwrights Foundation
1616 16th Street, Suite 350
San Francisco, CA 94103
Phone: (612) 332-7481
Fax: (612) 332-6037
info@pwcenter.org
www.playwrightsfoundation.org
Notes: Every year Playwrights Foundation produces the Bay Area Playwrights Festival (BAPF) in July. For submission information and deadlines please refer to our website.
Agent Only: No

Playwrights Gallery
Deborah Savadge, Literary Manager
119 W. 72nd St., #2700
New York, NY 10023
Phone: (612) 332-7481

info@pwcenter.org
www.playwrightsgallery.com
Notes: Est. 1989. Ongoing workshop. Company of professional actors reads new work by NYC-based playwrights twice monthly. Sept.-June. Public readings 2-3 times/year. Meet September-June. Two sessions: Tuesdays, Wednesdays, noon-2pm. Response Time: 9 months.
Preferred Length: Full-length
Submission Materials: 15-20 pg sample
Submission Fee: No
Agent Only: No

Playwrights' Center of San Francisco Staged Readings
588 Sutter St., #403
San Francisco, CA 94102
Phone: (212) 564-1235
Fax: (212) 594-0926
literary@playwrightshorizons.org
www.playwrightscentersf.org
Notes: Est. 1980. The mission of the The Playwrights' Center of San Francisco (PCSF) is to encourage and develop local playwrights and promote script writing, audience development, and related arts. PCSF was established as a forum for playwrights to get together and hear their work read. Over the last 30 years it has grown to a membership organization that offers a number of successful programs that offer support and feedback to new and experienced playwrights alike and provides opportunities for actors and directors as well.
Preferred Genre: All genres
Preferred Length: Any length
Submission Materials: see website
Submission Fee: No
Agent Only: No

Playwrights' Platform
9 Cutter Lane
Quincy, MA 02171
Phone: (973) 514-1787
Fax: (973) 514-2060
www.playwrightsplatform.org
Notes: Est. 1976. Monthly developmental readings in Boston area and annual festival in Boston, Massachusetts. Response: 3 months.
Preferred Genre: All genres
Preferred Length: Any length
Submission Materials: see website
Submission Fee: Yes
Agent Only: No

Primary Stages Playwriting Workshops
307 W. 38th St., #1510
New York, NY 10018
Phone: (212) 840-9705
Fax: (212) 840-9725
info@primarystages.org
www.primarystages.org
Notes: Est. 2002. Each week, 8 writers bring 10-15 pages for instructor feedback and group discussion, completing first draft of new full-length in 10 weeks.
Preferred Genre: Plays (No Musicals)
Preferred Length: Full-length
Submission Materials: application
Submission Fee: Yes
Agent Only: No

Pulse Ensemble Theatre's Playwrights' Lab
Brian Richardson, Company Manager
248 W. 35th St., 15th Floor
New York, NY 10001
Phone: (212) 695-1596
brian@pulseensembletheatre.org
www.pulseensembletheatre.org
Notes: Develops work of each playwright in 4-month workshop. Group (limit 10) meets 3 hours/week to read scenes, with discussion afterward. Presents two showcases of 3 works/year. Some plays selected for further development. Group is under the leadership of Award winning playwright Lezley Steele. Fees $100/month.
Preferred Genre: All genres
Agent Only: No

Remembrance Through the Performing Arts New Play Development
Rosalyn Rosen, Artistic Director
P.O. Box 162446
Austin, TX 78716
Phone: (512) 329-9118
Fax: (512) 329-9118
remperarts@aol.com
Notes: Est. 1988. New plays (unoptioned/unproduced/unpublished) in workshop through work in progress productions. Production: cast limit 8. Response: 2 months.
Preferred Genre: Plays (No Musicals)
Preferred Length: Any length
Submission Materials: 10-pg sample, query letter, S.A.S.E., synopsis
Submission Fee: No
Agent Only: No

Sewanee Writers' Conference
735 University Ave., 123-D Gailor H
Sewanee, TN 37383
Phone: (931) 598-1141
Fax: (931) 598-1145
cpeters@sewanee.edu
www.sewaneewriters.org
Notes: Est. 1990. Workshop in late July led by two noted playwrights. Limited number of scholarships and fellowships available on a competitive basis.
Preferred Genre: All genres
Preferred Length: Any length
Submission Materials: see website
Submission Fee: Yes
Agent Only: No

Soho Rep Writer/Director Lab
Soho Repertory
401 Broadway, Suite 300
New York, NY 10013
Phone: (212) 941-8632
Fax: (212) 941-7148
wdlab@sohorep.org
www.sohorep.org
Notes: Est. 1998. Five or six writer/director pairs are selected to create plays from scratch. From October-April, the Lab meets on alternate weeks. Writers agree in advance to bring in work three times during the six-month cycle. At each meeting, Lab members read the plays aloud, then discuss the work. At the end of the cycle, the plays born from the Lab are presented in a public reading series at Soho Rep.
Preferred Genre: Plays (No Musicals)
Preferred Length: Full-length
Submission Materials: application, full script
Submission Fee: No
Agent Only: No

Sundance Institute Theatre Lab
180 Varick St.
Suite 1330
New York, NY 10014
Phone: (646) 822-9563
Fax: (310) 360-1975
theatre@sundance.org
www.sundance.org/programs/theatre-lab
Notes: The Sundance Institute Theatre Lab, the centerpiece of the Theatre Program, is a three-week play development retreat designed to support the creation of new work by playwrights, directors, composers and

librettists, and to provide a place where that work can be effectively mentored and challenged. Operated under the umbrella of Sundance Institute, founded by Robert Redford, the Theatre Lab offers an independent-minded community for artists — both emerging and established — to engage with their work, ask questions, build text, and take risks.
Submission Materials: see website
Submission Fee: Yes
Agent Only: No
Deadline(s): November 15, 2014

The Kennedy Center New Visions/New Voices Festival (NVNV)
Kim Peter Kovac, Director, KCTYA
Kennedy Center
P.O. Box 101510
Arlington, VA 22210
Phone: (202) 416-8830
Fax: (202) 416-8297
kctya@kennedy-center.org
www.kennedy-center.org/education/nvnv.html
Notes: Est. 1991. Biennial (even years) weeklong developmental residency in May, culminating in a national conference, to support new plays and musicals for young audiences.
Preferred Genre: Plays or Musicals
Special Interest: Theatre for Young Audiences
Preferred Length: One-Act
Submission Materials: see website
Submission Fee: No
Agent Only: No

The New Harmony Project
Joel Grynheim, Project Director
Box 441062
Indianapolis, IN 46244
Phone: (317) 464-1103
Fax: (317) 464-1103
jgrynheim@newharmonyproject.org
www.newharmonyproject.org
Notes: Est. 1986. Development thru rehearsals and readings in 14 day conference of scripts that explore the human journey by offering hope and showing respect for the positive values of life. See website for detailed submission information.
Preferred Length: Full-length
Submission Materials: see website

Submission Fee: No
Agent Only: No
Deadline(s): October 1, 2014

The PlayCrafters Group
James Breckenridge, Creative Writing Consultant
11 Golf View Rd.
Doylestown, PA 18901
Phone: (888) 399-2506
hbcraft@att.net
www.playcraftersgroup.com
Notes: We provide script analysis and private consultations to help writers better focus their creativity and present their work in compelling and commercially viable ways.
Preferred Genre: All genres
Submission Materials: see website
Submission Fee: No
Agent Only: No

The Scripteasers
Jonathan Dunn-Rankin, Corresponding Secretary
3404 Hawk St.
San Diego, CA 92103
Phone: (619) 295-4040
thescripteasers@msn.com
www.scripteasers.org
Notes: Est. 1948. Writers' development group with biweekly readings of original plays and facilitated discussion. Staff: Jonathan Dunn-Rankin (Secretary).
Agent Only: No

Urban Retreat
Young Playwrights Inc
P.O. Box 5134
New York, NY 10185
Phone: (212) 594-5440
Fax: (212) 594-5443
registration@youngplaywrights.org
www.youngplaywrights.org
Notes: July workshop: authors age 14-21 collaborate with professional dramaturges, directors, and actors on staged reading of a new play to be presented in an Off-Broadway theater.
Preferred Genre: Plays (No Musicals)
Special Interest: Theatre for Young Audiences
Submission Materials: 10-pg sample, application

Submission Fee: Yes
Agent Only: No
Deadline(s): May 1, 2014

Women's Project Playwrights Lab
Megan Carter, Associate Artistic Director
55 West End Ave.
New York, NY 10023
Phone: (212) 765-1706
Fax: (212) 765-2024
info@womensproject.org
www.womensproject.org
Notes: 2-year program for playwrights,
directors, and producers. Each Lab has 10
members who collaborate with guest artists,
WP staff, industry professionals, and other
Lab participants. Frequency: biennial
Agent Only: No

Write Now
Jenny Millinger
900 S. Mitchell Drive
Tempe, AZ 85281
Phone: (480) 921-5700
Fax: (480) 921-5777
jmillinger@childsplayaz.org
Notes: 1 week of development and staged
readings for young audiences grades K - 12.
Work must be unpublished, unproduced
(professionally).

Special Interest: Theatre for Young
Audiences
Preferred Length: Any length
Submission Materials: application, full
script
Submission Fee: No
Agent Only: No

Young Playwrights Inc. Advanced Playwriting Workshop
Nick Gandiello, Literary Manager
PO Box 5134
New York, NY 10185
Phone: (212) 594-5440
Fax: (212) 594-5443
literary@youngplaywrights.org
www.youngplaywrights.org
Notes: Advanced Playwriting Workshop
meets for 18 or younger in midtown
Manhattan every Tuesday, 4:30-7:00pm,
October - May. Exercises help members
develop and revise new plays.
Preferred Genre: Plays (No Musicals)
Preferred Length: Any length
Submission Materials: see website
Submission Fee: Yes
Agent Only: No
Deadline(s): September 16, 2014

Writer Resources

Emergency Funds

Change Emergency Funds
Change, Inc.
P.O. Box 54 , FL 33924
Phone: (212) 473-3742
Notes: Awards of up to $1,000 for medical, living, or other emergencies. Open to artists of all disciplines, with no U.S. geographical restrictions; students are not eligible. Each applicant must submit a detailed letter describing the financial emergency, copies of outstanding bills, medical fee estimates, etc., and current financial statements, along with a career resume, exhibition or performance announcements, slides or photos of work and two letters of reference from someone in the affiliated field (no video tapes). Only complete applications will be accepted. Change, Inc does not issue more than one grant per person.
Submission Materials: application
Submission Fee: No
Agent Only: No

Creative Resistance Fund
www.freedimensional.org
Notes: The Creative Resistance Fund (CRF) provides $1,500 distress grants to people in danger due to their use of creativity to fight injustice. The fund may be used to evacuate a dangerous situation or to cover living costs while weighing long-term options for safety. Discipline(s) and media are: Visual arts, Sculpture, Performing arts, Textile art, Music, Literature, Educational programs, New Media.
Submission Fee: No
Agent Only: No

Dramatists Guild Fund
Rachel Routh , Executive Director
1501 Broadway
Suite 701
New York, NY 10036
Phone: (212) 391-8384
Fax: (212) 944-0420
rrouth@dramatistsguild.com
Notes: The Dramatists Guild Fund awards one-time emergency grants to individual playwrights, lyricists and composers in need of temporary financial assistance due to unexpected illness or extreme hardship. To be considered for personal grant, you must have

had a play or musical either presented for a paying audience anywhere in the United States or Canada, and/or published by a legitimate publishing/licensing company; or be an active member of The Dramatists Guild.
Submission Materials: see website
Submission Fee: No
Agent Only: No

El Pomar Foundation
Board of Trustees
10 Lake Circle
Colorado Springs, CO 80906
Phone: 1 (800) 554-7711
www.elpomar.org
Notes: The Foundation promotes the current and future well being of the people of Colorado through grant making and community stewardship. Funding interests include health, human services, education, arts and humanities, and civic and community initiatives. The Foundation's current focus is on assisting those most affected by the difficult economic situation. Application guidelines are available on the Web site. Grant: $50,000
Submission Materials: see website
Submission Fee: No
Agent Only: No

John Anson Kittredge Educational Fund
Key Trust Company of Maine
P.O. Box 1054
Augusta, ME 04332
Notes: Submit Applications to: P.O. Box 382203, Cambridge, MA 02238-2203 Grants awarded to artists in very special circumstances. $1,000 - $10,000. Initial contact by letter stating purpose, amount requested, period of funding, supporting letter.
Submission Fee: No
Agent Only: No

Mary Mason Memorial Lemonade Fund
Dale Albright , Director of Field Services
1119 Market Street, 2nd Floor
San Francisco, CA 94103
Phone: (617) 858-2700
dan.blask@art.state.ma.us
www.theatrebayarea.org

Notes: Mail application through US mail.
Fund exists to support Bay Area theatre
artists that are critically ill or facing a life
threatening emergency.
Submission Materials: application
Submission Fee: No
Agent Only: No

Pen American Center Writer's Fund

588 Broadway, Suite 303
New York, NY 10012
Phone: (212) 334-1660
Fax: (212) 334-2181
pen@pen.org
www.pen.org/
Notes: Est. 1922. PEN American Center is
the U.S. branch of the world's oldest
international literary and human rights
organization. International PEN was founded
in 1921 in direct response to the ethnic and
national divisions that contributed to the First
World War. PEN American Center is the
largest of the 144 PEN centers in 101
countries that together compose International
PEN.
Submission Materials: see website
Submission Fee: No
Agent Only: No

PEN Writers Fund

588 Broadway, #303
New York, NY 10012
Phone: (212) 334-1660
Fax: (212) 334-2181
annmarie@pen.org
www.pen.org
Notes: Est. 1921. The PEN Writers Fund is
an emergency fund for professionally
published or produced-writers with serious
financial difficulties. Depending on the
situation, the fund gives grants or loans of up
to $1,000. The maximum amount is given
only under especially dire circumstances and
when monies are available. The PEN Fund
for Writers and Editors with HIV/AIDS,
administered under the PEN Writers Fund,
gives grants of up to $1,000 to professional
writers and editors who face serious financial
difficulties because of HIV or AIDS-related
illness. The Writers Fund does not exist for
research purposes, to enable the completion
of writing projects, or to fund publications or
organizations. The Writers Fund Committee
meets approximately every two months to
review applications.

Submission Materials: see website
Submission Fee: No
Agent Only: No

Santa Fe Arts Institute Emergency Funds

www.sfai.org/applications.html
Notes: As an outgrowth of our original
Emergency Relief Residencies, SFAI has
instituted an ongoing Emergency Relief
Residency to provide residencies for artists
and writers whose lives and work are
compromised by domestic strife, political
upheaval or natural disasters. Residencies are
by application only. In response to the
devastating effects of recent hurricanes, SFAI
is ready to make available its facility to
artists, writers and crafts people who lost
homes, studios, art work or jobs.
Submission Materials: see website
Submission Fee: No
Agent Only: No

SFWA Legal Funds

www.sfwa.org/org/funds.htm
Notes: The SFWA Legal Fund makes loans
available to authors who must take a writing-
related dispute to court. Loans are made on a
case-by-case basis, after review by the
Grievance Committee and the SFWA
attorney.
Submission Fee: No
Agent Only: No

Springboard Emergency Relief Fund

http://springboardforthearts.org/health/
    emergency-relief-fund/
Notes: Springboard's Emergency Relief Fund
exists to help meet the emergency needs of
artists in need of immediate monies to cover
an expense due to loss from fire, theft, health
emergency, or other catastrophic, career-
threatening event. The purpose of the
Emergency Relief Fund is to expedite
recovery from a specific economic crisis so
that the artist applicant may continue their
work. Artist applicants living in Minnesota,
Iowa, North Dakota, South Dakota or
Wisconsin may access up to $500 to meet or
defray unexpected "emergency" expenses.
Relief Fund payments are made directly to
the business that the artist owes money, not
to the artist applicant.
Submission Fee: No
Agent Only: No

TURN2US
www.turn2us.org.uk
Notes: Turn2us is a new independent charity
that helps people access the money available
to them - through welfare benefits, grants and
other help. Their free, accessible website is a
comprehensive and invaluable resource that
helps you find sources of financial support,
quickly and easily, based on your particular
needs and circumstances.
Submission Fee: No
Agent Only: No

**Writer's Trust Woodcock Fund -
Emergency Funds**
90 Richmond Street East
Suite 200
Toronto, ON M5C 1P1 Canada
Phone: (323) 866-0900
Fax: (323) 866-1899
info@wriart.com
www.writerstrust.com
Notes: Provides emergency funding for
established writers in mid-project who are
facing financial crisis. Since its inception, the
Woodcock Fund has supported 103 Canadian
writers in financial difficulty. The total
amount dispersed to date is $380,000.
Submission Fee: No
Agent Only: No

Membership & Service Organizations

Alliance of Artists Communities (AAC)
255 South Main St.
Providence, RI 02903
Phone: (401) 351-4320
Fax: (401) 351-4507
aac@artistcommunities.org
www.artistcommunities.org
Notes: The Alliance was created to recognize
creative process and the exploration of new
ideas as essential to human progress. We
advocate on behalf of the field of artists'
communities and creative environments in
general, to funders, policymakers,
researchers, and the public. We provide a
forum on support for today's artists,
professional development opportunities to the
field, research and benchmarking data,
funding partnerships, and bringing new
financial resources to the field. We connect
our members to each other through
networking opportunities, artists, students,
and others to information on artists'
communities, the field to other professionals
in the arts, sciences and beyond.
Submission Materials: see website
Submission Fee: No
Agent Only: No

**Alliance of Los Angeles Playwrights
(ALAP)**
Dan Berkowitz, Jonathan Dorf , Co-Chairs
7510 Sunset Blvd., #1050
Los Angeles, CA 90046
Phone: (323) 696-ALAP (2527)

info@laplaywrights.org
www.laplaywrights.org
Notes: Service and support organization for
professional needs of Los Angeles
playwrights.
Submission Materials: application
Submission Fee: Yes
Agent Only: No

Alternate ROOTS Inc.
Shannon Turner, Manager of Programs &
Services
1083 Austin Ave., NE
Atlanta, GA 30307
Phone: (404) 577-1079
Fax: (404) 577-7991
shannon@alternateroots.org
www.alternateroots.org
Notes: Service organization for resident
Southern playwrights, directors &
choreographers creating original, community-
based projects.
Submission Materials: application
Submission Fee: Yes
Agent Only: No

**American Alliance for Theatre &
Education (AATE)**
Jeremy P. Kisling , Project Coordinator
c/o 418 West Short Street
Lexington, KY 40507
Phone: (859) 254-4546
jkisling@lctonstage.org
www.aate.com

Notes: Plays should be intended for young audiences through high school age and have a minimum performance length of 45 minutes. Scripts may be previously unproduced, but must be unpublished and not committed to publications. Supporting materials (resumes, photos, reviews, ect.) should not accompany submissions. Playwrights may up submit up to 2 scripts. Please e-mail a PDF to the listed address. The playwright's name must NOT be visible anywhere on the script. Please include your name, phone, address, and play title in your email submission. If you choose to send a hardcopy, please note that scripts cannot be returned. You may include a S.A.S.E for confirmation of receipt. If submitting a musical, it must include three recordings of the music and lyrics but do NOT send a written score. Please note, playwrights shall allow the release of their names, addresses and play titles to producers, professional publications and AATE members. Playwrights also grant permission to AATE to read portions of their work in activities that promote AATE/UPRP, with proper credit given to the playwrights.
Preferred Genre: Plays or Musicals
Preferred Length: Any length
Submission Materials: E-mail only

American Association of Community Theatre (AACT)
Julie Crawford , Executive Director
1300 Gendy St.
Fort Worth, TX 76107
Phone: (817) 732-3177
Fax: (817) 732-3178
info@aact.org
www.aact.org
Notes: Recognizing that the community theatre repertoire is in need of fresh, new work, the American Association of Community Theatre has created one of the largest playwriting festivals in the country. Five or six community theatres around the country will produce the top five or six plays of the contest.
Submission Materials: see website
Submission Fee: Yes
Agent Only: No

Around the Block Urban Dramatic Literature Workgroup
Carlos Jerome, Workgroup Leader
5 E. 22nd St., #9-K
New York, NY 10010
Phone: (212) 673-9187
info@aroundtheblock.org
www.aroundtheblock.org
Notes: Est. 2001. Focusing on urban life. Special Interests: Urban life and dreams; Technology - community interface. Committed to color blind casting. Contact to participate. Response time: 2 weeks.
Preferred Genre: Plays (No Musicals)
Submission Materials: see website
Submission Fee: No
Agent Only: No
Deadline(s): November 30 , 2014

ASCAP (American Society of Composers, Authors & Publishers)
Michael Kerker, Director of Musical Theatre
1 Lincoln Plaza
New York, NY 10023
Phone: (212) 621-6234
mkerker@ascap.com
www.ascap.com
Notes: Est. 1914. Membership organization for composers, lyricists and publishers of musical works. Programs include winter and spring Musical Theater Workshops directed by Stephen Schwartz and Songwriters Showcases in NY and LA. Author must be published, recorded or performed.
Preferred Genre: Musical theatre
Submission Materials: application
Submission Fee: No
Agent Only: No

Association for Jewish Theatre (AJT)
Eli Taylor, Coordinator
1810 W. Farwell, #1A
Chicago, IL 60626
Phone: (312) 608-9781
elitaylor@sbcglobal.net
www.afjt.com
Notes: International network of Jewish theatre. Annual conference, newsletter, website, member pages. See submission guide on website.
Submission Materials: see website
Submission Fee: No
Agent Only: No

Association for Theatre in Higher Education (ATHE)
Box 1290
Boulder, CO 80306
Phone: (888) 284-3737
Fax: (303) 530-2168
info@athe.org
www.athe.org
Notes: Organization promoting excellence in theater education thru publications, conferences, advocacy, projects and collaborative efforts with other organizations.
Preferred Genre: Educational
Submission Materials: application
Submission Fee: Yes
Agent Only: No

Association of Authors' Representatives, Inc.
676A 9th Avenue, #312
New York, NY 10036
administrator@aaronline.org
www.aar-online.org
Notes: The Association of Authors' Representatives is a not-for-profit, volunteer-based, membership organization. We are active in all areas of the publishing, theater, motion picture and television industries and related fields.
Submission Fee: Yes
Agent Only: No

Authors League Fund
Isabel Howe, Administrator
31 E. 32nd St., Fl. 7
New York, NY 10016
Phone: (212) 568-1208
Fax: (212) 564-5363
staff@authorsleaguefund.org
www.authorsleaguefund.org
Notes: Interest-free loans for personal emergencies of immediate need (rent, medical, etc.).
Submission Fee: No
Agent Only: No

Beverly Hills Theatre Guild
Box 148
Beverly Hills, CA 90213
Phone: (310) 273-3390
www.beverlyhillstheatreguild.com/
Notes: Est. 1977. The Beverly Hills Theatre Guild was established to develop and maintain greater community interest in the theatre. BHTG is a non-profit organization

made up of a diverse group of members who work together to encourage new works in the theatre and musical theatre and to enrich theatrical experiences in the community. We welcome new members who are interested in participating in The Guild through either active or financial support. Please visit our website for more information.
Submission Materials: see website

Black Theatre Network
Artisia V. Green, President
8306 Bluebird Way
Lorton, VA 22079
Phone: (850) 656-9061
avgreen@wm.edu
www.blacktheatrenetwork.org
Notes: BTN's ongoing drive is to collect, process and distribute information that supports the professional and personal development of its members and therefore nurtures the growth of Black Theatre. To meet its goals, BTN has developed programs that target specific sectors of its constituency while operating under the conviction that we are all in this continuum together; and therefore we are to help each other. The network provides a development of excellence and the growth of new visionary theatre professionals through its student design and writing competitions. Through its Recognition Awards, BTN acknowledges exceptional accomplishments and participation in workshops designed to help others develop skills specific to Black Theatre.
Special Interest: African-American
Submission Materials: see website
Submission Fee: No
Agent Only: No

Black Women's Playwrights' Group
2229 Newton St, NE
Washington, DC 20018
Phone: (202) 635-2974
Fax: (202) 882-7239
info@blackwomenplaywrights.org
www.blackwomenplaywrights.org
Notes: The Black Women Playwrights' Group (BWPG) is a service and advocacy group for African American women playwrights writing for the professional theater. The mission of BWPG is to support and promote the work of our members as

well advocate on critical issues within the theater world.
Special Interest: Women's Interest
Submission Materials: see website
Submission Fee: No
Agent Only: No

Chicago Dramatists
Russ Tutterow, Artistic Director
1105 W. Chicago Ave.
Chicago, IL 60642
Phone: (312) 633-0630
bloevner@gmail.com
www.chicagodramatists.org
Notes: Est. 1979. Developmental theater and playwright workshop. See "Programs" chapter on website for details.
Preferred Genre: All genres
Submission Materials: see website
Submission Fee: Yes
Agent Only: No

Dramatists Guild of America Inc.
Rebecca Stump, Membership Associate
1501 Broadway, Suite 701
New York, NY 10036
Phone: (212) 398-9366
Fax: (212) 944-0420
info@dramatistsguild.com
www.dramatistsguild.com
Notes: Est. 1920. Works for the professional rights of writers of stage works and the conditions under which those works are created and produced. Also fights to secure fair royalties and protect subsidiary rights, artistic control, and copyright ownership.
Preferred Genre: All genres
Preferred Length: Any length
Submission Materials: application, full script
Submission Fee: Yes
Agent Only: No

Educational Theatre Association
2343 Auburn Ave.
Cincinnati, OH 45219
Phone: (513) 421-3900
Fax: (513) 421-7077
dlafleche@edta.org
www.edta.org
Notes: Join the Educational Theatre Association to enjoy professional support and outstanding educational and awards programs for teachers, students, artists, and arts advocates. We serve as the eyes, ears, and voice of the entire school theatre community, advocating for a stronger role for theatre education in the curriculum.
Submission Materials: see website
Submission Fee: Yes
Agent Only: No

FirstStage [CA]
Dennis Safren, Literary Manager
P.O. Box 38280
Los Angeles, CA 90038
Phone: (323) 850-6271
Fax: (323) 850-6271
firststagela@aol.com
www.firststagela.org
Notes: Est. 1983. Develops new, unproduced work for stage and screen. Response: 6 months.
Preferred Genre: All genres
Submission Materials: full script
Submission Fee: No
Agent Only: No

Fractured Atlas
248 W. 35th St., 10th Floor
New York, NY 10001
Phone: (888) 692-7878
Fax: (212) 277-8025
support@fracturedatlas.org
www.fracturedatlas.org
Notes: Est. 2002. Microgrants for creative and organizational development.
Submission Materials: see website
Submission Fee: Yes
Agent Only: No

Greensboro Playwrights' Forum
Stephen D. Hyers, Managing Director
200 N. Davie St., #2
Greensboro, NC 27401
Phone: (336) 335-6426
Fax: (336) 373-2659
stephen@playwrightsforum.org
www.playwrightsforum.org
Notes: Est. 1993. Aids area dramatists in publishling, producing, and learning theater writing with monthly meetings & workshops, staged readings, newsletter, and studio space.
Preferred Genre: All genres
Preferred Length: Any length
Submission Materials: application
Submission Fee: Yes
Agent Only: No

Hispanic Organization of Latin Actors (HOLA)
Manuel Alfaro, Executive Director
107 Suffolk St., #302
New York, NY 10002
Phone: (212) 253-1015
Fax: (212) 253-9651
holagram@hellohola.org
www.hellohola.org
Special Interest: Latino
Submission Materials: see website
Submission Fee: No
Agent Only: No

Inside Broadway
630 9th Ave., #802
New York, NY 10036
Phone: (212) 245-0710
Fax: (212) 245-3018
mpresser@insidebroadway.org
www.insidebroadway.org
Notes: Professional children's theater producing classic musicals in NYC public schools. Also offer hands-on, in-school residencies that enrich core curriculum through drama, dance, and music.
Preferred Genre: Musical theatre
Special Interest: Theatre for Young Audiences
Preferred Length: Any length
Submission Materials: see website
Submission Fee: No
Agent Only: No

International Center for Women
admin@womenplaywrights.org
www.womenplaywrights.org
Notes: Dedicated to the Support of Female Dramatists around the world - through encouraging attention, production, translation, publication, and international distribution, providing means for communication, assisting development of their craft and setting critical standards, encouraging scholarly and critical examination, supporting efforts to gain equality, and freedom of expression without danger or harassment. Membership allows for access to members-only area of website, participation in online forums, contact information of fellow members, opportunity to catalogue/archive scripts at various places, apply for readings and grants.
Special Interest: Women's Interest
Submission Materials: see website

Submission Fee: No
Agent Only: No

International Theatre Institute US Center (ITI/US)
520 8th Ave., Fl. 24
New York, NY 10018
Phone: (212) 609-5900
Fax: (212) 609-5901
iti@tcg.org
www.tcg.org
Notes: Founded in Prague in 1948 by UNESCO and the international theatre community. Today, over 97 ITI Centers exist throughout the world to promote the international exchange of knowledge and practice in theatre arts and to deepen mutual understanding and creative cooperation between all people in the theatre arts. See website for further information.
Submission Fee: No
Agent Only: No

LA Stage Alliance
Douglas Clayton, Director of Programs & Operations
4200 W. Chevy Chase Drive
Los Angeles, CA 90039
Phone: (213) 614-0556
Fax: (213) 614-0561
info@lastagealliance.com
www.lastagealliance.com
Notes: Est. 1975. Nonprofit service organization of groups /individuals providing Ovation Awards, LA Stage Times, networking opportunities, half-price ticket services, artist resource co-op, cooperative ads, info, and referrals.
Submission Materials: application
Submission Fee: No
Agent Only: No

League of Chicago Theatres
17 N. Wabash Ave., Suite 520
Chicago, IL 60602
Phone: (312) 554-9800
Fax: (312) 922-7202
info@chicagoplays.com
www.chicagoplays.com
Notes: Est. 1979. The League of Chicago Theatres is proud to serve a membership of more than 200 theaters, a rich and varied theater community ranging from storefront, non-union theaters with budgets under $10,000 to major cultural centers with multi-

million dollar shows. No other theater service organization in the country has such a diverse theater membership. Whether you call yourself a Chicagoan or are just visiting for the weekend, the League of Chicago Theatres is your source for Chicago theater.
Submission Materials: see website
Submission Fee: Yes
Agent Only: No

League of Professional Theatre Women
12 Stuyvesant Oval
apt 8-D
New York, NY 10009
Phone: (212) 414-8048
Fax: (212) 225-2378
lindanyc@rcn.com
www.theatrewomen.org
Notes: Nonprofit advocacy organization promoting visibility and increasing opportunities for women in the professional theater.
Submission Fee: Yes
Agent Only: No

Literary Managers & Dramaturgs of the Americas (LMDA)
Danielle Carroll, Admin Director
P.O.Box 36.20985, P.A.C.C.
New York, NY 10129
Phone: (800) 680-2148
lmdanyc@gmail.com
www.lmda.org
Notes: Est. 1985. Volunteer membership organization with conferences, quarterly journal, newsletter, advocacy caucuses, dramaturgy prize and more.
Submission Materials: application
Submission Fee: No
Agent Only: No

National Association of Women Artists
80 Fifth Ave
Suite 1405
New York, NY 10011
Phone: (212) 675-1616
Fax: (212) 675-1616
office@nawanet.org
www.nawanet.org
Notes: Promotes women artists of all backgrounds and traditions through exhibitions, programs, and its historic archive.
Special Interest: Women's Interest

Submission Fee: No
Agent Only: No

New Dramatists
Emily Morse, Director of Artistic Development
424 W. 44th St.
New York, NY 10036
Phone: (212) 757-6960
Fax: (212) 265-4738
newdramatists@newdramatists.org
www.newdramatists.org
Notes: Est. 1949. New Dramatists is dedicated to the playwright, and pursues a singular mission: To give playwrights time and space in the company of gifted peers to create work, realize their artistic potential, and make lasting contributions to the theatre. Submissions accepted between July 15th & August 15th.
Preferred Length: Full-length
Submission Materials: see website
Submission Fee: No
Agent Only: No
Deadline(s): August 15, 2014

New Playwrights Foundation
Jeff Bergquist, Artistic Director
P.O. Box 54
Santa Monica, CA 90406
Phone: (310) 393-3682
dialogue@newplaywrights.org
www.newplaywrights.org
Notes: Est. 1969. A non-profit 501(c)3 corporation. The writers workshop meets every other Thursday, usually in Santa Monica. NPF has produced members' works for stage, film and video. Writers, actors, directors, producers, composers, and others are encouraged to attend workshop meetings free of charge. Submissions accepted year-round.
Preferred Genre: All genres
Preferred Length: Any length
Submission Fee: Yes
Agent Only: No

North Carolina Writers' Network (NCWN)
Ed Southern
P.O. Box 21591
Winston-Salem, NC 27120
Phone: (336) 293-8844
ed@ncwriters.org
www.ncwriters.org

Notes: Nonprofit to connect, promote and lead North Carolina writers thru conferences, contests, newsletter, website, member pages, member book catalog, critique and consultation, etc.
Preferred Genre: All genres
Submission Materials: application
Submission Fee: Yes
Agent Only: No

OPERA America
330 7th Ave., Fl. 16
New York, NY 10001
Phone: (212) 796-8620
Fax: (212) 796-8631
frontdesk@operaamerica.org
www.operaamerica.org
Notes: National service organization promoting creation, presentation and enjoyment of opera. Provides professional development resources for composers, librettists, educators, etc.
Preferred Genre: Opera
Submission Materials: application
Submission Fee: Yes
Agent Only: No

Orange County Playwrights Alliance (OCPA)
Eric Eberwein, Director
21112 Indigo Circle
Huntington Beach, CA 92646
Phone: (714) 902-5716
firenbones@aol.com
www.ocplaywrights.org
Notes: Est. 1995. Member organization workshop of Orange County dramatists. Develops new works, staged readings, occasional productions.
Submission Materials: see website
Submission Fee: Yes
Agent Only: No

Pacific Northwest Writers Assn.
PMB 2717
1420 NW Gilman Blvd, St 2
Issaquah, WA 98027
Phone: (425) 673-2665
pnwa@pnwa.org
www.pnwa.org
Notes: Est. 1956.
Submission Materials: application
Submission Fee: No
Agent Only: No

Philadelphia Dramatists Center (PDC)
P.O. 22666
Philadelphia, PA 19110-2666
director@pdc1.org
www.pdc1.org
Notes: Membership organization for improving the craft, opportunities and conditions of dramatic writers. Members/non-members can sign up for e-mailing list.
Submission Materials: application
Submission Fee: Yes
Agent Only: No

Playformers
30 Waterside Plaza, #7D
New York, NY 10010
Phone: (917) 825-2663
playformers@earthlink.net
Notes: Est. 1987. Playwright Group. Monthly meetings (September-May) to read new work by members. Response: 2 months.
Preferred Genre: All genres
Preferred Length: Any length
Submission Materials: full script, S.A.S.E.
Submission Fee: Yes
Agent Only: No

Playwrights Guild of Canada (PGC)
215 Spadina Ave. Suite 210
Toronto, ON M5T-2C7 Canada
Phone: (415) 820-3206
www.playwrightsguild.ca
Notes: Est. 1972. National nonprofit offering triannual directory of Canadian plays/playwrights and quarterly magazine. Response: 3 weeks.
Submission Materials: application, resume
Submission Fee: Yes
Agent Only: No

Playwrights' Center (MN)
Hayley Finn, Associate Artistic Director
2301 Franklin Ave. E.
Minneapolis, MN 55406
Phone: (415) 626-2176
Fax: (415) 575-1355
erin@playwrightsfoundation.org
www.pwcenter.org
Notes: Provides services that support playwrights and playwriting. Programs include listed submission opportunities, fellowships, workshops, readings, classes and online member-to-member networking services.
Submission Materials: application

Submission Fee: Yes
Agent Only: No

Playwrights' Forum [MD]
Box 5322
Rockville, MD 20848
membership@playwrightsplatform.org
www.playwrightsforum.org
Notes: Est. 1982. Author must be a Mid-
Atlantic resident.
Submission Materials: application
Submission Fee: Yes
Agent Only: No

Saskatchewan Writers Guild (SWG)
Box 3986
Regina, SK S4P 3R9 Canada
Phone: (306) 757-6310
info@skwriter.com
www.skwriter.com
Notes: Est. 1969. Membership is open to all
writers, teachers, librarians, publishers,
booksellers, students and others interested in
Saskatchewan writing.
Submission Materials: see website
Submission Fee: Yes
Agent Only: No
Deadline(s): June 30 , 2014

The Actors Fund
Barbara Davis, Chief Operating Officer
729 7th Ave., Fl. 10
New York, NY 10019
Phone: (212) 221-7300
Fax: (212) 746-0238
info@actorsfund.org
www.actorsfund.org
Notes: The Actors Fund is a nationwide
human services organization that helps all
professionals in performing arts and
entertainment (including writers). The Fund
is a safety net, providing programs and
services for those who are in need, crisis or
transition.
Submission Fee: No
Agent Only: No

The Field
Kelley Girod, Artist Services Associate,
Membership
161 6th Ave., Fl. 14
New York, NY 10013
Phone: (212) 691-6969
Fax: (212) 255-2053
kelley@thefield.org

www.thefield.org
Notes: Est. 1986. Founded by artists for
artists. The Field is dedicated to providing
strategic services to thousands of performing
artists and companies in New York City and
beyond. We foster creative exploration,
steward innovative management strategies,
and are delighted to help artists reach their
fullest potential. The Field offers
Membership, Fiscal Sponsorship, arts
management workshops, creative
opportunities, and residencies to artists
working in any performing arts discipline.
Preferred Genre: All genres
Preferred Length: Any length
Submission Fee: Yes
Agent Only: No

The New American Theatre
Hayworth Theatre Center, 2511 Wilsh
Los Angeles, CA 90057
Phone: (310) 701-0788
jeannine@NewAmericanTheatre.com
www.circustheatricals.com
Notes: Est. 1983. Membership company of
actors, directors and writers.
Preferred Genre: All genres
Preferred Length: Any length
Submission Materials: see website
Submission Fee: Yes
Agent Only: No

The Purple Circuit
Bill Kaiser, Co-founder/Editor
921 N. Naomi St.
Burbank, CA 91505
Phone: (818) 953-5096
purplecir@aol.com
www.buddybuddy.com/pc.html
Notes: Service group to promote Lesbian,
Gay, Bisexual, & Transgender (LGBT)
performing arts worldwide. Maintains
California show listings hotline (818-953-
5072), directory of Lesbian, Gay, Bisexual, &
Transgender-friendly venues, and free listing
of playwrights.
Special Interest: LGBT
Submission Fee: No
Agent Only: No

The Theatre Museum
40 Worth Street
Suite 824
New York, NY 10013
Phone: (212) 764-4112

information@thetheatremuseum.org
www.thetheatremuseum.org/
Notes: Est. 2003. The only non-profit
museum in America with the mission to
preserve, perpetuate and protect the legacy of
the theatre.
Submission Fee: No
Agent Only: No

The Writers' Guild of Great Britain
40 Rosebery Avenue
London United Kingdom
Phone: (212) 254-6995
Fax: (212) 533-6059
writersroom@writersroom.org
www.writersguild.org.uk
Notes: Trades Union Commission (TUC)-
affiliated union for professional writers living
or working in United Kingdom.
Submission Materials: see website
Submission Fee: Yes
Agent Only: No

The Writers Room
Donna Brodie, Executive Director
740 Broadway, Fl. 12
New York, NY 10003
Phone: (442) 078-3307 Ext 77
Fax: (442) 078-3347 Ext 77
anne@writersguild.org.uk
www.writersroom.org
Notes: Est. 1978. Large loft with 44 work
stations, library, storage area, kitchen/lounge
and phone room. Open 24/7. 1 month list for
full-time membership; no wait list for part-
time.
Submission Materials: see website
Submission Fee: Yes
Agent Only: No

Theater Resources Unlimited (TRU)
Bob Ost, Executive Director
Players Theater
115 MacDougal St.
New York, NY 10012
Phone: (212) 714-7628
Fax: (212) 864-6301
trustaff1@gmail.com
www.truonline.org
Notes: Nonprofit created to help producers
produce, emerging theater companies to
emerge healthily and all theater professionals
to understand and navigate the business of
theater. Membership includes self-producing
artists as well as career producers. Programs

include monthly educational panels, producer
boot camp workshops, a new plays and new
musicals reading series, monthly programs
for actor members, a producer mentorship
program, a monthly community newsletter
and much more.
Preferred Genre: Plays or Musicals
Preferred Length: Full-length
Submission Materials: see website
Submission Fee: Yes
Agent Only: No

Theatre Bay Area (TBA)
Brad Erickson, Executive Director
1119 Market Street, 2nd Floor
San Francisco, CA 94103
Phone: (415) 430-1140
Fax: (415) 430-1145
tba@theatrebayarea.org
www.theatrebayarea.org
Notes: Nonprofit organization, individuals,
and theater companies for Bay Area resident
authors offering grants, publication and more.
Submission Materials: application
Submission Fee: Yes
Agent Only: No

Theatre Communications Group (TCG)
520 8th Ave., Fl. 24
New York, NY 10018
Phone: (212) 609-5900
Fax: (212) 609-5901
tcg@tcg.org
www.tcg.org
Notes: National service organization for
nonprofit US professional theater. Services
include grants, fellowships, workshops,
conferences, advocacy, research, ticket
discounts.
Submission Materials: application
Submission Fee: Yes
Agent Only: No

Theatre Development Fund (TDF)
David LeShay, Director of Communications
520 8th Ave. #801
New York, NY 10018
Phone: (212) 912-9770 Ext 320
Fax: (212) 768-1563
dleshay@tdf.org
www.tdf.org
Notes: Est. 1968. Enabling a diverse
audience to attend live theatre and dance
through discount ticket booths, memberships.
Submission Materials: application

Submission Fee: Yes
Agent Only: No

Theatre West
John Gallogly, Executive Director
3333 Cahuenga Blvd. W.
Hollywood, CA 90068
Phone: (323) 851-4839
Fax: (323) 851-5286
theatrewest@theatrewest.org
www.theatrewest.org
Notes: Est. 1962. Member organization.
Author must be a resident of Southern
California. Mandatory 6 hours/month
volunteering in 1st year of membership.
Scripts accepted for membership only, not
production. Theatre West is a membership
company and we select work based on
member interest.
Preferred Genre: Plays or Musicals
Preferred Length: Full-length
Submission Materials: full script
Submission Fee: No
Agent Only: No

United States Copyright Office
101 Independence Ave., SE
Washington, DC 20003
Phone: (202) 707-3000
www.copyright.gov
Notes: Though registration isn't required for
protection, copyright law provides several
advantages to registration.
Submission Materials: see website
Submission Fee: Yes
Agent Only: No

Women In Theatre
11684 Ventura Blvd
Studio City, CA 91604
Phone: (818) 763-5222
julia@lct2039.com
www.womenintheatre.com
Notes: WIT's programming and activities
evolved as a two-fold purpose: to both
enlighten the power center in the Los
Angeles theatre community of the
contribution women can make, and to
encourage women to explore opportunities
for involvement. Activities include Quarterly
Mixers, Luncheons with special guest
speakers, workshops, seminars and symposia
on various topics are produced regularly. A
weekly e-letter, monthly play readings,
discounted theatre tickets and socials provide

networking opportunities. WIT's membership
uses its varied activities to educate and
empower women in theatre, to bring various
elements of theatre into the community
though outreach programming and to develop
works and audiences for theatre in the future.
Special Interest: Women's Interest
Submission Materials: see website
Submission Fee: No
Agent Only: No

Women Playwrights International
Phone: (407) 380-1812
womenplaywrights@gmail.com
www.wpinternational.net
Notes: The mission of Women Playwrights
International is to further the work of women
playwrights around the world by promoting
their works, encouraging and assisting the
development of their works and bringing
international recognition to their works.
"Women Playwrights" shall be understood to
include all women working in the theater of
all races, classes, ages, ethnic or religious
background, sexual preferences, and women
with disabilities.
Special Interest: Women's Interest
Submission Materials: see website
Submission Fee: No
Agent Only: No

Women Playwrights' Initiative (WPI)
P.O. Box 1546
Orlando, FL 32802
wpintl@wpinternational.net
www.womenplaywrights.wordpress.com
Notes: Setting new stages for women's
voices. Our mission is to foster the
development and production of plays written
by women, through educational outreach,
workshops, readings and productions.
Special Interest: Women's Interest
Submission Materials: see website
Submission Fee: No
Agent Only: No

Women's Theatre Alliance
Brenda E. Kelly, President
2936 N. Southport Ave.
Chicago, IL 60657
Phone: (212) 765-1706
Fax: (212) 765-2024
info@womensproject.org
www.wtachicago.org

Notes: Membership organization devoted to supporting, promoting, and showcasing Chicago's female theatre artists.
Special Interest: Women's Interest
Submission Materials: see website
Submission Fee: No
Agent Only: No
Deadline(s): February 28 , 2014

Writers Guild of America, East (WGAE)
555 W. 57th St., #1230
New York, NY 10019
Phone: (323) 951-4000
Fax: (323) 782-4800
www.wgae.org
Notes: Est. 1954. The Writers Guild of America, East, (WGAE) is a labor union of thousands of professionals who are the primary creators of what is seen or heard on television and film in the U.S., as well as the writers of a growing portion of original digital media content.
Submission Materials: see website
Submission Fee: Yes
Agent Only: No

Writers Guild of America, West (WGAW)
7000 W. 3rd St.
Los Angeles, CA 90048
Phone: (212) 206-6060
Fax: (212) 206-6114
writers@artomi.org

www.wga.org
Notes: The Writers Guild of America, West (WGAW), is a labor union composed of the thousands of writers who write the content for television shows, movies, news programs, documentaries, animation, and Internet and mobile phones (new media) that keep audiences constantly entertained and informed.
Submission Materials: see website
Submission Fee: Yes
Agent Only: No

Young Playwrights Inc.
Sheri Goldhirsch, Artistic Director
P.O. Box 5134
New York, NY 10185
Phone: (212) 594-5440
Fax: (212) 594-5443
artistic@youngplaywrights.org
www.youngplaywrights.org
Notes: Est. 1981. Young Playwrights Inc. has been the only professional theatre in the United States dedicated to identifying, developing, and promoting playwrights ages 18 and under: onstage, in the classroom, and in the artistic community.
Preferred Genre: Plays (No Musicals)
Submission Materials: see website
Submission Fee: Yes
Agent Only: No

Grant Writing

Without funding, your play or musical will never impact society the way you always dreamed. But have no fear, grant writing resources are here (literally, a few inches down)! With the help of these eager professionals, you can learn the ins and outs of crafting the perfect grant-seeking proposal. You have the creativity and drive; now you need the inside knowledge on how to find the right market for your project, speak the language of grant organizations, and focus your proposal to give it maximum strength. Once you have this inavaluable skill set, you can even pay it forward and help other people make their dreams come true (not to mention get paid yourself).

—Hallie Steiner

Deborah Kluge
www.proposalwriter.com/contact.html
Notes: Personal advice website/blog from Deborah Kluge, Proposal Development Consultant/International Development Consultant.

ECS Grants, Inc.
Dr. Bruce Sliger
Phone: (770) 714-3336

dr.sliger@gmail.com
www.grantwriting.com/home.html
Submission Fee: Yes
Notes: ECS Grants works with various organizations and can help your school, nonprofit, or community group learn the grant writing skills your team needs so you can continue offering the level of service you provide.

Education to Go: Instructor-Facilitated Online Courses
Student Support: PO Box 760
Temecula, CA 92593-0760
ed2go.classes@cengage.com
www.ed2go.com/online-courses/grant-
　writing-a-to-z.html
Submission Fee: Yes
Notes: A to Z Grant Writing is an invigorating and informative course that will equip you with the skills and tools you need; online course on grant writing.

Federal Grants
www.federalgrants.com/grant-writing.html
Notes: Advice, resources, articles etc. relating to researching and writing grants, particularly federally funded grants.

Foundation Center
Phone: (800) 634-2953
onlinelibrarian@foundationcenter.org
foundationcenter.org
Notes: Established in 1956 and today supported by close to 550 foundations, the Foundation Center is the leading source of information about philanthropy worldwide. Through data, analysis, and training, it connects people who want to change the world to the resources they need to succeed.

Fundraiser Help
708 Lanham Place
Raleigh, NC 27615
Phone: (919) 870-8889
Fax: (919) 870-6466
www.fundraiserhelp.com/grant-writing.htm
Notes: Fundraiser Help is a web-based business that provides free fundraising information to site visitors. The website also provides an e-book (electronic book) for sale that contains all of the information on the website.

Government Grants
18340 Yorba Linda Blvd
Suite # 107-326
Yorba Linda, CA 92886
Phone: (714) 577-5386
Fax: (714) 961-1412
customersupport@grantseekerpro.us
www.grants.biz/grant_writing.htm
Notes: Tips and strategies on writing grants.
Submission Fee: Yes

Government Grant Money.Net
governmentgrantmoney.net
Notes: Grants offered, as well as advice on applying and obtaining grants.

GrantLinks
2151 Consulate Dr.
Unit 13
Orlando, FL 32837
Phone: (877)-857-9002
grantlinks.net
Notes: Our mission is to help non-profit organizations, churches, small businesses and individuals with grant writing services. Whether you need a grant to fund new nonprofit programs, start your business or further your education, we have you covered!

Grant Training Center
P.O Box 2223
Arlington, VA 22202
Phone: (866) 704-7268
Fax: (571) 257-8865
granttrainingcenter.com
Notes: The Grant Training Center's mission is to train educators, researchers, non-profit professionals, and public sector administrators to advance their knowledge of federal, foundation, corporate and individual giving, and to submit winning proposals.
Submission Fee: Yes

Grant Writing Training
Phone: (480) 768-7400
grantsconsulting@aol.com
www.grantwritingbootcamp.us
Notes: The mission of the Grant Writing Training Foundation (GWTF) is to provide affordable and relevant training in grant seeking and proposal writing. Classes, articles and other resources available.

Grant Writing USA
Phone: (800) 814-819
cs@grantwritingusa.com
www.grantwritingusa.com
Notes: Grant Writing USA delivers training programs across America that dramatically enhance performance in the areas of grant writing, grants management and grant maker research.
Submission Fee: Yes

Grantwriters
grantwriters.com

Notes: Free tips and hints to writing grants. Books and other resources for sale.

Non-Profit Blog.com
www.nonprofitgrantblog.com
Notes: Everything about finding grants and how to write grant proposals that are effective.

Non-Profit Expert.com
www.nonprofitexpert.com/grant.htm
Notes: Advice and articles on the ins and outs of non profit organizations.

Resource Associates
Phone: (505) 326-4245
www.grantwriters.net
Notes: Free grant writers/grant writing opportunities.

U.S. Environmental Protection Agency
www.epa.gov/ogd/recipient/tips.htm
Notes: Tips on Grant Writing.

Books and Software

Art, Craft, Theory, and Business

The following list was designed to aid writers in selecting the scriptwriting, craft and business books that best fit their individual needs. Readers can generally assume that playwriting craft books will explore action, character and dialogue. Specific aspects of craft that are emphasized by the author are listed under features. Chapter or section titles that suggest further distinguishing features are listed in quotes.

The 2011 Screenwriter's and Playwright's Market
By: Chuck Sambuchino
Publisher: Writers Digest Books
Publication date: 3rd ed, November 26, 2010
Features: 978-1-58297-957-1 Business strategies, Business resources

American Theatre Magazine
www.tcg.org
Contact: Theatre Communications Group
520 8th Avenue, 24th floor
New York, NY 10018-4156
Phone: 212-609-5900
custserv@tcg.org
Features: Features: National monthly magazine for American professional not-for-profit theatre featuring articles on important issues, productions and developments in contemporary theatre.

The Art and Craft of Playwriting
By: Jeffrey Hatcher
Publisher: FW Publications
ISBN: 978-1-884910-46-3
Features: Aristotle's theories, Interviews, "Space, Time, and Causality," Structure

The Art of Dramatic Writing
By: Lajos Egri
Publisher: Simon and Schuster

Publication date: June 1, 1960
ISBN: 978-0-671-21332-9
Features: Character behavior, Dialectics, "Orchestration," Premise, "Unity of Opposites"

The Art of the Playwright: Creating the Magic of Theatre, Second edition
By: William Packard
Publisher: Thunder's Mouth Press
Publication date: May 5, 1997
ISBN: ISBN: 978-1-56025-117-0
Features: Business resources, "Contemporary and Avant Garde Playwrights," "Dramatic Versus Narrative"

The art of playwriting: being a practical treatise on the elements of dramatic construction; intended for the playwright, the student, and the dramatic critic
By: Alfred Hennequin
Publisher: Nabu Press
Publication date: September 8, 2010
ISBN: 978-1-171-70855-1
Features: Reproduction of playwriting guide pre-1923

The Art of Writing Drama
By: Michelene Wandor
Publisher: A&C BLACK
Publication date: September 2008
ISBN: 978-0-413-77586-3

An Artist's Guide to the Law
By: Richard Amada
Publisher: Focus Publishing /R. Pullins Co., Inc.
Publication date: February 1, 2010
ISBN: 978-1-58510-356-0
Features: Copyright, intellectual property, contracts

A More Perfect Ten: Writing and Producing the Ten Minute Play
By: Gary Garrison
Publisher: Focus Publishing/R. Pullins Co., Inc.
Publication date: November 30, 2008
ISBN: 978-1-58510-327-0
Features: Formatting for submission, list of theatres and festivals

Backwards & Forwards: A Technical Manual for Reading Plays, First edition
By: David Ball
Publisher: Southern Illinois University Press
Publication date: July 7, 1983
ISBN: 978-0-8093-1110-1
Features: Literary analysis

Blunt Playwright: An Introduction to Playwriting
By: Clem Martini
Publisher: Consortium Book
Publication date: September 30, 2007
ISBN: 978-0-88754-894-9
Features: Exercises, Play analyses, Rewriting, Workshopping

Business and Legal Forms For Theater, Second edition
By: Charles Grippo
Publisher: Allworth Press
ISBN: 978-1-58115-323-1
Features: 40 fill in the blank contracts with guidelines of how to use (Simple Production License, Collaborations, Song Licensing and much more)

Characters in Action: Playwriting the Easy Way, First Edition
By: Marsh Cassady (Author), Theodore O Zapel (Editor), Tom Myers (Designer)
Publisher: Meriwether Publishing Ltd.
Publication date: September 1, 1995
ISBN: 978-1-56608-010-1
Features: Playwriting

Collaborative Playwright: Practical Advice for Getting Your Play Written
By: Bruce Graham, Michele Volansky
Publisher: Heinemann
Publication date: March 30, 2007
ISBN: 978-0-325-00995-7
Features: Collaboration, Interviews, "Prewriting and Outlines," Rewriting

The Crafty Art of Playmaking
By: Alan Ayckbourn
Publisher: Palgrave Macmillan
Publication date: September 30, 2008
ISBN: 978-0-230-61488-8
Features: Directorial perspectives

Creating Unforgettable Characters
By: Linda Seger
Publisher: Henry Holt
Publication date: July 1, 1990
ISBN: 978-0-8050-1171-5
Features: Character psychology, "Creating Nonrealistic Characters," Research

Developing Story Ideas, Second edition
By: Michael Rabiger
Publisher: Focal Press
Publication date: November 4, 2005
ISBN: 978-0-240-80736-2
Features: Artistic identity, Exercises, Generating ideas

Dramatic Writer's Companion: Tools to Develop Characters, Cause Scenes and Build Stories
By: Will Dunne
Publisher: University of Chicago Press
Publication date: April 15, 2009
ISBN: 978-0-226-17253-8
Features: Character development, Structure

Dramatists Toolkit: The Craft of the Working Playwright
By: Jeffrey Sweet
Publisher: Heinemann
Publication date: November 1, 1993
ISBN: 978-0-435-08629-9
Features: "Negotiations," "Violating Rituals"

The Elements of Playwriting
By: Louis E. Catron
Publisher: Waveland Press
Publication date: November 1, 2001
ISBN: 978-1-57766-227-3
Features: Basic principles, Creating characters, Step-by-step advice

The Female Dramatist: Profiles of Women Playwrights from Around the World from the Middle Ages to the Present Day
By: Elaine T. Partnow, Lesley Anne Hyatt
Publisher: Facts on File
Publication date: June 1998
ISBN: 978-0-8160-3015-6
Features: Theatre history

Final Draft
26707 Agoura Road
Suite 205
Calabasas, CA 91302
Phone: (818) 995-8995
Fax: (818) 995-4422
sales@finaldraft.com
www.finaldraft.com
Notes: For over 20 years, Final Draft, Inc. has published Final Draft® software - the number-one selling screenwriting application in the world. Final Draft software paginates and formats your script to industry standards allowing the story to be the writer's main focus. Our other resources for writers include the Big BreakContest - an annual screenwriting contest designed to launch careers, and ScriptXpert coverage services. The recently launched Final Draft Writer® and Final Draft Reader® allow you to write, edit, read and annotate FDX files easily anywhere, anytime.

How to Write a Play (Teach Yourself)
By: David Carter
Publisher: NTC Publishing Group
Publication date: Publication date: January 11th, 1999IBSN-13: 978-0-8442-0231-0
Features: Features: Writing of Stage, Film, TV, Radio Plays, Self-production, Marketing and Financial Guidance

In Their Own Words: Contemporary American Playwrights
By: David Savran
Publisher: Theatre Communications Group
Publication date: January 1, 1993
ISBN: 978-0-930452-70-4
Features: Interviews, Essays

Insight for Playwrights Magazine
www.insightforplaywrights.com
Contact: Insight for Playwrights
11309 E Petra Ave
Mesa, AZ 85212

Features: Monthly publication featuring submission guidelines on theatres seeking new works, grants, contests, festivals, etc.

Making Musicals: An Informal Introduction to the World of Musical Theater, First Limelight edition
By: Tom Jones
Publisher: Limelight Editions
Publication date: August 1, 2004
ISBN: 978-0-87910-095-7
Features: History, How-to, Memoir

The Making of a Musical, First Limelight edition
By: Lehman Engel
Publisher: Limelight Editions
Publication date: January 1986
ISBN: 978-0-87910-049-0
Features: History, Musical writing advice, Producing

Musical Theatre Writer's Survival Guide
By: David Spencer
Publisher: Heinemann
Publication date: July 1, 2005
ISBN: 978-0-325-00786-1
Features: Musical writing, Collaboration, Business strategies, "Presentation, Formatting and Packaging," "The Spirit of the Thing, or: Adaptation"

Naked Playwriting: The Art, the Craft, and the Life Laid Bare
By: Robin U. Russin and William M. Downs
Publisher: Silman-James Press
Publication date: December 15, 2004
ISBN: 978-1-879505-76-6
Features: Business strategies, Generating ideas, Rewriting

The New, Improved Playwright's Survival Guide: Keeping the Drama in Your Work and Out of Your Life
By: Gary Garrison
Publisher: Heinemann Drama
Publication date: October 14, 2005
ISBN: ISBN:978-0-325-00816-5
Features: Dramatic structure, Synopsizing a play, Uncovering inspiration, Dealing with criticism

New Playwriting Strategies: A Language-Based Approach to Playwriting
By: Paul C. Castagno
Publisher: Theatre Arts Book

ISBN: 978-0-87830-136-2
Features: "On Multivocality and Speech Genres," Play analyses

New Tax Guide for Writers, Artists, Performers and Other Creative People, 2012
By: Peter Jason Riley
Publisher: Focus Publishing/R. Pullins Co., Inc.
Publication date: January 1, 2012
ISBN: 978-1-58510-469-7
Features: Record-keeping, deductions, sample tax forms

Notes from a Practicing Writer: The Craft, Career, and Aesthetic of Playwriting
By: Ed Shockley
Publisher: Lightning Source
Publication date: January 30, 2007
ISBN: 978-0-9726906-3-8
Features: Business strategies, "Compression," "The Magic What-If," "Projection," Play analyses, "Reduction"

Play-Making: A Manual of Craftsmanship
By: William Archer
Publisher: Nabu Press
Publication date: September 8, 2010
ISBN: 978-1-171-75598-2
Features: Historical text

Playwrights on Playwriting: From Ibsen to Ionesco
By: Toby Cole, John Gassner (Introduction)
Publisher: Rowman & Littlefield Publishers, Inc.
Publication date: May 2001
ISBN: 978-0-8154-1141-3
Features: Interviews, Essays

Playwright's Guidebook
By: Stuart Spencer
Publisher: Farrar Straus and Grioux
Publication date: April 1, 2002
ISBN: 978-0-571-19991-4
Features: Exercises, Generating ideas, Rewriting, Structure, "High Stakes and High Hopes," "Writing from an Image"

The Playwright's Handbook, Revised edition
By: Frank Pike, Thomas G. Dunn
Publisher: Plume
Publication date: April 1, 1996
ISBN: 978-0-452-27588-1
Features: Rewriting, Business strategies, Workshops, "Sight, Hearing, Touch, Taste,

Smell," "Understanding the Relationship of Ritual and Dram"

The Playwright's Process: Learning the Craft from Today's Leading Dramatists
By: Buzz McLaughlin
Publisher: Back Stage Books
Publication date: May 1, 1997
ISBN: 978-0-8230-8833-1
Features: Interviews, Rewriting, Development, "The Play Idea Worksheet," "The Short-form Biography," "The Long-form Biography"

Playwrights Teach Playwriting
By: Joan Harrington (Editor) and Brian Crystal (Editor)
Publisher: Smith & Kraus
Publication date: September 30, 2006
ISBN: 978-1-57525-423-4
Features: Essays, Interviews, Teaching methods

Playwrights' Voice, First edition
By: David Savran (Editor)
Publisher: Theatre Communications Group
Publication date: April 15, 1999
ISBN: 978-1-55936-163-7
Features: Interviews, Essays

Playwrights at Work
By: Paris Review (Author), George Plimpton (Editor), John Lahr (Introduction)
Publisher: Modern Library
Publication date: May 30, 2000
ISBN: 978-0-679-64021-9
Features: Interviews, Essays

The Playwright's Workbook
By: Jean-Claude Van Itallie
Publisher: Applause
Publication date: 1997
ISBN: 978-1-55783-302-0
Features: Exercises, Play analyses, Images, Various forms and genres

The Playwright's Workout
By: Liz Engelman, Michael Bigelow Dixon
Publisher: Smith and Krause Publishers
ISBN: 978-1-57525-617-7
Features: Exercises

Playwriting: A Complete Guide to Creating Theatre
By: Shelly Frome
Publisher: Mcfarland & Co Inc Pub

Publication date: March 1990
ISBN: 978-0-89950-425-4
Features: Quotations, Interviews, Submissions, Grants, Contests, Festivals, Agents, Examples

Playwriting: A Practical Guide
By: Noel Greig
Publisher: Routledge
Publication date: February 28, 2005
ISBN: 978-0415310444
Features: Generating ideas, Rewriting

Playwriting: A Study in Choices and Challenges (Lillenas Drama Resource How to Book)
By: Paul McCusker
Publisher: Lillenas Publishing Company
Publication date: May 1995
ISBN: 978-0-415-31044-4 Specialty: Christian writing

Playwriting, Brief and Brilliant
By: Julie Jensen
Publisher: Smith & Kraus
Publication date: October 30, 2007
ISBN: 978-1-57525-570-5
Features: Beginning, Re-writing, Writer's block, Marketing

*Playwriting for Dummies*by Angelo Parra
Publisher: Wiley Publishing, Inc.
ISBN: 978-1-118-01722-7
Features: Features: Practical (and fun) step-by-step coaching from idea to script to production.

Playwriting: From Formula to Form, First edition
By: William M. Downs (Author), Wright (Author)
Publisher: Wadsworth Publishing
Publication date: August 14, 1997
ISBN: 978-0-15-503861-5
Features: Fundamentals of formula, Marketing

Playwriting in Process – Thinking and Working Theatrically, Second edition
By: Michael Wright
Publisher: Focus Publishing/R. Pullins Co., Inc.
Publication date: Sept. 1, 2010
ISBN: 978-1-58510-340-9
Features: Character, plot, collaboration, unblocking, exercises

Playwriting Master Class – The Personality of Process and the Art of Rewriting
By: Michael Wright
Publisher: Focus Publishing /R. Pullins Co., Inc.
Publication date: August 1, 2010
ISBN: 978-1-58510-342-3
Features: Case studies, individual approaches, post-creative self-analysis

Playwriting: The First Workshop
By: Kathleen George
Publisher: Allworth Press
Publication date: August 1, 2008
ISBN: 978-1-58115-658-4
Features: Basic principles, Alternative approaches, Using autobiographical materials, Play analysis

Playwriting: The Fundamentals
By: Effiong Johnson
Publisher: Xlibris, Corp.
Publication date: February 16, 2011
ISBN: 978-1-4535-8490-3
Features: Nigerian theatre

Playwriting: The Structure of Action
By: Norman A. Bert, Sam Smiley
Publisher: Yale University Press
Publication date: October 30, 2005
ISBN: 978-0-300-10724-1
Features: Aristotle's principles, Generating ideas

Playwriting: Writing, Producing and Selling Your Play
By: Louis E. Catron
Publisher: Waveland Press
Publication date: July 1990
ISBN: 978-0-88133-564-4
Features: Business strategies, Aristotle's principals, Workshops

Practical Playwriting
By: David Copelin
Publisher: Writer, Inc.
Publication date: September 1998
ISBN: 978-0-87116-185-7
Features: Play development

The Power of the Playwright's Vision: Blueprints for the Working Writer
By: Gordon Farrell
Publisher: Heinemann Drama
Publication date: September 6, 2001
ISBN: 978-0-325-00242-2

Features: Blueprints of various playwrights' techniques

Reminiscence Theatre : Making Theatre from Memories
By: Glenda Jackson, Pam Schweitzer
Publisher: Jessica Kingsley Publishers
Publication date: January 15, 2006
ISBN: 978-1-84310-430-8
Features: Community building, Documentary, Teaching methods, Therapy

Script is Finished, Now What Do I Do: The Scriptwriter's Resource Book and Agent Guide
By: K. Callan
Publisher: SCB Distributors
Publication date: January 15, 2007
ISBN: 978-1-878355-18-8
Features: Business resources, Business strategies

Solving Your Script : Tools and Techniques for the Playwright
By: Jeffrey Sweet
Publisher: Heinemann
Publication date: February 15, 2001
ISBN: 978-0-325-00053-4
Features: "Negotiation Over Objects," "Different Relationships, Different Roles," "Disruption of a Ritual"

So You Want to Be a Playwright? : How to Write a Play and Get It Produced
By: Tim Fountain
Publisher: Nick Hern Books
Publication date: April 1, 2008
ISBN: 978-1-85459-716-8
Features: Finding the story, Construction, Strategies for production

Spaces of Creation: The Creative Process of Playwriting
By: Suzan Zeder (Author), Jim Hancock (Author)
Publisher: Heinemann Drama
Publication date: July 1, 2005
ISBN: 978-0-325-00684-0
Features: Exercises, Movement-based mind-body disciples, Creative process

The Stage Producers Business and Legal Guide
By: Charles Grippo
Publisher: Allworth Press
ISBN: 978-1-58115-241-8

Features: Organizing a theater company, Renting spaces, Licensing plays and musicals, Taxes, Managing a Non Profit Theater Company, Joint Ventures and much more

Stage Writers Handbook: A Complete Business Guide for Playwrights, Composers, Lyricists and Librettists
By: Dana Singer
Publisher: Theatre Communications Group
Publication date: May 1, 1996
ISBN: 978-1-55936-116-3
Features: Business resources, Business strategies

Stage Writing
By: Val Taylor
Publisher: Crowood Press
Publication date: September 1, 2002
ISBN: 978-1-86126-452-7
Features: Building relationships, Understanding physical space, Developing story, Creating characters and dialogue, Building a strong structure, Writing effective stage directions, Textual analysis

Strategies for Playbuilding : Helping Groups Translate Issues into Theater
By: Will Weigler
Publisher: Heinemann
Publication date: March 15, 2001
ISBN: 978-0-325-00340-5
Features: Community building, Documentary, Teaching methods

Teaching Young Playwrights
By: Gerald Chapman, Lisa A Barnett
Publisher: Heinemann
Publication date: November 26, 1990
ISBN: 978-0-435-08212-3
Features: Exercises, Teaching methods

Teach Yourself Writing a Play
By: Ann Gawthorpe, Lesley Brown
Publisher: McGraw-Hill
Publication date: October 26, 2007
ISBN: 978-0-07-149697-1
Features: Business strategies, Generating ideas, Genres, Rewriting

Theory and Technique of Playwriting
By: John Howard Lawson
Publisher: Hill & Wang Pub
Publication date: 1961
ISBN: 978-0-8090-0525-3

Features: Historical text

To Be a Playwright, New edition
By: Janet Neipris
Publisher: Theatre Arts Book
Publication date: September 28, 2005
ISBN: 978-0-87830-188-1
Features: "Twelve Habits of Successful Playwrights," "Adapting from Fact and Fiction," "Critics"

The Way of Story: The Craft & Soul of Writing
By: Catherine Ann Jones
Publisher: Ingram Publisher Services
Publication date: August 1, 2007
ISBN: 978-1-932907-32-2
Features: Dialogue Structure, Rewriting, Generating ideas

Words with Music: Creating the Broadway Musical Libretto, Updated & revised edition
By: Lehman Engel
Publisher: Applause Books
Publication date: January 1, 2006
ISBN: 978-1-55783-554-3
Features: Musical theatre writing

Worlds in Words: Storytelling in Contemporary Theatre and Playwriting, New edition
By: Mateusz Borowski (Author, Editor), Malgorzata Sugiera (Editor)
Publisher: Cambridge Scholars Publishing
Publication date: October 1, 2010
ISBN: 978-1-4438-2109-4
Features: Essays on technique

Working on a New Play: A Play Development Handbook for Actors, Directors, Designers and Playwrights, Second edition
By: Edward M. Cohen
Publisher: Limelight Editions
Publication date: July 1, 2004
ISBN: 978-0-87910-190-9
Features: Play development

Write Brothers Inc.
Chris Huntley, Vice President
348 E. Olive Avenue. Suite H
Burbank, CA 91502
Phone: (818) 843-6557
Fax: (818) 843-8364
chris@screenplay.com
www.screenplay.com

Notes: Since 1982, Write Brothers Inc. (Formerly called Screenplay Systems) has been a world leader in film and television scriptwriting and production software. We are the only company to receive a Technical Achievement Award from the Academy of Motion Picture Arts & Sciences for scriptwriting software. We have developed software for all phases of writing: creativity, brainstorming, outlining, and formatting. Our top-selling Movie Magic Screenwriter, Dramatica, and Outline 4D writing programs are used by leading novelists, fiction writers, screenwriters, and playwrights.

"Writer's Block" Busters : 101 Exercises to Clear the Deadwood and Make Room for Flights of Fancy
By: Velina Hasu Houston
Publisher: Smith & Kraus
Publication date: September 16, 2008
ISBN: 978-1-57525-597-2
Features: Exercises

Writing For The Stage: A Practical Playwriting Guide
By: Leroy Clark
Publisher: Allyn & Bacon
Publication date: September 23, 2005
ISBN: 978-0-205-41297-6

The Writer Got Screwed (but didn't have to): Guide to the Legal and Business Practices of Writing for the Entertainment Industry
By: Brooke A. Wharton
Publisher: Harper Paperbacks
Publication date: March 14, 1997
ISBN: 978-0-06-273236-1
Features: Business strategies

The Writer's Journey: Mythic Structure for Writers
By: Christopher Vogler
Publisher: Ingram Publisher Services
Publication date: November 1, 2007
ISBN: 978-1-932907-36-0
Features: Mythic structure, Mythic characters

Writing 45-minute One-act Plays, Skits, Monologues, & Animation Scripts for Drama Workshops : Adapting Current Events, Social Issues, Life Stories, News & Histories
By: Anne Hart
Publisher: ASJA Press
Publication date: March 14, 2005
ISBN: 978-0-595-34597-7
Features: One-act plays, Documentary

Writing Dialogue for Scripts: Effective Dialogue for Film, TV, Radio, and Stage, Third edition
By: Rib Davis
Publisher: A&C Black
Publication date: January 1, 2009
ISBN: 978-1-4081-0134-6
Features: Dialogue

Writing the Broadway Musical
By: Aaron Frankel
Publisher: Perseus Books Group
Publication date: August 17, 2000
ISBN: 978-0-306-80943-9
Features: Musical writing

Writing Musical Theatre
By: Allen Cohen, Steven L. Rosenhaus
Publisher: St. Martins Press
Publication date: February 7, 2006
ISBN: 978-1-4039-6395-6
Features: Musical writing, Adaptations, Business strategies

Writing Your First Play
By: Stephen Sossaman
Publisher: Prentice Hall
Publication date: August 11, 2000
ISBN: 978-0-13-027416-8
Features: Step-by-step, Critical revision, Exercises

Writing: Working in the Theatre
By: Robert Emmet Long (Editor), Paula Vogel (Foreword)
Publisher: Continuum
Publication date: January 15, 2008
ISBN: 978-0-8264-1807-4
Features: Production, Recent shows

You Can Write a Play!, Revised edition
By: Milton E. Polsky
Publisher: Applause Books
Publication date: February 1, 2002
ISBN: 978-1-55783-485-0
Features: Exercises

Young At Art : Classroom Playbuilding in Practice, First edition
By: Christine Hatton and Sarah Lovesy
Publisher: David Fulton Publish
Publication date: November 24, 2008
ISBN: 978-0-415-45478-0
Features: Exercises, Teaching methods

Index of Special Interests

African-American

American

Asian-American

Deaf

Disabled

Jewish

Latino

LGBT

Multi-Ethnic

Native American

Theatre for Young Audiences

Women's Interest

Submission Calendar

January

February

March

April

May

June

November

December

Index of Unsolicited Opportunities

190

Index of No Fee Opportunities

Index of Listings

Dramatists Guild of America

Membership Application

I am a. . . (please check all that apply)

☐ Playwright ☐ Composer ☐ Lyricist ☐ Librettist

Mr/Ms
Dr/Mrs   First Name   Middle   Last Name

Pseudonym or Alternate Professional Name

Address (Street)

City/State/Zip or Postal Code

Country

Home Phone

Cell Phone

E-mail Address

Date of Birth

Agent/Agency Name

Agent/Agency Phone & Address

I have enclosed the appropriate support materials with my application

☐ **MEMBER:**
any one of the following:
1. a copy of a **review** or a **program** from a production of my work before a paying audience.
-or-
2. a copy of a published **script** by a legitimate widely-recognized publisher.

☐ **ASSOCIATE:**
any one of the following:
1. a copy of a **script**
-or-
2. a **program** from a reading or workshop of my work

☐ **FULL-TIME STUDENT DISCOUNT**
please submit the following:

a **letter** from my professor on University letterhead.

GRADUATION DATE:

MO / DAY / YEAR

I qualify for the following level of membership (please check only one)

☐ Member $130/yr.   ☐ Associate $90/yr.   ☐ Student Discount
50% off either Associate or Member dues, depending on eligibility

RESIDENTS OF CANADA PLEASE ADD $10 TO MEMBERSHIP FEE. RESIDENTS OUTSIDE THE U.S. AND CANADA, PLEASE ADD $20 TO MEMBERSHIP FEE.

☐ Enclosed is my check made payable to Dramatists Guild of America, Inc.

☐ Please bill my credit card ☐ VISA ☐ MasterCard ☐ Discover Card ☐ AMEX

Account Number   _____ / _____ Exp. Date

Signature

Mail to: The Dramatists Guild of America; Attn: Membership Dept.; 1501 Broadway, suite 701; New York, NY 10036